The New Goliaths

The
New
Goliaths

How Corporations Use Software to
Dominate Industries, Kill Innovation,
and Undermine Regulation

James Bessen

Yale UNIVERSITY PRESS
New Haven & London

Published with assistance from the foundation established in memory of Philip Hamilton McMillan of the Class of 1894, Yale College.

Yale University Press books may be purchased in quantity for educational, business, or promotional use. For information, please e-mail sales.press@yale.edu (U.S. office) or sales@yaleup.co.uk (U.K. office).

Set in Galliard type by IDS Infotech Ltd., Chandigarh, India.
Printed in the United States of America.

Library of Congress Control Number: 2021946319
ISBN 978-0-300-25504-1 (hardcover : alk. paper)

A catalogue record for this book is available from the British Library.

This paper meets the requirements of ANSI/NISO Z39.48-1992 (Permanence of Paper).

10 9 8 7 6 5 4 3 2 1

To Jonas and Micah

Contents

Preface

Two decades ago, the business world was abuzz with talk of a New Economy. *Fast Company,* one of the magazines created to herald this change, declared in August 2001 that this "democratic capitalist" movement was about "the expansion of individual opportunity, the disruptive energy of ceaseless innovation, and the transformative power of information technology and communications." Individuals could access inexpensive new computer and networking technology, learn valuable skills, innovate, create new companies based on their innovations, grow these companies rapidly by focusing on their "core competencies," outsource other tasks to global partners thanks to the communications-enabled "death of distance," and ultimately disrupt entrenched old economy companies.

Many people were skeptical, none more so than leading economists. While recognizing that new information technology helped deliver strong productivity growth (growth in output per worker) in the 1990s, Martin Feldstein, who had been chairman of the Council of Economic Advisers under Ronald Reagan, asserted that it did not fundamentally transform the "relationships that govern economic processes in the United States." Alan Greenspan, chairman of the Federal Reserve, agreed, arguing that new technology was just continuing its role in Schumpeterian "creative destruction," replacing older technologies with newer, more productive ones. Indeed, if anything, he saw information technology accelerating the process of creative destruction that had been under way at least since the Industrial Revolution.

But neither the New Economy vision nor the views of the economist critics has aged well. Information technology (IT) is indeed fundamentally transforming economic processes, although not along the lines of the New Economy. Not only did that vision fail, but the actual effect of information technology has been the opposite of what was predicted in many areas. And rather than accelerating creative destruction, information technology is suppressing it today. Information technology is changing the nature of markets, innovation, and firm organization, exacerbating economic divisions, and undermining government regulation. It is, in fact, changing the basic nature of capitalism.

The origins of this book date back thirty years to when I was running a software company. During the 1980s and 1990s, low-cost computers did indeed level the playing field, allowing individuals and small firms to access powerful technology. For instance, bar code scanning allowed small retail stores to use advanced merchandising and inventory control tools. New companies sprung up, taking advantage of new opportunities, sometimes growing to disrupt entrenched, old technology firms.

I ran one of those new companies, a startup that developed one of the first desktop publishing programs. My experience made me aware of a nascent trend. Our customers used our technology to customize print publications in order to target individuals or small demographic groups. For instance, the grocery chain A&P used our publishing software to produce different weekly ad circulars targeting the dozens of store shopping zones within each metropolitan area. Software gave them the flexibility to use the individual and demographic data they were now collecting on a large scale. I wrote about this trend in 1993 in an article in the *Harvard Business Review* titled "Riding the Marketing Information Wave."

When I left business and became an academic researcher, I wanted to explore this trend further, but at the time there was little evidence to suggest that it led to far-reaching change in the economy. That changed. Walmart took that same basic bar code scanner technology and used it to build a massive logistics and inventory management system connecting stores, suppliers, and warehouses with the enormous flow of data from its scanners. This system, deployed with a new business model and organizational structure, allowed Walmart to offer greater selection in stores, to respond more rapidly to changing demand, and to do this with less inventory and lower transportation costs. Using this advantage, Walmart grew to dominate the retail sector. Other companies in other sectors also built large IT systems and used them to achieve industry dominance. Automobile companies and aircraft manufacturers built multi-billion-dollar systems to design new cars and jets, which themselves now depend heavily on software; banks developed systems to use financial data to target consumers with tailored credit card offers while managing risk; Google and Facebook developed systems to use data from online activity to target consumers with advertising. These systems involved a major shift of investment into proprietary software and the persistent dominance of leading firms within their industries.

What these disparate systems have in common is that they allow firms to better address highly heterogeneous and sometimes rapidly changing demands of their customers. They do this by adding features or selection that increase the complexity of their offerings. Compared to its rivals, Walmart efficiently manages far greater selection in its stores and does so more efficiently; leading automobiles and jets have far more features; leading banks and advertisers do far more detailed targeting. When people think about the economic impact of computers, they often focus on prices, the rapidly falling prices of computer hardware, or the low cost of reproducing software. Here another, less remarked characteristic of software is also at play: compared to tangible systems, it is relatively inexpensive to add a feature to a software system; hence, complexity can be managed cost-effectively at a much larger scale. Firms compete on complexity.

Although this technology helped firms succeed, until I started thinking about historical context, I still did not see that it fundamentally changed economic processes. New technologies do not typically change basic economic and social relations, but beginning in the late nineteenth century, they did. Firms in many industries began to achieve major gains in efficiency by producing at large scale. The building blocks of industry, steel and electricity, became much more affordable. New types of large firms emerged and came to dominate their industries, changing competition, labor markets, economic integration, and innovation processes. And with great economic power came opportunities for abuse and political corruption. The Progressive Era response was to counterbalance growing corporate power with new regulatory power of the state over competition, food and medicine safety, employment abuses, child labor, political corruption, and more.

Because these technologies operated at a larger scale, they required new organizations and new institutions, changing the economy and society. Yet they also had important limitations. Large firms gained economic efficiencies at the expense of variety and flexibility. Standardization was essential to mass production because it was costly to manage too much variety or too many features. But information technology can substantially reduce these costs. Today, software revisits the tradeoff between efficiency and heterogeneity, allowing firms to achieve a degree of both. And because this tradeoff not only occurs across the economy but involves new types of organization and institutions, it does indeed have far-reaching effects.

This book makes that case. Information technology no longer levels the playing field; instead, innovative challengers face strong headwinds to growth. Now, only the top firms have access to key frontier technologies. A growing gap in revenue per employee has emerged between the superstar firms that have the technology and those who don't, slowing economic growth. Moreover, only select workers have access to the new technology to learn the skills that bring high pay. Superstar firms pay more, especially in some cities and some occupations. Because pay increasingly depends on whom you work for and not just how hard you work, inequality fuels a politics of resentment. As economic divisions and inequality grow, social cohesion is undermined. Also, the balance of power between large corporations and the rest of society has shifted, as it did in the past. When technology makes products and services dramatically more complex, government loses its ability to regulate. Volkswagen fiddles its software and governments cannot regulate diesel emissions; financial institutions fiddle models of mortgage risk and regulators cannot manage systemic risk. As regulation becomes more complex in response, moreover, agencies become subject to capture by industry experts and indirect corruption facilitated by lobbying and campaign contributions.

Our society faces another, different challenge from technology today. New technology is creating a new economy, a superstar capitalism. Understanding this change is critical to developing policies that can restore economic dynamism, a fairer sharing of wealth, and a more cohesive society.

Acknowledgments

I have long been interested in the interaction between economic complexity and information technology. Complexity featured in my last book, *Learning by Doing: The Real Connection between Innovation, Wages, and Wealth;* the complexity of technology meant that key skills for using new technologies had to be learned through experience, and that had strong implications for the way new technologies were adopted and the workforce acquired skills. But I had not seen the connections among complexity, software, and the big economic changes occurring in recent years. All this started to change about five years ago. After reading new studies on the rise in industrial concentration in the United States, I realized that software might be playing a role. I began research that showed this to be true.

The ideas of other researchers—to whom this book owes a lot—helped connect the dots between the new generation of software and broader economic changes. Jonathan Haskel and Stian Westlake drew out implications of the rising use of intangible capital. Chiara Criscuolo and her colleagues at the Organisation for Economic Co-operation and Development found rising concentration in other developed countries, and they also related this rise to digital technology. These researchers also discovered a rising productivity gap since 2000 between the best and the rest. David Autor, David Dorn, Larry Katz, Christina Patterson, and John van Reenen documented the rise in industry concentration in the United States and related it to the growth of superstar firms. Robert Frank and Philip Cook highlighted a winner-take-all society, and Erik Brynjolfsson and Andy

McAfee linked this to IT. But the exact mechanism linking technology to firm dominance was not clear to me until Georg von Graevenitz reminded me of the work of John Sutton and Avner Shaked on natural oligopolies. Another influence was James Beniger, who described the link between information and technology in an earlier era.

Of course, the actual work of doing the research and providing the feedback and discussion needed to mature these ideas fell substantially to my colleagues at the Technology & Policy Research Initiative. Thanks go to Boston University School of Law, our funders, and Erich Denk, Maarten Goos, Stephen Michael Impink, Sina Khoshsokhan, Joowon Kim, James Kossuth, Chen Meng, Mike Meurer, Lydia Reichensperger, Cesare Righi, Anna Salomons, Tim Simcoe, and Victoria Smith.

Thanks also to various coauthors, commenters, providers of data, and other helpful people: Daron Acemoglu, Philippe Aghion, David Autor, Stefan Bechtold, Victor Bennett, Seth Benzell, Pietro Biroli, Peter Blair, Dennis Carlton, Marcus Casey, Jorge Contreras, Claude Diebolt, Josh Feng, Martin Fleming, Richard Freeman, Walt Frick, Maarten Goos, Dietmar Harhoff, Philipp Hartmann, Ricardo Hausmann, Joachim Henkel, Ke-Wei Huang, Andrea Ichino, Stephen Michael Impink, Egbert Jongen, Brian Kahin, Sina Khoshsokhan, Megan MacGarvie, Michael Mandel, Joe Mazur, Kristina McElheran, Mike Meurer, Filippo Mezzanotti, Guy Michaels, Joel Mokyr, Tim O'Reilly, Emilie Rademakers, Pascual Restrepo, Daniel Rock, Nancy Rose, Ronja Röttger, Bob Rowthorn, Anna Salomons, Mike Scherer, Dick Schmalensee, Rob Seamans, Carl Shapiro, Tim Simcoe, Ken Simons, John Turner, Helene Turon, Gabriel Unger, Wiljan van den Berge, Jeroen van den Bosch, Bas van der Klaauw, Rory van Loo, John van Reenen, Hal Varian, and Georg von Graevenitz.

Other people provided valuable insights in interviews, including Paul Blaha, Iain Cockburn, Daniel Dines, Dan Faulkner, Ian Hathaway, Sue Helper, Bob Hunt, Bill Janeway, and Frank Wnek. Elias Wolfberg and Halle Gordon answered questions and provided access to a number of Amazon executives.

Thanks finally to Lisa Adams, my agent, who helped me cobble together a book proposal; Erich Denk, who served as an able research assistant; Mike Meurer, my always available sounding board; Eric Maskin, my mentor; and, of course, my wife and family, who put up with me during the writing.

The New Goliaths

1

Introduction

When Sharon Buchanan came to work on June 26, 1974, she noticed a larger than normal group of people milling about. Sharon worked at a Marsh Supermarkets grocery store in Troy, Ohio, not far from Dayton. The previous night, engineers and technicians had installed a bar code scanner in her checkout lane, and they were eager to see how it worked in practice. Joining them were executives from the grocery chain and from local companies that had developed the technology. Clyde Dawson, a Marsh executive, was Sharon's first customer, and when she scanned his sixty-seven-cent pack of Wrigley's Juicy Fruit gum, it marked the first commercial use of bar code scanners in retail.[1] Since that initial scan, use of this technology has become ubiquitous. More than five billion bar codes are scanned each and every day. The technology has transformed not just the retail industries but many other industries as well. That pack of gum is now in the National Museum of American History in Washington, D.C.

Notably, Marsh Supermarkets was not a major national chain but a modest-sized regional grocer. Like many digital technologies of the 1970s and 1980s, the bar code scanner was affordable and helped small companies compete against larger rivals. This was especially true as the prices of digital hardware plummeted. Greater affordability to a much broader market made many new digital technologies "disruptive innovations."[2]

That would soon change. Walmart—then another regional chain—had also adopted the bar code scanner early on. But it was able to build a large system based on the technology, and it would eventually come to dominate the industry. Whereas bar code scanners initially allowed smaller firms to compete with big ones on a more equal footing, new systems have allowed large firms to dominate their markets. The technology is now tilting the playing field instead of leveling it. The story of bar code technology illustrates deep economic changes taking place that affect many industries and society more generally.

Rise of the Chains

The retail playing field began tilting toward larger firms during the early twentieth century with the rise of chain stores.[3] In the grocery segment, this chain store revolution was led by John Hartford of A&P, who introduced the cash-and-carry economy store in 1912. At the turn of the twentieth century, consumers typically purchased groceries from an array of specialty shops (butcher, baker, candlestick maker) that were supplied by a network of middlemen wholesalers and jobbers. These shops sold on credit and provided delivery. Hartford eliminated credit and delivery, standardized the format of A&P's stores as well as the selection of goods sold in them, introduced centralized accounting, control, and purchasing, and built central warehouses and a distribution network that used the company's own trucks in order to cut out the middlemen. In addition, A&P purchased in bulk quantities, extracting the most favorable prices from manufacturers or, in many cases, providing its own store brands at lower cost.

This business model innovation gave A&P several advantages over the independent grocery shops. Distribution costs were lower thanks to standardization, economies of scale, and a centralized warehousing and delivery network; the markups of middlemen were eliminated; and with better accounting and inventory management, the chain could better forecast demand for each product and keep stores shelves full of the items that were selling. The chain stores passed part of these lower costs on to consumers. Studies of the 1920s and 1930s find that chain store prices were 4.5 percent to 14 percent lower than the prices charged by independent stores.

The chain store business model was not an engineering or scientific innovation. Instead, the innovation was in the organizational technology of bureaucratic control. As historian James Beniger argues, beginning in the nineteenth century, faster industrial production demanded new methods to control the flow of information in order to manage greater and greater volumes in the production and distribution of goods.[4] In Hartford's model at A&P, information about sales and inventory flowed to central head-quarters, where managers made decisions about what to stock, where to place it, and how to price it. Standardization limited the amount of information that had to be managed. Centralized decision-making with stan-dardized products and stores meant that A&P could invest profitably in the large fixed costs of warehouses and trucking fleets. And these provided economies of scale that meant lower costs and lower prices.

These advantages allowed the chain to grow. During the early decades, A&P opened a new store every three days on average, growing from 650 stores in 1914 to more than 15,000 stores by the Great Depression. The chain accounted for over 11 percent of the grocery business in the United States. Other chain stores, including Kroger, American Stores, Safeway, and First National, also grew rapidly. These top five chains grew to account for over 29 percent of grocery sales by 1931.

The growing dominance of chain stores was devastating to small inde-pendents, driving thousands of stores out of business. Some formed co-operatives to gain the advantages of scale and centralized distribution. And political backlash was strong. Beginning in 1922, the National Association of Retail Grocers pushed for laws to restrain chain stores, including taxes on chain store locations and merchandise and zoning laws to limit the number of chain outlets. Most states passed laws inhibiting chain store growth, and in 1936 Congress passed the Robinson-Patman Act, designed to protect small retailers by restricting the discounts that large chains could exact from manufacturers. Nevertheless, ever since the 1920s and continu-ing through the era of supermarkets and shopping centers, large chain stores have commanded a substantial share of the grocery market.

Levelers

When it was introduced, then, bar code scanner technology pre-sented a real opportunity for midsized grocery firms: it was a technology they could afford but also one that provided significant benefits. Before this possibility could be realized, however, the industry had to solve a chicken-and-egg problem. The scanner was most useful when manufacturers printed the bar codes on the item packaging. So, the benefit to grocers grew as more manufacturers signed on. But manufacturers were reluctant to alter their packaging until they were sure that sufficient numbers of grocers really wanted the bar code. Furthermore, bar codes needed to be standardized so that the codes on packages would all be readable by the particular scanners the grocers installed.

Six trade associations—representing both manufacturers and grocers—formed a committee to develop such a standard, and in 1973, they released the universal product code (UPC).[5] This is the bar code standard we use today and the one that was first scanned in Marsh Supermarkets' Troy store in June 1974. But initial adoption of the bar code scanner was slow, as is typical of many new technologies. In part this was because of limitations and cost of the initial technology, and in part it was because only two thousand food and beverage manufacturers initially printed bar codes on their products. Gradually, though, a trickle of grocers installed the equipment and more and more manufacturers added bar codes to their packaging. By 1984, thirteen thousand manufacturers had signed up, and by 1985, 29 percent of supermarkets used the scanners.[6]

The early adopters tended to be large independents or regional chains, and in fact, the large national chains were relatively slow to adopt the technology.[7] The smallest stores were even less likely to adopt bar code scanners because the technology was still relatively costly.

For midsized chains, the bar code scanner made economic sense because it delivered real benefits. Consider, for example, Dick's Supermarkets in southern Wisconsin. Dick's installed scanners in 1978 when the company had five stores and 325 employees. Bill Brodbeck, son of the founder of the chain, told the local newspaper: "Scanners reduce the time spent in checkout lines and provide customers with a receipt tape that identifies each item purchased in addition to its price."[8]

A major benefit of the new system was that it saved costs by automating tasks. Indeed, the main reason early adopters gave for installing the new technology was its labor-saving potential. With scanners, less of the cashier's time was required to check out a customer's groceries. A study by the U.S. Department of Agriculture found that scanners could reduce checker time by 18–19 percent.[9] In addition, at many stores the labor required to put price stickers on each item was eliminated. And because the scanners were connected to computers that kept a real-time inventory, frequent manual store inventories were no longer needed. Economist Emek Basker estimates that scanners reduced labor costs per dollar of revenue by 4.5 percent.[10]

Perhaps an even greater benefit of the new system was the improved service that stores could provide their customers. Shoppers benefited from faster checkout times and the receipt tape, of course. But the system also let the store provide different consumers the products they wanted when they wanted them. In a 1987 interview, Dave Hymer, senior vice president of sales of Dick's Supermarkets, said, "We could not effectively merchandise our stores without the scanner information. What sells in Platteville does not necessarily sell in Prairie du Chien. So we use data on an individual store basis to set shelves and arrange the product facings so that we attain maximum sales and productivity from every foot of display space." In addition to tailoring the product offerings in different stores, the system allowed store managers to discover which products were dogs and which ones were moneymakers. The slow movers could be weeded out to make way for new products, so that a store's product mix constantly changed. Moreover, the inventory could be managed efficiently to reduce stockouts of high-selling products and stock a greater variety of items. "We don't believe in shooting from the hip," Hymer said. Store managers were encouraged to be creative with merchandising and to use the scanner information to make the store more profitable.[11]

According to the *Progressive Grocer,* the combination of leading-edge technology and talented personnel made Dick's Supermarkets "one of the savviest food retailers anywhere" and an effective competitor against even national chain stores. In 1985, Dick's opened a store in Prairie du Chien, population six thousand, competing against a store in the national Piggly Wiggly franchise chain. "The competition was well-established, but did not have the variety or the style that we have," Dave Hymer told the *Progressive Grocer.*[12]

As the basic technology improved, the scanners could read smaller bar codes and wet or damaged labels. And the number of manufacturers providing bar codes increased dramatically. Perhaps most important, the price of the hardware, including computers, dropped sharply, making installation much more affordable to smaller stores.

The Age of Disruption

The emergence of the personal computer (PC) and the sharp fall in computing prices spurred the adoption of new digital technologies across many industries. And in many, these technologies allowed small companies to compete on a level playing field or even to displace less nimble, established large firms. In 1995, *Inc.* magazine enthused:

> Can information technology (IT) make a David seem like a Goliath? According to the CEOs and company presidents we spoke with, the answer is an unqualified yes. In today's world of networked databases, E-mail, CD-ROM subscriptions, and teleconferencing, success is determined less by size than by technological muscle. Even companies of 15 or 20 can gather market data in all parts of the world, establish long-distance strategic partnerships, advertise anywhere via the World Wide Web, or hold international sales meetings—and their employees never have to leave the office.
>
> Competing with big business is easier than ever now that IT is so affordable. Ten years ago, purchasing a high-powered computer system could set a small company back half a year's revenues.[13]

At first, many of the new technologies were simply cheaper versions of technologies that ran on expensive mainframe or minicomputers. Basic accounting and payroll programs had run on mainframe computers since the 1950s. Now they became available on desktop computers for a few hundred dollars. The same was true for tax preparation software. During the 1970s, companies such as Wang provided word processor systems on dedicated minicomputers. Comparable software programs soon became available on PCs.

And a whole slew of niche applications was ported to personal computers, making them more affordable. For example, Primavera Systems introduced a PC-based project management system in 1983 that was ported from a minicomputer program. This program allowed managers to plan, implement, and track detailed plans for complex projects in construction and other fields. These systems had formerly been too expensive for many companies. Now large numbers of small and large general contractors began using PC-based project management systems.

Many applications soon went beyond their mainframe or minicomputer ancestors. They became interactive, they incorporated graphical user interfaces that made it easier for people to learn the systems, and they added new and important features. Although it had been possible to compute a spreadsheet in batch mode on a mainframe computer since 1969, with the introduction of VisiCalc in 1979, spreadsheets could be entered interactively on a personal computer, providing much greater ease of use, real-time adaptability, and other powerful tools for customizing spreadsheets to a wide variety of uses.

Not only did these changes upend the software industry, but many companies began to create custom applications for their specific needs using inexpensive off-the-shelf spreadsheet programs and desktop computers. All sorts of businesses, large and small, were able to use the new tools in innovative ways. The exuberance of the *Inc.* writer about the opportunities for small firms was real and widely experienced.

I experienced that exuberance firsthand. In 1983 I was managing a small weekly newspaper in Philadelphia, the first bilingual paper serving the city's Hispanic population. As at many small publications, composing ads was a pain in the neck. Many ads came in just at deadline. They had to be composed quickly and pages assembled around them. Any mistakes and we might not get paid.

The first IBM PC had just been announced, and I realized I could program it to compose the text graphically on screen (with the help of a specialized Hercules graphics adapter card) and output it to a phototypesetting machine. I did that and built the first what-you-see-is-what-you-get (WYSIWYG) desktop publishing program. Soon we were using it to produce ads and assemble pages for our publications.

At the time I wrote this software, I was vaguely aware that there were advanced systems built on minicomputers or engineering workstations that could do similar things. The Atex system had been widely adopted at large newspapers during the 1970s. This was a specialized word-processing system running on a Digital minicomputer that was specifically tailored to the needs of daily newspapers. But Atex did not have WYSIWYG page composition. There were also specialized advertising composition workstations that did offer WYSIWYG displays. But they cost $100,000 or more, putting them far out of the reach of small newspapers and magazines.

I first tried to sell my program to a typesetting company. It turned me down and decided to develop a similar product of its own. Plan B was to sell it myself. In April 1984, I purchased a ten-by-ten-foot booth at the back of the exhibit hall of a trade show for printing and typesetting. My wife and I staffed the booth, showing our product in action. We were soon mobbed, much to the chagrin of the large typesetting companies across the aisle. And we were exuberant.

Our company and others soon made desktop publishing widely available, and all sorts of people became familiar with fonts, kerning, and the argot of typesetting.[14] An array of newsletters and other publications that were once composed on a typewriter were now designed with highly styled type. *Desktop Publishing* magazine appeared in 1985, the publishers claiming, "It has become cost-effective for almost anyone using a personal computer to prepare documents that appear professionally published. The new publishing tools put book making, newsletter publishing, magazine design, ad layout, manual production, and promotional literature publishing into the hands of personal computer users who never before had the opportunity to do these things." They also quoted the journalist A. J. Liebling's statement that "freedom of the press is guaranteed only to those who own one."[15] Liebling had made the remark in 1960 while reporting on the American Newspaper Publishers Association annual meeting, noting how consolidation of the newspaper industry was limiting the range of views that newspapers represented.

Desktop publishing did indeed allow more people to own the press. The number of weekly newspapers had been falling for decades, from 11,516 in 1939 to 6,798 in 1984. But over the next five years, the net number of weeklies grew by over 824. The number of monthly periodicals grew by 349. Even the number of daily newspapers increased from 1,646 in 1987 to 1,788 in 1990. Decades of industry consolidation dominated by large newspaper and magazine chains gave way to a brief renaissance of new publications. The renaissance was short-lived, however, because the Internet grew rapidly in the 1990s, taking advertising away from print publishers, large and small.

The rapid growth of inexpensive computers and the flood of new software packages likely contributed to a general increase in industry dynamism in other industries, too. One way to measure industry dynamism is to look at the turnover rate of dominant firms within each industry—how often the dominant firms get displaced by up-and-coming firms. An industry where the top firms are under constant competitive threat from rising rivals is one where firms will innovate to stay ahead. An industry where established firms are not under threat of being displaced is one with at best weak incentives to innovate. As economist John Hicks once noted, "The best of all monopoly profits is a quiet life."[16] In 1970, dominant firms did have a relatively quiet life on average. Across all narrowly defined industries, the probability that a firm would fall out of the top-four ranking by sales in its industry was about 6 percent. By the late 1990s, that turnover rate had doubled to 12–13 percent. Those decades appear to have been a period of increasing disruption as innovative firms leapfrogged established incumbents, a kind of renaissance for startups and smaller firms.

A New Goliath

Like the renaissance for small publications, the renaissance for small retailers brought by the bar code scanner was short-lived. A few firms were able to build new systems and organizations using bar code technology to great effect, and they grew to dominate the various retailing segments. Neither small retailers nor large established chain stores could compete with them.

Walmart provides the most dramatic example. Here is a summary from the *Harvard Business Review:*

> In 1979, Kmart was king of the discount retailing industry, an industry it had virtually created. With 1,891 stores and average revenues per store of $7.25 million, Kmart enjoyed enormous size advantages. This allowed economies of scale in purchasing, distribution, and marketing that, according to just about any management textbook, are crucial to competitive success in a mature and low-growth industry. By contrast, Wal-Mart was a small niche retailer in the South with only 229 stores and average revenues about half of those of Kmart stores—hardly a serious competitor.
>
> And yet, only ten years later, Wal-Mart had transformed itself and the discount retailing industry. Growing nearly 25% a year, the

company achieved the highest sales per square foot, inventory turns, and operating profit of any discount retailer. Its 1989 pretax return on sales was 8%, nearly double that of Kmart. Today [1992] Wal-Mart is the largest and highest profit retailer in the world.[17]

In 1982, Walmart accounted for 3 percent of the sales of U.S. general merchandise retailers; thirty years later, Walmart's U.S. sales comprised 52 percent of industry sales. Kmart, on the other hand, merged with Sears in 2004, and the new company declared Chapter 11 bankruptcy in 2018.

And the impact was at least as devastating for small retailers. One study finds that each new Walmart store reduces the number of small retailers (those with fewer than one hundred employees) by 4.7 stores on average.[18] Between 1977 and 2007, Walmart opened three thousand stores. Another study finds that Walmart's expansion explains approximately half of the decline in single-store general merchandisers in the United States between 1987 and 1997. Moreover, when Walmart enters a market, the profits of more than half of the stores fall so that they can no longer recover their sunk costs.[19] In other words, if they were starting over again, they would choose not to enter the market because profits were so low.

Walmart was a relatively early adopter of bar code scanning in the general merchandise industry.[20] By the late 1980s, the company had the technology in all of its distribution centers. These scanners generated a firehose of information—every purchase of every item at every checkout lane in every store. But rather than just direct that information to headquarters for centralized decision-making as in the chain store model, Walmart turned the flow around to support decentralized decision-making by individual store managers and even by suppliers. By the late 1970s, all distribution centers were linked by a computer network.[21] In 1987, Walmart completed its own $24 million satellite network to facilitate communications between stores and headquarters. This was the largest private satellite communication system in the United States at the time.[22] In 1990, Walmart introduced Retail Link—software connecting its stores, distribution centers, and suppliers and providing detailed inventory data "to bring our suppliers closer to our individual stores."[23] Suppliers could track sales at individual stores and generate orders to restock shelves quickly. In some cases, computers generated the new orders using automated purchasing technology.

Perhaps the biggest single benefit was that Walmart stores could dramatically increase the number of products offered, facilitating one-stop shopping. By using information technology to decentralize decision-making, Walmart reduced the cost of managing an additional product line, allowing the stores to handle many more items. Although Walmart began as a purely general merchandise discount store, with this technology it soon expanded its product lines, initially experimenting with different store formats. In 1988 it introduced the Supercenter format that not only sells general merchandise but also includes a full-service supermarket selling dry and frozen goods, meat, poultry, fresh seafood and produce, and a range of other services including pharmacies, optical stores, photography services, tire and lube services, hair and nail salons, cellular phone stores, banks, and fast food providers.

With greater variety, Walmart is more likely to have the goods the consumer wants, and one-stop shopping makes it easier to purchase a range of products and services. Walmart had long touted one-stop shopping as the reason why "customers choose our Supercenters."[24] And consumers agree; in a poll asking the "best thing about Wal-Mart," 22 percent named its broad selection and variety.[25] One study finds that consumers are willing to pay a premium to shop at Walmart because of this advantage.[26]

It is, of course, costly to handle more items and more product lines in a store. While John Hartford's chain store strategy had been to limit and standardize the number of products in order to make centralized decision-making feasible and cost effective, Walmart turned that model on its head by using information technology to manage complexity efficiently. This provided a strong competitive advantage that differentiated Walmart from its rivals.

The greater number of products per store and the large volume of the stores in each region also created significant economies of scale. Walmart abandoned the traditional chain store warehouse model in favor of a logistics practice called cross-docking. In the traditional warehouse system, when product would come in from suppliers, these trucks would be unloaded, and the items would be stored on warehouse shelves. Later, when stores needed resupply, workers would fetch the items off the shelves and load them on trucks for delivery to the stores. In Walmart's system, supplier trucks unloaded at the warehouse, but the goods, rather than being stored on shelves for later retrieval, were directly loaded on delivery trucks for distribution to the stores. The Walmart approach eliminated much of the cost of warehousing labor. In order for this system to work, supply trucks had to arrive at roughly the same time as the trucks that would take the goods the last miles to the stores. Rich data flows and information technology made this coordination possible. As one study noted, "Cross-docking enables Wal-Mart to achieve the economies that come with purchasing full truckloads of goods while avoiding the usual inventory and handling costs."[27] In the grocery segment, the savings meant that Walmart Supercenters (which include groceries) charge about 10 percent less for the same products in the same markets relative to traditional supermarkets.[28] These savings allowed Walmart to pursue an Everyday Low Prices strategy, charging less than competitors and bringing in additional retail traffic. They also saved the expense of frequent promotional sales, making sales more predictable with fewer stockouts and lower inventory.

Walmart could realize these benefits only by sending a steady flow of information on individual stores' sales outward to suppliers and store managers. The inward flow of products also brought time savings. Suppliers could respond more quickly as the demand for individual products waxed and waned, making sure that the hot items of the moment were in stock in each store and that they didn't end up with excess inventory when fads faded. With its dedicated fleet of company-owned trucks Walmart could get goods from warehouse to store in less than forty-eight hours. The company managed to replenish stores' shelves twice a week on average, compared to an industry norm of once every two weeks.

Last, this system meant that the flow of goods was highly tailored to each specific store, giving each store the variety of products that were in demand in that local market.

This system was not just about the information technology. To be sure, many large retailers invested heavily in technology. Walmart wasn't alone in investing in technology to manage retail information. Sears was a leader in many retail technologies. The company was IBM's largest customer during the late 1980s and pioneered e-commerce on its Prodigy system. But Walmart did something different, marrying information technology to a new type of organization. It turned the chain store model of John Hartford around and used information technology to decentralize decision-making, allowing countless decisions to be made quickly and efficiently, creating stores that better met customer needs. It was this combination of technology and organization that allowed Walmart to grow while Sears and Kmart and countless smaller retailers struggled and often failed.

Information and Technology

The cost of computing has had an extraordinary fall; the cost of reproducing software is often negligible, leading to free or nearly free services. These changes are important, but my focus in this book is on another phenomenon: information technology is changing the economy because it is changing the way economic actors use information. Because information is so important to the nature of markets and economic institutions, the technology of information affects key aspects of how the economy works.

Indeed, one of the major achievements of economic analysis since World War II is the understanding that information—what economic actors know and what they don't—has profound effects on the workings of the economy. Information is understood to play a role in why markets fail. It affects the boundaries and organizations of firms, how contracts are made, how institutions are designed to provide the best incentives, and how regulation can be designed. A casual look at the list of economics Nobel laureates shows that it is dominated by people who have contributed to the economics of information.

This research agenda began with a critique of socialist economic planning initially by Ludwig von Mises and later by Friedrich Hayek.[29] Socialists were advocating central planning boards that would control the economy by allocating resources to production and distribution. Mises and then Hayek, critiquing socialist economic planning, argued that prices were needed to run an economy. In a seminal paper, "The Use of Knowledge in Society," published in 1945, Hayek posed the question of how to organize an economy, arguing that a critical problem was information or knowledge:

> The peculiar character of the problem of a rational economic order
> is determined precisely by the fact that the knowledge of the cir-
> cumstances of which we must make use never exists in concentrated

or integrated form, but solely as the dispersed bits of incomplete and frequently contradictory knowledge which all the separate individuals possess. The economic problem of society . . . is a problem of how to secure the best use of resources known to any of the members of society, for ends whose relative importance only these individuals know. Or, to put it briefly, it is a problem of the utilization of knowledge not given to anyone in its totality.[30]

The challenge, moreover, was not just obtaining the knowledge but also inducing disparate economic agents to act in the socially optimal way.[31] Socialist central planning might promise a fairer economy, but it would fail because planners could neither know the disparate and changing needs of a complex economy nor effectively guide disparate economic actors to address those needs.

Other economists developed this notion further and extended the analysis of information and knowledge into other areas.[32] Two closely related problems of economic knowledge are related to Hayek's question. First, much of this knowledge is broadly dispersed, highly local, and changes frequently, making it difficult or impossible for a central planner to acquire, for a single mind to know. Second, many economic actors won't truthfully reveal their knowledge to planners or to other economic actors. For instance, a manufacturer has information about the quality of its product but may be reluctant to reveal that information to prospective customers, especially if the product's quality is not good. This is known as private or asymmetric information (one party has more relevant information than the other), and it affects a wide range of economic interaction.

Such information concerns explain a lot about the rise of chain stores and the subsequent rise of Walmart. Retailers seek to acquire the best-quality goods from manufacturers at the best price. But they lack information about the quality of different manufacturers' offerings. Manufacturers might have varying reputations, but retailers basically have to learn the quality of goods through experience.[33] They have to stock them, see how they sell, and see how customers like the goods or if they return them. This learning is costly and time-consuming, especially when many new products are becoming available all the time. As a result, an independent retailer must choose between offering a limited selection or stocking goods of uncertain quality.

Chain stores realize economies of scale through standardization, in addition to other economies, such as those affecting distribution costs. This means that chain stores can provide an assured level of quality and offer a somewhat greater selection of goods. Of course, this centralization of decision-making has a downside—the chain ignores much local information, it has a limited ability to tailor offerings to different areas that might have varying tastes, and it is slow to respond to local changes. The chain store model trades the ability to adapt to local information for a reduction in the costs of obtaining information about product quality. Chain stores and other large enterprises introduce an element of central planning into capitalism, and by doing so, they suffer from Hayek's problem of local information known to dispersed individuals.

The Walmart business model also saves learning costs by sharing information about product quality between outlets, but because it decentralizes decision-making, it can adapt better to local information. By decentralizing critical information, Walmart permits store managers to adjust to local demand under the watchful monitoring of central headquarters, and it handles the complex distribution of varied goods to different stores. At the same time, it facilitates sharing of information between stores about new products and changing demand. The technology also manages to distribute the changing goods to the stores quickly and efficiently. These advantages mean that Walmart can cost-effectively offer far greater selection in its stores, providing the product quality that consumers want.

Information technology can adapt to local information because it permits basic economies of scope. Well-designed software is modular; code to handle an additional product or feature can be developed largely independently at relatively low cost compared to physical systems.[34] With these scope economies, information technology breaks the deadlock between local information needs and the cost savings that come with standardization. This change to the economics of information fundamentally alters the economic order.

Walmart is not an isolated example. Other firms in other industries are using information technology to adapt to individual or local information. And the playing field has tilted in other industries, too: similar stories can be told about other firms coming to dominance and then using new information technology to remain on top. These narratives run counter to a widely held view that we live in an age of hypercompetition. Joseph Schumpeter's notion of creative destruction and Clayton Christensen's ideas about corporate disruption have wide currency. Many experts, such as Alan Greenspan, believe that we live in a time of accelerated creative destruction.

I contest this disruption myth, and in the chapters that follow we'll explore why it has become a myth. In chapter 2 I present evidence that the rate of disruption of leading companies has sharply declined over the past two decades and show that firms have become dominant by making major investments in proprietary software. These new systems enable leading firms to compete by leveraging complexity—that is, to offer dramatically greater variety, more features, or more product versions.

But why should investments in proprietary software lead to the persistent dominance of large firms? In chapter 3 I argue that competing on complexity changes the nature of markets and industry structure. Complexity in products and services allows firms to differentiate their offerings from those of rivals. Following the ideas of John Sutton, such competition gives rise to "natural oligopolies," industries where a few "superstar" firms—the ones that have made the investments and mastered the technology—dominate.[35] The dominance of the top firms is not just a matter that they have better managers or higher-quality workers. It's also that the nature of competition has changed in many industries, magnifying performance differences and changing firm behavior.

A key implication of this new kind of competition is that knowledge of new technologies does not spread through society as rapidly as it has in the past. In chapter 4 we'll explore a puzzle about how firms manage to maintain dominant positions based on new technology. In the past, knowledge of major new technologies spread to rival firms, increasing competition. New knowledge was shared, it was licensed, it was copied, and it was independently developed. That appears to be happening to a lesser extent or more slowly today. I suggest two major reasons: dominant firms don't have incentives to license their technology because doing so would reduce their differentiation from rivals; and the complexity of the technology limits how easily rival firms can imitate or develop independently. This slower "diffusion" of technical knowledge is critical to the impact of the superstar economy. In chapters 6, 7, and 8 I'll spell out how slower diffusion is changing industry dynamism, the growth prospects of startup firms, productivity growth, income inequality, and even the ability of regulators to govern.

But before that, in chapter 5, I confront a common misconception: that the effects of new technology are mainly about automating work, threatening to create unemployment. I contend that automation does not necessarily lead to mass unemployment; it is not doing so today, nor is it likely to do so in the next couple decades. Although automation does compel many workers to undergo costly transitions to new jobs requiring new skills, the far bigger impact of new technology lies elsewhere.

The significance of slower diffusion goes far beyond industry structure. The fingerprints of superstar capitalism are all over today's economy. In chapter 6 we'll look at industry dynamism and the fate of smaller, innovative firms. A critical factor is that smaller firms now see headwinds to growth; lacking access to the most advanced technologies, highly productive small firms have grown more slowly on average since 2000. It's not that the number of innovative startups has declined. Instead, they enter the marketplace but grow more slowly. The net effect, however, is to reduce aggregate productivity growth.

Also, because access to the new technologies is limited, workers face greater difficulty acquiring skills related to these technologies, creating a skills gap for employers and greater income inequality for employees. In chapter 7 I explore how these gaps are exacerbating income differences between workers at different firms, diverse occupations, and varied places.

Limited access to the data and software used in products and services has another effect: it undermines government regulation. In chapter 8 we'll see how the growing dependence regulators have on information limits their abilities to govern, leading to major failures such as the diesel emissions scandal, the Boeing 737 MAX catastrophe, and the subprime mortgage market collapse leading to the Great Recession.

These problems with industry dynamism, productivity growth, inequality, and regulation arise substantially from slow diffusion or limited access. But these outcomes are not technologically determined. Firms, guided by laws and institutions, make their own choices about licensing or sharing data, software, or related knowledge. The key policy challenge is to encourage firms to license or share more, diffusing knowledge more rapidly, ameliorating these problems, and allowing the considerable benefits of the new technology to be shared throughout society.

In chapter 9 we'll look specifically at the role of digital platforms, which have been a subject of particular concern regarding antitrust law and a focus of congressional hearings. Digital platforms complicate antitrust analysis, making it harder to manage competition policy. But although Big Tech platforms deserve close antitrust scrutiny, the challenge that dominant firms pose today concerns much more than a handful of digital platform companies and goes far beyond competition policy. Strengthening antitrust enforcement is a good idea, but it is likely not enough to remedy the challenge of the superstar economy. Nor is breaking up big firms likely to remedy the problems that have much more to do with access to knowledge than with firm size per se.

Indeed, in chapter 10 I argue that open platforms should be encouraged; they are essential to undoing some of the damage superstar capitalism has done to productivity, inequality, safety, and security. The creation of open platforms when IBM unbundled its software and when Amazon unbundled its IT infrastructure and its website unleashed highly dynamic industry growth that worked to level the playing field for small firms, creating opportunities for growth in productivity, skills, and pay. However, significant policies, particularly regarding intellectual property, diminish the incentives for dominant firms to unbundle.

In concluding, I suggest in chapter 11 that with the right policy balance we can move toward a new economic order, one that excels at meeting disparate consumer demands but with greater opportunity for workers and innovative firms and a fairer, more cohesive, and better managed society. A sustainable information economy is not merely one where large numbers of people work with information; it is one where new knowledge is actively developed and widely shared.

2

Disruption Lost

The *Economist* called Clayton Christensen, who died in early 2020, "the most influential management thinker of his time."[1] Christensen's seminal work is *The Innovator's Dilemma,* published in 1997. In this book, he argues that good managers at leading firms can be "disrupted" by new technologies that they don't see initially as a serious threat. By focusing on the needs of their most profitable customers, leading companies can miss new technologies that are initially cheap and inferior but that become better over time until firms using these technologies supplant the leaders.

This notion of disruption has powerful appeal. Historian and journalist Jill Lepore writes in the *New Yorker:*

> Ever since "The Innovator's Dilemma," everyone is either disrupting or being disrupted. There are disruption consultants, disruption con-ferences, and disruption seminars. This fall, the University of Southern California is opening a new program: "The degree is in disruption," the university announced. "Disrupt or be disrupted," the venture cap-italist Josh Linkner warns in a new book, "The Road to Reinvention," in which he argues that "fickle consumer trends, friction-free markets, and political unrest," along with "dizzying speed, exponential com-plexity, and mind-numbing technology advances," mean that the time has come to panic as you've never panicked before.[2]

This concept of disruption and the belief that the pace of disruption is dramatically increasing have become core tenets of thinking about technology. Many economists and businesspeople adhere to the view of Joseph Schumpeter that capitalism is all about disruption; it is a process of "industrial mutation . . . that incessantly revolutionizes the economic structure *from within,* incessantly destroying the old one, incessantly creating a new one. This process of Creative Destruction is the essential fact about capitalism. It is what capitalism consists in and what every capitalist concern has got to live in."[3]

And this view captured an element of reality. When Christensen published his book, the pace at which industry-leading firms were disrupted had been increasing for decades. Yet a strange thing happened shortly after *The Innovator's Dilemma* was published: the rate of disruption of market leaders declined sharply.

Today the likelihood that a top firm in any industry will be displaced by a rival is less than half of what it was in the late 1990s. Figure 1 shows the probability that a firm ranked in the top four by sales in its industry is bumped out of the top four in any four-year period.[4] The rate of disruption increased from the 1970s to the late 1990s. The increase in disruption and the corresponding decrease in the persistence of firm profits was noted by researchers, leading some to claim that we had entered an era of "hypercompetition."[5] But the rate of disruption sharply reversed trend around 2000. If we look at other ways of measuring these displacement rates, the basic pattern is the same: the displacement of industry leaders happened more and more frequently until sometime in the late 1990s or early 2000s; then it began happening much less often.[6]

This finding seems surprising because in many ways technology *is* disrupting our lives, or at least changing them in important ways. We now fill our hours connected to the Internet; we read our news online; we entertain ourselves differently with games and videos; we shop online. Because we change our behavior in response to new technology, we disrupt industries in a sense. Online advertising disrupts the newspaper industry; e-commerce disrupts retail. However, while these changes have driven some retailers and some newspaper companies out of business, the industry leaders remain firmly entrenched. Although struggling in e-commerce, Walmart still dominates retail; News Corp., Gannett, and the *New York Times* still dominate the newspaper industry. So, while technology is still highly disruptive in a general sense, the dis-

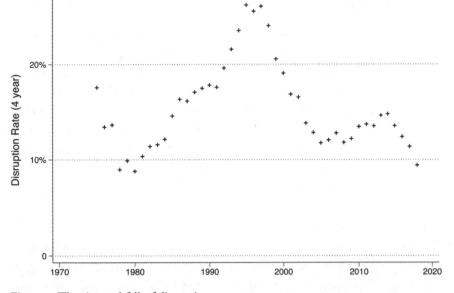

Figure 1. The rise and fall of disruption
Source: Bessen et al., "Declining Industrial Disruption."

placement of industry-leading firms is far lower despite the hype about disruption.

Walmart is one data point illustrating the changing trend. Walmart disrupted Sears to become the largest U.S. retailer by sales in 1990. Yet in the thirty subsequent years, Walmart has become increasingly entrenched. No other brick-and-mortar retailer comes even close to it in sales. But the change in disruption rates occurred not just in retail and not just in Big Tech but through most sectors of the economy, including wholesale, finance, manufacturing, transport, mining, and communications. This reversal in the probability of disruption of industry leaders is substantial, it is happening across the economy, and it represents a fundamental change in the nature of capitalist competition.

What is the chief driver of this change? A new generation of software-enabled business models that allows firms to compete in a different way. In industry after industry, new software empowered firms to compete on complexity—that is, to offer greater selection, more features, customized offerings, and/or greater targeting to better meet consumer needs.

Software Feature Wars

It is helpful to look at examples of firms that use proprietary software and how this changes the nature of competition. Some technologies such as electrical or steam power generation are called general purpose technologies because they can be used in a variety of industries.[7] But typically, such technologies must be adapted to each different industry, and this often takes decades, making their impact substantial but gradual.[8] While computer technology has been evolving for decades, some recent development appears to have allowed large firms in many different industries to take advantage of software in a new and distinct way within a relatively short time.

Walmart provides a critical clue as to what is going on. Recall that Walmart's advantage over other retailers was that its software allowed it to manage complexity more efficiently. Walmart stores could offer greater selection, facilitating one-stop shopping, and Walmart could coordinate the complex flow of these many goods from manufacturers to stores efficiently and quickly, reducing costs and increasing responsiveness to changing demand. Walmart bested its rivals by competing on quality enabled by complex software. During the 1990s software systems emerged, allowing leading firms to manage complexity in a variety of industries in order to deliver better-quality products and services than their rivals. These systems allowed leading firms to compete in a new and different way to become more dominant in their markets.

We can glimpse this new kind of competition in the early years of the personal computer software industry. The first major successful PC software product was VisiCalc, an electronic spreadsheet program introduced in 1979 for the new Apple computer. VisiCalc was the killer app for the Apple computer, the program that provided a reason for thousands of people to buy the computer to run the software.[9]

VisiCalc's success and rapid growth promoted entry into the market. By 1982 there were at least eighteen PC spreadsheet programs for sale. Although the market was growing rapidly, competition was fierce, and each new product sought to distinguish itself with distinctive new features. Indeed, competition in spreadsheet programs, word processors, and other popular PC products took the form of feature wars. Firms rapidly added new features, and each new generation of products was rated on the features and how well they were integrated. Typical was a review of eleven of the most popular PC spreadsheets in the issue of *PC Magazine* of October 27, 1987.[10] The programs were evaluated side by side on more than sixty features.

Firms raced to upgrade quickly, adding new features, sometimes those seen in competing products. This led to a kind of feature inflation, or bloat, as hundreds of features were added, not always well integrated. But it also led to aggressive competition. As one firm after another was able to come up with the best combination of features and to integrate them well, leadership of the industry shifted. VisiCalc was the early leader, but VisiCalc lacked an integrated ability to produce figures and charts. Lotus 1-2-3 introduced just such an integrated graphics capability in 1983 and rapidly displaced VisiCalc, gaining a 70 percent market share by 1988. But Lotus had a text-based interface, as was true of almost all applications running on the IBM-PC compatibles. Apple introduced the Macintosh, with a now-familiar graphical user interface, and Microsoft introduced the Excel spreadsheet program for it in 1985. Because Macintosh sales were limited, Excel was slow to catch on, but in 1988 the Microsoft Windows graphical user interface allowed Excel to run on the large base of IBM-PC compatibles. In 1991, Microsoft then delivered Microsoft Office, which bundled the spreadsheet program with a word processor (Word) and a presentation program (PowerPoint). Excel became the leader of the spreadsheet market in 1993 and has remained there since.

This pattern of competition was novel. To be sure, firms have competed on quality and features in many industries. One example is the well-known competition between Ford and General Motors in the 1920s. Henry Ford decided to make his cars highly standardized. Standardization reduced the variety, but it facilitated efficiency at scale, much as the standardization of products at A&P facilitated scale economies. Ford famously declared that customers could have "any color so long as it is black." He was intensely focused on driving down costs to make automobiles affordable, and allowing for multiple colors would have added equipment, labor, and a degree of complexity to the marketing and manufacturing process, increasing costs. Alfred Sloan at General Motors realized an opening, and beginning in 1923, GM introduced cars with multiple colors and stylish bodies that changed each model year. Consumers valued this variety, helping GM displace Ford as the automotive market leader.

But the software feature wars are very different from this kind of competition in the automobile industry. GM added just a few features, these were largely cosmetic, and auto production at GM was still highly standardized. In contrast, software firms added many substantive features and added them quickly. This is because the economics of adding software features is different. First, because of the nature of software code, many new features can be developed quickly and often without great cost. Indeed, the entire initial VisiCalc product was created by two guys (Dan Bricklin and Bob Frankston) in an attic in a matter of months. This property derives from the modular nature of software—modular systems can be designed so that each feature can be developed independently of the others as long as basic rules of interaction are followed.[11] In contrast, new features that involve physical transformations of material typically take much longer to develop and incur greater expense. Second, once a software feature is designed and developed and the integrated product is tested, there is little additional cost per unit sold.[12] That is not so for all features in physical products; the body styling of GM's cars required additional metalworking, likely increasing unit costs. These two properties make software extensible— that is, new features can be added at large scale without great cost.

This extensibility alters the nature of markets. It means that firms can rapidly increase features. By adding features, the product can better meet the needs of more individual customers, improving quality. Better quality gives firms a competitive edge, differentiating them from rivals. They leverage complexity to compete better. But this is a different sort of competition. For one, it can be highly dynamic when each new generation of product rapidly builds on and improves the previous generation by adding new features. The Nobel Prize–winning economist Eric Maskin and I first argued back in 1998 that this sort of sequential innovation explained a puzzle about the early software industry—namely, why it was highly innovative even though software could not generally be patented by itself.[13] Many economists contended that patents or some equivalent intellectual property protection were required to provide strong incentives to innovate. The software industry seemed to contradict that view. We showed that with sequential innovation, the expansion of demand via feature improvement could be so great that firms earn profits even if their technology is imitated. When an imitator copies a firm's product, the firm earns less from the product. But if the imitator adds important new features, the size of the market will increase and the imitated firm can incorporate the new features in its future products, increasing profits. Indeed, in the spreadsheet feature war the market grew dramatically: the number of spreadsheet units shipped increased tenfold from 1979 to 1983 and then tenfold again to 1993.

But competing on complexity means that eventually the leading products become highly complex, involving large numbers of features that require large initial fixed costs that rivals cannot profitably duplicate. When Microsoft became the market leader in 1993 with Excel 5.0, the product specification documents were 1,850 pages long, and the entire Microsoft Office Suite required large numbers of specialists to design the products, develop them, and test and support them.[14] This meant that few firms could compete in the spreadsheet market. Dozens of firms exited along the way, and Microsoft has solidified its market dominance since then, not only in the market for Windows spreadsheets, where it arguably could leverage its operating system dominance, but also in the Mac spreadsheet market. Microsoft is unlikely to be disrupted anytime soon.

The large investment required to produce a top-of-the-line product limits competition. It is not the only factor that allows Microsoft Office to continue to dominate; for instance, once users learn to use the product, they are reluctant to switch to a new one, although such switching costs did not prevent Lotus from replacing VisiCalc or prevent Excel from replacing Lotus.[15] But the large investment required to build the top-quality product is a key obstacle to rivals, and it plays a prominent role in shaping industry structure.

Competing on Complexity

In industries where software is not the product, large software systems allow firms to compete by leveraging complexity to improve the quality of products and services in a variety of ways. They can increase the features of the product to meet more heterogeneous needs. Or they can increase the varieties of product they offer, tailoring different products to different customers. Or, like Walmart, they can increase the selection available to consumers, also meeting diverse needs. Or they can customize products or marketing to target individual customers with well-matched products. Firms use software to manage greater complexity of products, of services, of distribution, and of marketing.[16] And they can take advantage of their software capabilities to rapidly change their products, services, distribution, and marketing as demand changes. These tactics use complex software to improve quality, but ideally, they do not make the products and services more complex for consumers to use. Of course, people have different preferences regarding quality; some prefer to shop at stores with less variety and more personal contact; some prefer to purchase products with fewer features that might be easier to operate. Nevertheless, complex software allows firms to compete more effectively for those customers who prefer more features and variety.

Firms that best manage this complexity differentiate their products from rivals and come to dominate their markets. Walmart excels at managing complex merchandising, logistics, and inventory control. That is true for retailers in other segments such as Amazon and for wholesalers. Waste management companies also use logistics to streamline garbage hauling and to respond more rapidly to changing customer demand. These companies have also been making large investments in information technology.

Manufacturers also leverage complexity for competitive advantage. The automobile has gotten much more complex since the days of competition over colors and body styles in the 1920s. Thirty years ago, cars had ten thousand components. Today, they have thirty thousand. But the biggest difference is in software. Today's automobiles contain fifty, one hundred, or more computers, all networked together. An average model contains more than one hundred million lines of software code. By comparison, the space shuttle has only four hundred thousand lines of code; Google Chrome and a Boeing 787 each have a bit over six million lines of code.

Yet it is not the sheer amount of code but the interactions among the various modules that really heighten the complexity. Consider automobile transmissions. In the days before electronic control, a transmission needed to adjust gearing based on the engine speed and torque. But today's transmission control modules—the computers that control transmissions—adapt to a wide range of sensors, and to optimize drivability, fuel economy, emissions, and safety, they interact with a variety of other modules. Typical transmission control modules take inputs from vehicle speed sensors, wheel speed sensors, throttle speed sensors, turbine speed sensors, transmission fluid temperature sensors, and switches detecting braking, full pedal position, and fluid pressure in various hydraulic lines, as well as inputs from the traction control system, cruise control system, and other control modules. In turn, transmission control modules send output signals to solenoids to shift gears, and to lock the shift lever if the brake is not depressed, to multiple pressure control solenoids to control the working of the transmission, to the torque converter clutch, and to the engine control unit and other controllers. All of these multiple inputs and outputs enable a wide variety of interactions. For instance, the signals that the transmission control unit sends to the engine control unit might be used to retard ignition timing a few milliseconds when heavy throttle conditions are detected. This helps reduce load on the transmission and allows for smooth shifting even under heavy torque conditions that might otherwise risk damage to the gearbox. The result is a transmission with far better quality performance than a purely mechanical transmission.

But there is thus far more to the design of a vehicle with so many possible interactions, enabling substantial improvements in performance, safety, and reliability. There is also far more that can go wrong. And when each module affects the performance of many others, debugging can become a major problem. Because of the complex interactions, things can go wrong in strange and unpredictable ways. Volkswagen recalled Passats and Tiguans for a software bug that caused the engine to unexpectedly rev when the air conditioning was turned on. Mercedes-Benz reportedly had a problem that the seats moved when a navigation button was pressed. Vehicle recalls are increasingly being caused by software-related bugs. IBM estimates that 50 percent of the warranty costs of cars comes from software and electronics.

Debugging becomes a costly problem with increased complexity, contributing to the rising cost of designing a new car model. Because of the complexity, the cost of designing a new model using major existing components (engine, platform, and so on) begins at around $1 billion and can take five years. Designing a new car from scratch costs as much as $5 or $6 billion. The cost of software code alone can reach $1 billion.[17]

And automakers compete on their ability to deliver the combinations of new features that consumers want. It's not just the number of features that matters but also the ability to flexibly rearrange combinations of features to produce a variety of products or versions. For example, "As soon as Toyota bosses spot a gap in the market or a smart new product from a rival, they swiftly move in with their own version. The result is a bewildering array of over 60 models in Japan and loads of different versions in big overseas markets such as Europe and America."[18] Toyota was able to overtake General Motors to become one of the top global car manufacturers because it can produce new models in under two years and at lower cost. James P. Womack, coauthor of *The Machine That Changed the World*, a book about Toyota's lean production methods, explains how Toyota pulled ahead: "GM and Ford can't design vehicles that Americans want to pay 'Toyota money' for. And this is not a matter of bad bets on product concepts or dumb engineers. It's a matter of Toyota's better engineering system, using simple concepts like chief engineers with real responsibility for products, concurrent and simultaneous engineering practices, and sophisticated knowledge capture methods."[19] While Toyota has long had superior product design and development approaches, the growing complexity of automobiles has allowed the automaker to leverage its capabilities into competitive advantage.

Competing on complexity has put General Motors and Ford at a disadvantage, but it has also put extreme pressure on smaller automakers that cannot afford these large costs of new models. Increasingly, small automakers have sought to merge, and a common rationale given is that mergers are necessary to economize on the high costs of developing new products and speeding them to market. For example, Fiat-Chrysler justified its proposed merger with Renault, saying, "Broader collaboration through a combination would substantially improve capital efficiency and the speed of product development." This proposal is the latest example of established automakers seeking partnerships to share the costs of developing new technologies, including electric vehicles and autonomous driving systems.[20]

Other manufacturing industries have also seen consolidation resulting from rising complexity of product design and development. It now costs $25 to $30 billion to develop a major new jumbo jet. By the mid-1990s, only three manufacturers were left in the commercial market for large jets:

Boeing, Airbus, and the Douglas Aircraft Division of McDonnell Douglas. Airbus received European subsidies for developing new planes, but McDonnell Douglas could not keep up.[21] In 1996, McDonnell Douglas began jointly designing a new aircraft with Boeing, and in 1997, Boeing acquired McDonnell Douglas.

Industries in service sectors also leverage complexity for competitive advantage. Using large amounts of data and sophisticated software systems, Google and Facebook provide advertisers an unprecedented level of targeting, allowing them to target ads to very narrowly defined groups, increasing the effectiveness of advertising. These systems, too, are highly complex. Google, for instance, has been tweaking its search algorithms for two decades, conducting more than ten thousand experiments annually in recent years to refine their search efficacy.[22] Financial institutions compete on complexity by tailoring both their products and their marketing. For example, four large banks dominate the U.S. credit card industry by marketing tailored credit offerings to highly targeted groups of prospective customers, thus managing risk while maximizing market reach. These systems, too, are built using large amounts of data endlessly tweaked to optimize performance. Insurance companies also use technology to tailor and market health plans to individuals. And pharmacy benefit managers use technology to handle the complexity of drug reimbursement plans.

Thus, across a range of industries we see large firms making big investments in proprietary systems that allow them to compete on complexity more effectively. In total, these investments appear as a major surge in aggregate investment statistics. Private investment in proprietary software—software that firms develop on their own or by contracting others, excluding purchases of prepackaged software and excluding software products—grew to $234 billion in 2019.[23] That is about as much as firms' net investment in equipment. Moreover, this investment is dominated by the largest firms, and it is occurring in every major sector of the economy. It is hard to think of another technology that brought such a large shift in investment across all major sectors of the economy in such a short time. And, concentrated among the largest firms, it appears linked to a change in the nature of competition.

But the investment in software is only a part of the total investment in these systems. The entire technology investment that firms make in these proprietary systems goes well beyond just software code to include data, workforce skills, and investments in alternative organizational structures. A substantial literature finds that these complementary investments are critical to the success of narrowly defined information technology invest-ments, and by some measure, the software expense comprises a minority of the investment.[24] Walmart's software enables a system that includes cross-docking facilities, training for store managers and suppliers, and a satellite communications system. Citibank's software enables a system that includes a range of personnel to develop products and marketing programs, to ensure regulatory compliance, and to administer and manage ongoing loans. Often these systems take the form of a platform, something I discuss further in chapter 9.

Moreover, these systems are proprietary in the sense that at least some critical part is not available to rivals and thus helps to differentiate the firm. We will explore the ways that firms keep their investments as a source of proprietary advantage in chapter 4. It is important to note that not all of the associated investments need to be proprietary. Sometimes critical soft-ware components are made freely available as open-source software but the data are kept secret. For example, Google released its proprietary MapReduce software used in big data analysis, now available as Hadoop open-source software. But much of Google's data remain proprietary. I use the term "proprietary software" loosely to refer to the software code, data, and organization that provide competitive advantage, and this may include cases where the software itself is open sourced.

Accounting for Declining Disruption

These proprietary systems do appear to give large firms competi-tive advantages, but they are clearly not the only reason that some firms dominate their industries. For instance, some firms have come to lead their industries by acquiring their rivals. Does firm investment in proprietary systems substantially account for the decline in disruption or do these other factors account for the change?

We can gain important clues to what is going on by looking at what dominant firms are actually *doing* to establish and maintain their domi-nance.[25] Figure 2 shows the mean cumulative investments (stocks) of

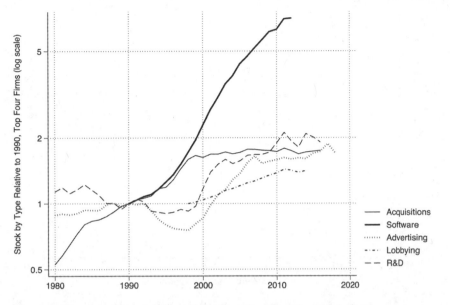

Figure 2. The rise of intangible capital of top four firms in each industry
Source: Bessen et al., "Declining Industrial Disruption."

each type of asset for firms ranked in the top four of their industries
by sales.

The figure includes research and development (R&D) and advertising
and marketing stocks, which come from firm financial statements. It also
includes nonstandard measures of investment in acquisitions, in corporate
lobbying, and in software development. The software development investment is based on the number of software developers employed.[26] For comparison, the chart shows each type of stock relative to the level of the stock
in 1990. Generally, investments in all types of intangibles have increased
substantially, as other researchers have documented.[27] While several of the
stocks have almost doubled since 1990, the stock of own-developed software
increased eightfold for top-four firms, clearly outstripping the rest. Moreover,
the investments in software by the top four firms even doubled relative to
the mean investments made by second-tier firms ranked fifth through eighth.
Investment in own-developed software is dominated by large firms. Note
that these investments happened across industries, excluding the software
industry and other industries where software is a major part of the product.

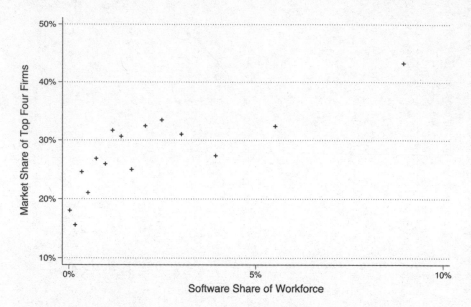

Figure 3. IT-intensive industries are more dominated by top firms
Source: James Bessen, "Information Technology and Industry Concentration,"
Journal of Law and Economics, University of Chicago Press, vol. 63(3). Copyright
2020 by The University of Chicago. All rights reserved.

Moreover, when we look across firms, we find, not surprisingly, that both tangible and intangible investments decrease the likelihood that a top firm will fall out of the top four. But software turns out to be the most important intangible asset type. Investments made by top-four firms in own-developed software significantly decreased the probability that a second-tier firm would leapfrog into the top four within its industry.[28] Moreover, this effect is substantial; proprietary software investment accounts for most of the decline in the leapfrogging probability since 2000.

In effect, investments in proprietary software by top firms suppress the relative growth of second-tier firms. As a result, the largest firms grow faster than their challengers, decreasing the likelihood that they will be leapfrogged and increasing their share of industry revenues. We see the latter relationship in figure 3, which shows that the market share of the largest four firms in each industry increases with the portion of the workforce involved in software development.[29] Note that the chart excludes industries where software is part of the product so that it reflects only the development of software for internal use. The growth in the market share of the top four firms since 2000—a measure of industry concentration and widely documented at the national level—is largely explained by the rise in the IT share of the workforce, a measure of firm investment in proprietary software. This account is supported by other research showing that investments in information technology are associated with growing industry concentration and market power.[30]

Moreover, a variety of tests show that both the link between software and the decline in leapfrogging and the link to the rise in industry concentration are causal. That is, it was no mere coincidence that the abrupt decline in disruption of leading firms beginning in the late 1990s was matched by an abrupt increase in software investment by top firms. Nor was it coincidence that the market shares of the dominant firms grew in industries that invested in software. Careful analysis suggests that the investments in software actually caused these trends.[31]

What about other factors? One prominent line of thought argues that competition has declined because antitrust enforcement has been weakened.[32] During the 1980s, under the influence of Robert Bork and other laissez-faire scholars of the Chicago School, antitrust authorities at the Department of Justice and the Federal Trade Commission changed the standards they used to judge mergers and acquisitions. As a result, large firms could more easily buy out their rivals and thereby preserve or increase a dominant market position.

Some evidence lends support to this view. Since the 1980s, the ratio of prices to unit costs—called the markup—has been rising in the United States and Europe.[33] Also since the 1980s, industry concentration, the market share of the top firms in each industry, has been rising in many industries in the United States and Europe at the national level.[34] Some economists see these trends as evidence of declining competition.

But this explanation and the supporting evidence have a number of problems when it comes to accounting for the decline in the disruption of industry leaders. First, after rising since 1980, the rate at which dominant firms have acquired other companies has actually declined since the late 1990s.[35] The stock of acquisitions has been flat since 2000 (see fig. 2). In the econometric analysis mentioned above, the rate of acquisitions by top firms is uncorrelated with both disruption and leapfrogging rates. This makes it difficult to argue that top firms have avoided being disrupted since 2000 by acquiring their rivals at an increased rate. While some firms in some industries have surely used acquisitions to obtain or maintain a dominant position, acquisitions do not appear to account for the dramatic decline in disruption.

Second, markups and industry concentration rose in Europe as well as the United States, although perhaps not quite as much.[36] Nevertheless, it is hard to attribute the worldwide changes to shifts in strictly U.S. antitrust policy during the 1980s. Furthermore, as above, the rise in concentration is largely explained by proprietary software and associated investments. In any case, markups are not a good indicator of the kind of competition that leads to displacement of top firms.[37] While there *is* some evidence that antitrust enforcement might be too lax, it seems that shifts in U.S. competition policy cannot account for much of the dramatic decline in the disruption of dominant firms.[38]

Finally, the timing of this account is off. The relevant changes in antitrust policy occurred in the 1980s, and that is when markups, industry concentration, and acquisitions all began rising. But industrial disruption *rose* substantially during the 1980s and 1990s, only declining sharply after that. It seems hard to attribute a sharp drop after 2000 to factors that appear to have contributed to rising rates of displacement for two decades before that.

Timing is also a problem for other possible explanatory factors. For example, some economists see the rising dominance of large firms arising from the fall of long-term interest rates.[39] They argue that a low interest rate environment advantages larger firms by allowing them to invest more economically. However, real long-term interest rates have been falling since 1983, so while low interest rates may have contributed to large firm dominance, they cannot easily explain the sharp reversal in disruption rates that occurred around 2000. And figure 2 clearly indicates there has been not just an increase in investment but a major shift in investment into software. Other economists see the aging of the baby boomers as a cause of slowing labor force growth that contributed to large firm dominance.[40] But the growth of the labor force also began slowing during the 1980s, so this factor cannot be decisive in explaining the decline in disruption either.

Other explanations fail because they apply only to limited industries. For example, in some industries, digital platforms give rise to "network effects" (see chapter 9) that tend to create winner-take-all industries. But the decline in disruption has occurred across all industries, few of which exhibit such significant effects. The China Shock—a flood of imports from China—also occurred around 2000. But again, disruption declined in many industries not affected by imports.

More Than Bigness

In summary, the large shift of investment by dominant firms into proprietary software and the associated systems accounts substantially for the sharp drop in industry disruption rates beginning around 2000. Acquisitions, interest rates, and other factors surely affect the dominance of certain firms in some industries at some times but do not seem to account for the reversal in disruption. Software systems emerged in a wide range of industries that helped firms to manage complexity better. Where firms could improve the quality of their products and services by increasing complexity, these systems provided competitive advantage. This happened in different ways in different industries. In retail and wholesale industries, systems allowed firms to offer greater selection while streamlining logistics and inventory; in manufacturing and software industries, software allowed firms to increase the features of their products, appealing to a larger market; in services and finance, firms could target their marketing and their product offerings to different customers. While the mechanisms differ from industry to industry, in all these cases, leading firms competed more effectively by taking advantage of software-enabled complexity. To do so, they often had to change their organizations and make deep investments in the capabilities of their employees.

In each of these cases, technology allowed firms to reduce the information costs of addressing a wide range of customers or locales. Walmart replaced the standardized product selection of chain stores with greater variety; auto manufacturers replaced standardized models—every color so long as it is black—with more models and more features in each model; banks replaced standardized mortgages with a wide variety of financial vehicles tailored to different needs and risk tolerances; advertisers tailored their ads to finely defined groups.

Of course, some IT systems serve other needs of the firm and don't provide competitive advantage. Much of that kind of software can be purchased from independent vendors. But it does appear in example after example that the big, proprietary, mission-critical systems involve delivering greater complexity because they address disparate customer needs. This link between own-developed software and the decline in disruption is distinctive, and it is different from the role of past technologies. We are accustomed to thinking of technology as a force creating disruption. Here, it seems, technology may be *suppressing* disruption.

When the quality of products or services can be improved at the cost of greater complexity, then these new systems provide competitive advantage. Initially, this meant greater industrial disruption as firms that harnessed the technology displaced those that did not. Walmart overtook Sears and Kmart; Toyota overtook GM and Ford; Lotus overtook VisiCalc but was later overtaken by Microsoft. But once the new leaders emerged, they were not easily dislodged, and disruption of industry leaders has declined. And this new pattern of competition has major implications not only for industry structure but for productivity growth, wage inequality, and policy.

Yet a puzzle remains unexplained. Why, exactly, has this shift to software led to the persistent dominance of top firms? Indeed, if software *reduces* the cost of managing complexity, then more firms should be able to purchase or develop it, leveling the playing field instead of tilting it. Sears and Kmart and GM and Ford are not small companies, yet the change in the economy has worked against them.

The key to solving this puzzle is the nature of human demand. Too often, technology is seen as purely a matter of production efficiency, a supply-side issue. Yet demand is key to understanding the ultimate effect of new technologies on the economy. The next chapter explores how the scope of demand affects the dominance of large firms when they compete on complexity.

3

The Superstar Economy

In November 1957, Mao Zedong, chairman of the People's Republic of China, attended the celebration of the fortieth anniversary of the Russian Revolution in Moscow. While there, he was excited to hear Nikita Khrushchev, premier of the Soviet Union, claim that the USSR would overtake the United States in steel production within fifteen years. Mao, who was formulating his own plans for China's industrial development, was captivated by this idea of overtaking the West. Within the month he declared that "China will overtake Britain" in steel production. "The east wind will overwhelm the west wind."[1]

Pursuing this ambition of rapid growth, Mao's economic planners raised the target for steel production in the five-year economic plan beginning in 1958. Initially, the plan called for production of ten million tons of steel by 1962. They upped the target to thirty million tons, the level Britain was expected to reach that year. Then, further enthusiasm tripled that target to ninety million tons by 1962. This push to dramatically expand steel production was a core part of the so-called Great Leap Forward.

But how was China to do this? After all, China had produced only five million tons of steel in 1957. China had some steel mills, but it lacked the capital to rapidly expand them. Rather than follow a Soviet-style path of heavy investment in large enterprises, Mao turned to what he saw as China's greatest strength, its Revolutionary Masses. By the end of 1958, more than sixty million peasants were ordered to build backyard furnaces to produce iron and steel.

The result was disastrous. For one, diverting so many agricultural labor-ers meant that, according to Bo Yibo, one of the chief economic planners, "many food crops and other agricultural products were left in the field without being harvested," contributing to the Great Famine that followed.[2] But despite these horrendous social costs, steel output rose only modestly for a couple years before declining. There are multiple reasons for these poor results. Expert knowledge needed to produce high-quality steel was in short supply. Many areas lacked access to coal or coke and used wood instead, denuding the forests.

But a key contributor to the failure was this: making steel in small fur-naces is very costly and inefficient. Steel production is subject to economies of scale, meaning that unit costs decrease with the scale of production, at least up to a point. The brutal arithmetic of scale economies doomed the production of steel in the Great Leap Forward; the inefficiency of backyard furnaces made production expensive at a time when inputs were scarce.

Bigness and Technology

The arithmetic of scale economies has shaped not only the devel-opment of the steel industry and other industries in the United States but also basic features of the modern economy, including the nature of the firm, the role of modern management, the process of innovation, and the balance of power between corporations and government. During the lat-ter half of the nineteenth century, new technologies brought major economies of scale to many industries, dramatically changing the industry structure and leading to the emergence of the first large firms.[3] These new firms were organized differently, with managerial hierarchies. And they came to dominate in steel and other industries, forcing small producers out of the market. These large firms gained substantial power over society, which became a political concern and contributed to the development of the modern regulatory state.

It is tempting to interpret the recent decline in the disruption of dom-inant firms in terms of economies of scale. The scale of investment in new software systems does indeed seem to matter. Smaller automobile manu-facturers are forced to merge in order to afford the investments needed to design and develop new car models. McDonnell Douglas was forced to

merge with Boeing when it could no longer afford the large-scale investments needed to design new commercial airliners.

But we already have industries with scale economies. What is different
now? Scale economies do not completely explain what is happening. Product differentiation is the key to understanding why the disruption of leading firms has declined and industries have become more stagnant. The
new systems combine the advantages of large scale with the advantages of
mass customization. While the quantity of demand is key to understanding
why scale economies affect industry structure, it is the *scope* of demand
that is key to understanding why top firms have recently become more
persistently dominant. New information technology allows firms to become
dominant by leveraging complexity, creating a new, powerful generation
of IT superstar companies. With this type of competition, leading firms
can remain dominant even as their markets grow dramatically, and rival
firms face strong headwinds that deter them from growing to challenge
the leaders.

We tend to think the advantages of bigness arise from scale economies.
Historically that has been true. Since the latter half of the nineteenth century,
economies of scale enabled large firms to dominate their industries and to
acquire substantial economic, social, and political power. But today the
structure of industries and the nature of competition are changing in other
ways, for other reasons, leading to a more ossified version of capitalism.
Now, with information technology, both economic growth and rising economic inequality tend to further entrench the superstar firms. And the
changing nature of competition affects the diffusion of technology, productivity growth, economic inequality, and more. It is helpful to begin by looking at how technology affected the emergence of dominant firms in the past.

Economies of Scale

Technologies with economies of scale were a key feature of the
Industrial Revolution, and these led to stark changes in industry structure.
Economies of scale are also well identified in many modern industries, such
as steelmaking or electric power generation. But the industry structures that
result from simple economies of scale are not the same as what we observe
with those industries competing with large software investments today.

Consider steelmaking. Primary steel products are generally made from raw materials in three stages.[4] First, iron is smelted from ore in blast furnaces. Second, iron is refined into steel by removing excess carbon and other impurities. Third, steel ingots are shaped into the final delivered form such as rails or steel sheet produced in rolling mills. At the beginning of the nineteenth century, these stages were typically performed by different firms.[5] While blast furnace firms were some of the largest firms in the United States before the Civil War, employing fifty to one hundred people, there were many such producers and the market was not dominated by a few large mills. Steel was mostly refined using the puddling process, in which workers would stir molten iron in a small furnace, gradually incorporating air to burn off impurities.

The technology changed dramatically after the Civil War with the U.S. introduction of the Bessemer process, invented by Henry Bessemer in England. In this process, crude smelted iron is melted in a large vessel and then oxygen is forced through it to remove impurities. This approach allowed for much larger quantities of steel to be produced at once. In addition, the Bessemer steel producers in the United States developed a series of innovations to further increase efficiency in plants that integrated the blast furnaces, the Bessemer converters, and rolling mills. To gain a sense of the changes in scale, the entire U.S. production of steel in 1860 was 13,000 short tons. By 1878, the ten operating Bessemer mills produced 650,000 tons; on average, each Bessemer mill produced five times the entire national output of just eighteen years earlier.

This huge increase in scale changed the nature of business organizations. As Alfred Chandler relates, the extreme increase in the volume of throughput meant that the entire process of production had to be actively managed rather than relying on markets to coordinate activity.[6] The steel mills needed to secure regular inputs of iron ore and coke of the right quality and chemical composition, and they needed to manage the production of rails and fabricated steel; these tasks required sales and marketing. Business organizations split internally into multiunit enterprises where professional managers handled the details of these different aspects. The occupation of middle manager was created to staff these hierarchies. In some cases, the firms vertically integrated; Andrew Carnegie bought up iron ore and coke firms to secure a reliable supply of the right quality.

The economies of scale also changed industry structure. To see how, it is helpful to look at how large size created efficiencies. The Bessemer process realized efficiencies in part because smelting was no longer limited by the need for manual manipulation of the molten iron; it automated that task. But the process also critically benefited from the physical properties of heat dissipation in large furnaces and other containers.[7] Because large vessels can be heated more efficiently than smaller ones, many industrial processes exhibit economies of scale, including steel production, electric and steam power generation, many chemical processes, and cement production.

However, this property also implies diminishing returns—that is, the relative payoff from a further increase in size diminishes as the size increases. At the same time, there are typically other diseconomies of scale. For instance, larger vessels mean that larger quantities of inputs are needed at once. Managing the logistics and traffic on a larger scale creates congestion costs, such as the costs of coordinating the rail traffic to bring a greater volume of inputs to the furnaces. Also, larger quantities of outputs need to be processed, creating congestion costs. Typically, this means that the scale economies end after the firm reaches a certain minimum efficient scale. Beyond this size, unit costs no longer decrease with size, and they might even begin increasing. Economists have calculated the minimum efficient scale for plants in industries with scale economies. For example, one estimate of the minimum efficient size for an integrated steel mill in the 1970s was about six million tons per year.[8] An estimate of the minimum efficient size for an electricity generating plant in 1972 was about twenty billion kilowatt-hours.[9]

Economists have long understood that large plant scale has direct implications for industry structure. Joe Bain, a pioneer of industrial analysis, emphasized that economies of scale served as barriers to entry into an industry.[10] If the most efficient steel mill costs, say, $5 billion, additional firms will not enter in a small market because doing so would drive prices down, making it impossible to recoup the cost of entry. This happens in niche markets and in regional markets. For example, transportation costs mean that cement plants or hospitals tend to serve limited geographical areas. In the more limited, less densely populated markets, one or a few firms can dominate, limiting competition.

But in larger markets, economies of scale do not, by themselves, promote the dominance of a few firms. The size of today's steel market in the United

States is much larger than the output of a plant of minimum efficient size.[11] Although a few firms dominate the steel industry today, that is not because of economies of scale. Those firms contain many plants of minimum efficient size or larger. In larger markets, more firms can profitably enter at the minimum efficient scale, making competition more intense unless firms can find a way, perhaps via collusion, to soften competition. Generally, economists find that larger markets are less likely to be dominated by a few firms.[12] Hence, economies of scale do not necessarily mean that the industry will be highly concentrated.

Moreover, as market size grows, the dominance of the top firms tends to erode. Something like this happened in the U.S. steel industry in the nineteenth century. Initially, the Bessemer firms rapidly outstripped the smaller producers, driving many out of the market, because Bessemer costs were much lower. By 1873, the U.S. steel market was dominated by just seven Bessemer mills. But the lower costs meant lower prices, and this meant a dramatic growth in the size of the market. As costs came down, the price of steel plummeted from $166 per ton in 1866 to under $30 per ton in 1885. In 1860, the market for steel was 111,000 tons.[13] This increased more than tenfold by 1885 and a hundredfold by 1899.

The growth in the market opened the door to many more entrants, raising the prospect of greater competition. In 1878, the Bessemer mills produced an average of 65,000 tons each. This meant that in that year, seven mills produced 79 percent of the total output. But as the market grew rapidly, more firms chose to enter. Between 1873 and 1876, three new Bessemer mills began production. At this point, the mills began to worry about competition with each other. They tried to form a cartel in 1875 that could restrict output by giving each mill a quota. They hoped that the restricted output would allow them to maintain high prices. But the pool fell apart when Andrew Carnegie failed to go along. Another pool that was formed in 1877 was a bit more successful, but it could not prevent further entrants, and it did not help producers outside of the rail market segment.

Ultimately, it was not economies of scale but industry financial consolidation that allowed a large firm to dominate the steel industry.[14] The successful mills began vertically integrating, combining steel production facilities with coke and iron ore production and steel fabrication, and they also acquired rivals. The Illinois Steel Company was formed in 1889 by the merger of three Bessemer producers. These firms also began vertically integrating, buying up coke and iron ore companies as well as secondary product manufacturers. The investment banker J. P. Morgan underwrote some of these mergers. Meanwhile, Carnegie began buying rival mills near Pittsburgh and buying up vertically related companies. In 1901, facing the threat of intensified competition between his merged companies and Carnegie Steel, Morgan bought out Carnegie, merging it with the Illinois group as well as with secondary producers. The resulting company was United States Steel, the world's largest industrial corporation. It produced two-thirds of all the steel made in the United States during its first year of operation.

Economies of scale don't explain the creation of a single dominant steel producer; mergers and acquisitions do. While the large scale of the mills helped in the sense of requiring fewer acquisitions, the emergence of this behemoth was mainly the result of financial combination. The creation of U.S. Steel was part of a broader trend toward the creation of large trusts that dominated their industries such as Standard Oil or the American Sugar Refining Company. But there was a reaction to the trusts as well, resulting in the Sherman Act of 1890 and the creation of antitrust law. The federal government took note of U.S. Steel and in 1911 brought suit to break it up, unsuccessfully as it turns out. I will return to antitrust law in chapter 9.

Economies of scale allowed a small number of mills to dominate the steel industry for a short term. A similar pattern was seen in other industries, such as petroleum refining, sugar, and meatpacking. But as these markets grew—and the cost savings of the new technology propelled rapid growth—scale economies by themselves no longer served to reduce competition. Firms turned, instead, to financial consolidation or predatory acquisitions to maintain or expand their power. Nevertheless, economies of scale had played a role in critically transforming the economy, changing the nature of firm organization, and providing the initial dominance of large firms.

Do economies of scale explain the decline in industrial disruption of the last two decades? It is true that the dominant firms have spent large sums building their internal IT systems. But the story appears different from the nineteenth-century story of scale economies for two reasons: these investments are not particularly large, and dominant firms seem to maintain their dominance despite industry growth.

First, the scale of the IT systems used by the top firms is not large compared to the scale of other investments undertaken in today's capital-intensive industries. In 2018, the ten largest IT spenders invested between $6.6 billion and $13.6 billion on information technology. This is small compared to the capital expenditures of the big energy companies, which have exceeded $30 billion in recent years, and in the same range as capital expenditures by GE, Toyota, and Intel.[15] It is hard to see how the introduction of smaller-scale economies can account for the sharp change in industrial disruption rates especially in industries that already had major-scale economies. Indeed, we are seeing declines in disruption rates even in industries that have well-recognized economies of scale in production such as durable manufacturing, petroleum, and utilities.[16]

Second, unlike the dominant firms in steel and other scale industries, today's dominant firms do not appear to lose their dominance as markets grow. Many are in rapidly growing markets, yet they maintain a dominant share of the market. Walmart maintained its dominance in general merchandise retail as that market grew 50 percent in inflation-adjusted terms; Amazon has maintained its leading share of e-commerce as that market has grown twentyfold. Moreover, as we saw in the last chapter, these dominant firms have not been growing mainly by aggressively merging with or acquiring other companies. More generally, while we might expect industries operating with scale economies to see declining industry concentration as the industry grows, in fact, more rapidly growing industries tend to increase industry concentration.[17]

There is a corresponding difference in the way challenger firms fare. In steel, although the investment required to enter the market was huge, anyone could enter if they had the resources. But today, firms that are large enough to make the investments have also fallen behind. Sears was much larger than Walmart in the 1980s and could afford whatever technology Walmart could afford. Sears was no technological slouch. Even though it was IBM's largest customer during the 1980s and it pioneered e-commerce, Sears fell behind. Similarly, Microsoft was not too small to make investments in search technology, nor does Microsoft lack technological capabilities, yet

Microsoft has been a laggard to Google in search engines. These firms could certainly afford the technology and they had technical expertise, but they became at best also-rans in these areas.

The difference between the behavior of today's dominant firms and those of the past lies in the nature of competition. The steel firms made large investments that lowered their costs, allowing them to compete effectively on price. Today's firms make large investments in systems that combine the advantages of large scale with the advantages of mass customization. These systems allow firms to compete by differentiating the quality of their offerings, and this makes all the difference. What matters in this competition is not the absolute scale of critical investments; what matters is the scale relative to rival firms, and this helps explain the new persistent dominance of large firms and much more about today's economy. It is helpful to look at how quality differentiation differs from simple price competition.

Quality Competition and Superstars

In 1981, economist Sherwin Rosen wrote a paper about the phenomenon of superstars, "wherein relatively small numbers of people earn enormous amounts of money and dominate the activities in which they engage, [which] seems to be increasingly important in the modern world."[18] The number of comedians was smaller than during the days of vaudeville, most making very little money, but the top performers, especially those appearing on television, earned extraordinary sums. Something similar was seen with opera stars, sports figures, newscasters, and textbook authors. Olympic gold medalists won lucrative endorsement deals while silver and bronze winners did not. The rewards paid to the top performers seemed to be out of all proportion to the quality of their performances, which was only marginally better than that of the runners-up, sometimes by only a few hundredths of a second.

This phenomenon is a bit disconcerting to economists who like to think that pay is proportional to performance. Of course, in many markets it is. Weavers vary in their ability and effort, some producing more than others in a day's work. In the early textile mills, the weavers were paid, not by the number of hours they worked, but by the yards of cloth they produced.

Economists often assume that something similar operates throughout the economy so that workers who produce greater quantities are paid more.

But clearly for some categories of workers, differences in *quality* correspond to huge differences in pay. Rosen identified a key reason for this. Quantity and quality cannot be easily traded off in these cases: "Hearing a succession of mediocre singers does not add up to a single outstanding performance. If a surgeon is 10 percent more successful in saving lives than his fellows, most people would be willing to pay more than a 10 percent premium for his services."[19] In economics jargon, different-quality services are imperfect substitutes. When consumers differentiate services in this way, what matters is not the absolute level of quality but the quality *relative* to the next-best provider. And the effects on pay can be disproportionate. When most people prefer the best surgeon to the second-best, the market demand for that best surgeon is drastically higher.

Moreover, this effect is stronger in larger markets. As the number of prospective patients grows, the competition between them to gain the services of the top surgeon becomes fiercer. In this way, Rosen was prescient. Digital technologies lowered communication and reproduction costs for all sorts of media, making markets for many performance-related services global. As a result, the superstar effect mushroomed for movie actors, sports stars, and top authors.[20] In 1990, the highest-paid basketball player, Patrick Ewing of the New York Knicks, earned $8.4 million in inflation-adjusted dollars. Since then, NBA revenues have increased nearly tenfold. Now, the highest-paid player, Steph Curry, earns $40.2 million a year. And this applies to corporate talent as well. Reed Hastings, CEO of Netflix, explained why his firm pays top-of-the-market salaries: "When you're looking at great sports teams, they're often the teams that can pay high for the best players. We want to have the absolute best players and compensation is one part of that. We'd rather have three outstanding people than four OK people."[21] So, unlike markets with substantial scale economies, the leaders in these superstar markets increase their market power as the size of the market grows.

But comedians, opera singers, and basketball players are not major firms. Nevertheless, a body of economic research finds a similar pattern in industry organization. When firms differentiate on quality, the growth of the market does not necessarily erode firm dominance. Economist John Sutton notes that in some industries, large firms maintain dominant market shares even when the size of the market increases.[22] In particular, these tend to be industries that invest significantly in advertising and/or R&D. The critical distinction here is that in these markets, fixed investments in advertising and R&D allow firms to differentiate on quality. Some consumers are willing to pay more for better quality (or perceived quality, in the case of advertising) than others.[23]

In Sutton's analysis, this gives rise to a "natural oligopoly" market structure where firms differ both in size and in the quality of their products. Because demand for quality varies from consumer to consumer, industry competition is distinctive. By differentiating themselves on quality, firms address different market segments and competition between them is soft, allowing them to earn profits. Dominant firms invest more in quality and attract the more quality-conscious consumers who are willing to pay more. Smaller firms invest less and attract less quality-conscious consumers.

Consider a hypothetical example. Suppose there are two computer manufacturers and they can each choose to invest in R&D to produce a better-quality product, say, one that is more user-friendly. Suppose that one company enters the market first and makes a big investment to produce a high-quality product. The second company can choose to make a computer of equal quality. If it does so, however, the only thing that distinguishes one offering from the other is the price. As a result, the manufacturers will compete intensely over price, driving the price down to the point that neither makes a profit. On the other hand, if the second company invests less in quality, it produces a lower-quality product for which it can charge a lower price. Then the two companies will appeal to different groups of customers. Because some customers are more budget conscious than quality conscious whereas other customers are relatively more quality conscious, the firms end up selling differentiated products to different market segments. They can earn positive profits by charging a bit more, knowing that they are still offering the best package to their particular segment of consumers.

Moreover, in a natural oligopoly, market structure tends to remain stable. This persistence arises because higher-quality firms have different incentives than their lower-quality rivals to innovate. Consider the above hypothetical. Suppose the second firm comes up with an innovation that improves product quality. Such an innovation is a mixed blessing. Although it increases the firm's appeal to quality-conscious consumers, it also brings it more into direct competition with the first firm, reducing the price it can charge. By comparison, the firm with the higher-quality product faces no such disincentive to innovating. These asymmetric incentives make the lower-quality firm less interested in innovating and therefore less likely to develop an innovation that would allow it to leapfrog the higher-quality firm. In other words, a natural oligopoly has a lower rate of disruption, all else equal. Effectively, nondominant firms face headwinds to growth from innovation.

Because differentiated industries compete in a different way, the role of large fixed investments is different. In the traditional barrier-to-entry model, the minimum efficient scale is determined by forces outside the firm's control—for example, by the physics of heat dissipation in large furnaces. In these markets, when firms compete on price, a firm of minimum efficient size can charge lower prices than smaller firms and thus compete effectively. But the size of the needed investment for a minimum efficient steel mill stays unchanged as the market grows. As a result, more firms can enter at the minimum efficient size and the market share of any minimum efficient steel mill declines.

In natural oligopolies, firms differentiate themselves by making large investments in advertising and R&D. Here, what matters is not the *absolute* size of investment; what matters in this case is the size of investment *relative* to rivals' investments. Firms choose the level of investment with an eye to their competitors; the firm selling to the most quality-conscious consumers invests more than the next firm. When the size of the market grows in this kind of differentiated market, the payoff to quality also increases. So, firms invest *more* in advertising and R&D fixed costs. As Sutton and his coauthor, Avner Shaked, put it, the number of firms entering the aircraft or mainframe computer markets is limited, "not because the fixed costs of product development are so high, relative to the size of the market—but rather because the possibility exists, primarily through incurring additional fixed costs, of shifting the technological frontier constantly forward towards more sophisticated products."[24]

In this case, then, the top firms remain dominant as the market expands. In a series of case studies, Sutton shows how the market shares of the top

firms can remain large even as the size of the market grows. Other researchers have found evidence of this pattern in the supermarket industry, banking, among online booksellers, and in newspapers.[25]

IT Superstar Industries

It should be clear that the large upfront investments that top firms
are making today in software systems play the same role as investments in
advertising and R&D. These are large fixed investments that improve the
quality of the firm's products and services, differentiating it from rivals.[26]
Indeed, economist Paul Ellickson's studies of the supermarket industry
identify the source of the quality differentiation achieved by the dominant
firms: logistics and inventory management systems using data from optical
scanners and pioneered by Walmart.[27] These systems allow the dominant
firms to deliver much greater variety, differentiating their offerings from
rivals. Ellickson notes that the average number of products offered per
store increased from 14,145 in 1980 to over 30,000 by 2004.

Greater differentiation in stores corresponds to changes in consumer
behavior. Niches become more important. Consumers spend more of their
budget on a small number of preferred products, but these product selec-
tions differ more from consumer to consumer.[28] And, consistent with
theory, consumers at supermarkets have grown less price sensitive as goods
better match consumers' individual preferences.[29]

We can clearly see the difference in industry structure between industries
with strong scale economies and industries differentiated on quality.
Both the supermarket industries and the ready-mixed concrete industry
have geographically limited markets; transportation costs mean that establishments in these markets tend to serve distinct regional trading areas.
But the markets differ in size depending on the population density. Concrete producers have significant economies of scale, and the market share
of producers declines on average as market size increases. Supermarkets,
in contrast, differentiate, and market shares do not show that kind of
decline. On average, the top four firms in each supermarket trading area
account for about 60 percent of all grocery sales in both the smallest
and largest markets, even though the large markets are ten times bigger.[30]
This same distinction between dominance by scale and dominance by

differentiation applies as markets grow over time instead of across geographical regions.

Quality differentiation explains why industries are persistently dominated by a few firms when they compete on complexity. New software systems, developed beginning in the 1980s and 1990s, allowed firms to increasingly differentiate their quality from rivals by increasing features, product variety, targeting, and so on. These capabilities allowed firms to overcome the Hayekian dilemma, allowing the firms to address widely disparate needs and demands. In industries where firms differentiate on quality, those firms that were best able to manage complexity became dominant; other firms offered lower quality, fewer features, or less variety and remained smaller. Of course, not all industries have these properties and not all industries make the corresponding large investments in own-developed software. We can gain a rough sense of the size of this phenomenon by classifying industries according to their employment of software developers. Using the 2012 Economic Census, if we exclude industries where software is a major part of the product and count those industries that employ over five thousand software developers or those industries where software developers comprise over 2 percent of the workforce, then 45 percent of industries are software intensive. But these industries tend to be large, accounting for 71 percent of revenues. In words, the software-intensive industries comprise a very sizable chunk of the economy.[31]

A Different Kind of Industry

In one sense, large firms have become more dominant because they have excelled at using new software systems to better meet consumers' disparate needs. These firms deliver mass-customized products with more features, stores with greater selection, and highly targeted services. It is not surprising that they have grown. But that is only part of the story. Also, in this new type of competition, smaller, innovative firms experience headwinds to growth that slow their ability to disrupt incumbent market leaders.

It has long been recognized that some firms have persistently better performance or profits than others.[32] Economist Chad Syverson reviews the literature on firm differences in productivity and finds a variety of possible reasons why performance differences might persist, including: some firms have better-quality managers than others; some have better-quality workers, equipment, or technology; some are organized in superior ways to use their capabilities; and some have gained valuable knowledge through experience and thus have greater "organizational capital."[33] Moreover, it has long been known that more productive firms tend to grow faster.[34] Economists have called these high-performing, fast-growing firms "superstars."[35]

But the decline in disruption and the increased persistence of dominant firms is not just a matter of these firms having better managers or higher-quality workers or similar advantages. It's also that the nature of competition has changed since 2000 in many industries, magnifying performance differences and reinforcing the dominance of industry leaders. The story here is not so much about a crop of highly successful superstar firms; it is about the emergence of a different kind of competition, a new variant of capitalism. Critically, the superstar economy changes the relationship between firm productivity and firm growth. As above, in quality-differentiated markets, smaller firms have weak incentives to improve their quality—higher quality means that they will become *less* differentiated from their larger rivals; hence, they will face stronger competition and possibly lower profits. Also, large firm investments in system quality tend to undercut the growth of innovative smaller companies, stealing a portion of their business. We will explore how these effects work and show evidence of their highly significant impact in chapter 6, but these differences in industry structure are a key reason that follower firms, even rather large firms such as Sears and Kmart, have greater difficulty competing.

Yet it is important to note that the decline in disruption is not an inherent outcome of the new technologies of mass customization any more than the dominance of U.S. Steel at the beginning of the twentieth century was an inevitable result of scale economies in steel production. Rather, large firm dominance in both cases arose from specific policies and firm choices. In particular, disruption has declined because access to the new technologies is limited. Only select firms can develop and use the technology, hence the persistent differences. Of course, new technologies are often subject to intellectual property restrictions and other barriers to widespread use. But in the past, the spread of new techniques through the economy tended to happen faster than today. Even patented products and services were often widely licensed so that they became widely used. For example, the Bessemer process was initially subject to patents, but steel mills could readily obtain licenses. This process of diffusion today is occurring at a much slower pace. And it is this development that is behind the troubling trends the superstar economy exhibits regarding the pace of productivity growth, growing income inequality, and less effective government. Firms have choices in how they use these powerful new technologies. If the technology diffuses widely, then society benefits to the greatest degree. When firms limit access to the technology, they may benefit relative to their rivals, but society may not benefit so much; society as a whole might even be worse off.

4

From Open to Closed Capitalism

In industry after industry, dominant firms have used proprietary technologies to achieve persistent competitive advantages and persistent market dominance. Walmart and Amazon have used their unique logistics, inventory management, and fulfillment systems to dominate major retailing segments; major manufacturers have used specialized computer-aided design (CAD), computer-aided manufacturing (CAM), and other design technologies to win features wars; large banks have dominated consumer credit with proprietary marketing and risk management systems. And so on.

Yet what keeps these incumbents from being displaced? Capitalism has long been an open system where new technologies diffuse—the relevant knowledge spreads to other parties who can use the new technology, spreading its advantages. Then, often after a relatively short time, rival firms can access the technology and close in on market leaders, if not actually improving the technology and leapfrogging them.

Consider the diffusion of one invention, the automatic transmission for the automobile.[1] Earl Thompson at General Motors led a team that developed the first commercially successful automatic transmission, the Hydramatic. This transmission was initially made available as an option on the 1940 Oldsmobile, and a year later, it was adopted by GM's Cadillac division. World War II shut down most automobile production, but this automatic transmission was used in military vehicles and tanks. After the war, it became apparent that customers would buy this option even at a high price tag and that any model *not* offering the option would be at a competitive disadvantage. The automatic transmission significantly expanded the market for automobiles by making them accessible to people who had difficulty learning to drive with a manual transmission or who found manual transmissions cumbersome. During the postwar boom, other GM divisions adopted the Hydramatic. Then, in 1949, GM began providing the Hydramatic to other car manufacturers, including Ford's Lincoln division, Hudson, Nash, Kaiser, Bentley, and Rolls-Royce.

The Hydramatic transmission was protected by patents, preventing other manufacturers from directly imitating it unless they purchased it or licensed it from GM. However, the underlying gearing and hydraulic technologies used in the Hydramatic were widely known. Engineers from the various automobile manufacturers had actively exchanged information about these and other emerging technologies. Early in the history of the automobile industry, engineers recognized that they faced common design problems and that their field would benefit from common standards in all areas of technology. The Society of Automobile Engineers was founded in 1905 to promote the free exchange of ideas.[2] This group grew rapidly to over 5,000 members by 1920 and over 128,000 today. Transmission technologies, including gearing and hydraulic coupling, had been under development since the beginning of the twentieth century, and related knowledge was widely shared. Consequently, it was possible for other manufacturers to develop their own automatic transmissions—that is, they could invent around GM's Hydramatic patents. Packard introduced a version in 1949. Borg-Warner, an automotive supplier, developed another version and they licensed their design and/or supplied manufactured transmissions to Ford, American Motors, and Studebaker beginning in the early 1950s.

Thus, in a little over ten years, comparable technology was used throughout the automobile industry. While General Motors had a significant advantage for some years, diffusion of the technology prevented GM from becoming too entrenched, too dominant. In part, GM chose to sell its technology to some rivals; in part, other rivals were able to develop alternative technologies.

Technologies also diffuse in other ways. People with hands-on technical knowledge themselves diffuse to new firms. The semiconductor industry famously began with a series of spinouts. William Shockley developed the first transistor with John Bardeen and Walter Brattain at Bell Labs during the late 1940s and early 1950s. Shockley established Shockley Semiconductor Laboratory in California in 1956. However, Shockley alienated key employees. Eight of them left in 1957 to establish Fairchild Semiconductor. Fairchild, in turn, spawned a whole series of spinouts that became the foundation of the new semiconductor industry, including Intel. Gordon Moore, a Fairchild alumnus who cofounded the spinout Intel, noted, "It seemed like every time we had a new product idea we had several spin-offs. Most of the companies around here even today can trace their lineage back to Fairchild. It was really the place that got the engineer entrepreneur really moving."[3]

In short, technological knowledge is disseminated through a variety of channels. Sometimes a new technology is licensed; sometimes it is "embodied" and sold as a manufactured good; sometimes it is carried in the minds of relocating employees; sometimes it is shared in trade organizations or conferences. One study surveyed industrial R&D managers about where they obtained information derived from university research.[4] In order of descending importance they included: publications, informal exchange, meetings and conferences, consulting, contract research, new hires, joint research ventures, patents, licenses, and personal exchange. Broadly speaking, the channels of diffusion fall into two groups: (1) independent creation, including imitation, where rival firms can develop or acquire the knowledge and capabilities to implement a new technology; and (2) voluntary diffusion, where firms that have the technology license or share that knowledge.

The Technology Gap

The diffusion of new technologies has been a central pillar of capitalism's success. Yet, of late, somehow it doesn't seem to work so well. To be sure, licensing and spinouts still occur, but they seem to happen at a slower pace that is insufficient to dislodge dominant firms. Indeed, researchers at the Organisation for Economic Co-operation and Development first noticed a growing divergence in productivity between "the best and the rest," and they associated this divergence with use of information technology.[5] Macroeconomists Ufuk Akcigit and Sina Ates attribute a wide range of economic changes to a slowdown in diffusion, including growing industry concentration and rising profits.[6]

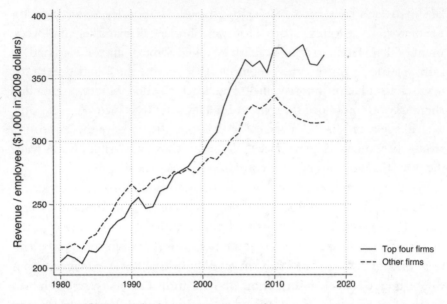

Figure 4. Top firms earn higher revenue per employee

We can see the emergence of a gap between the top firms and the rest by looking at constant-dollar revenue per employee for publicly listed firms.[7] Figure 4 shows separate averages for firms that are ranked in the top four by sales of their industries and for firms with smaller sales.[8] During the 1980s and 1990s, there was not a large difference between the industry leaders and the rest; if anything, the top four firms had slightly lower revenues per employee. But starting in the late 1990s, the averages diverged. A gap opened up, and today the top firms bring in substantially more revenue per employee than the rest.

Furthermore, analysis shows that information technology accounts for much of this difference.[9] We saw in chapter 2 that the top firms spend a lot more on information technology than do the smaller firms. Large firms appear to gain more from these technology investments. Information technology is associated with greater revenue per employee for both top and bottom firms. However, the association with IT is much stronger for the top four firms in each industry.

This gap in revenue per employee implies a technology gap. Dominant firms are using somewhat different technologies than smaller firms, this provides them a greater advantage, and these technologies do not appear to be diffusing as rapidly as technologies diffused in the past. Diffusion would have closed the gap. Yet, as I develop below, the technology gap is the source of some troubling developments.

Why Doesn't Technology Diffusion Topple Dominant Firms?

But why doesn't technology diffusion loosen the grasp of entrenched incumbent firms today? Why can't challengers access or acquire similar technologies to close the technology gap? Why don't leading firms license or sell their technologies to rivals to make extra profits? Why couldn't Sears or Kmart or even smaller firms acquire technology to allow them to compete effectively against Walmart? Why don't key technical personnel from dominant firms create spinouts to provide technology to the market?

I argue that two features of the superstar economy limit the diffusion of technology, each affecting both independent creation and voluntary diffusion. First, the ever-greater complexity of the technology makes independent creation difficult. Complexity makes it more difficult for rivals to independently develop the technology, it makes it more difficult for departing employees to re-create comparable technology, and it makes licensing more difficult.

Second, dominant firms often do not have the incentives to license their technology because that would undermine their degree of differentiation from rivals. In markets where product differentiation is critical for success, many dominant firms will not *want* to license or share their technology.

I first turn to complexity. Rising complexity is, of course, nothing new. Casual observation suggests that the technologies of today are more complex than the technologies of the Industrial Revolution, and these were more complex than what came before. Moreover, particular technologies appear to become more complex as they mature. Today's airplanes are orders of magnitude more complex than those of the Wright brothers. It is helpful to look at history to see how the growth and maturation of technology affects diffusion.

Major innovations often begin life as proprietary technologies. Only one or a few firms initially have the equipment and the knowledge to implement a brand-new technology. Often, major new technologies require new skills and new forms of organization in order to work well. This was the case, for example, with the power loom, introduced into the United States in 1814. Effective use required weavers, mechanics, and mill managers to learn new, specialized skills, and it required a new model of factory organization.[10] The early mills built their own looms, sometimes in close coordination with a local machine shop, and they trained their own workers and managers.

Because few people had the skills and the knowledge to implement the technology, diffusion was slow. Perhaps surprisingly, many nascent technologies have spread because firms freely *shared* knowledge, including many critical loom technologies.[11] Firms benefited from exchanging new knowledge as it was rapidly advancing, and because of skill shortages, helping rivals did little to reduce the firm's own market. Technology also spread as skilled workers migrated to new regions of the country. Economic historian Ross Thomson and sociologist David Meyer have traced how the growth of new mechanical industries followed the individual migrations of skilled mechanics.[12]

Gradually, technical knowledge in textiles and other mechanical industries became standardized. The equipment was standardized; mills that had formerly built their own equipment spun off their machine shops into independent textile equipment manufacturers that sold to any manufacturer. Training also became more standardized. Schools were established for skilled occupations and managers. Trade organizations coordinated on standard best practices for the mills. And as the knowledge became standardized, it spread.

And as knowledge diffused, the markets became more competitive. Rivals were able to enter, driving down prices and profits. Both textile manufacturers and manufacturers of textile equipment found competition substantially fiercer beginning in the 1830s. But this broad diffusion across a range of new technologies had another salutary effect: with the basic knowledge and tools widely available, a wide variety of people could improve upon the technology, making their own inventions. The independent inventors of the nineteenth century broadly spread new inventions across the young nation, raising it to technological leadership.

The Rise and Fall of the Independent Inventor

The late nineteenth century was a golden age for individual inventors in the United States. Mechanics, farmers, small manufacturers, and other Americans were obsessed with inventing and patenting. As one English observer put it, "The true genius of the American people is inventive and mechanical . . . and it would appear as though invention, relatively speaking, has flourished more in the United States than in all the rest of the world."[13] One such inventor was Rufus W. Porter, an itinerant mural painter who wandered across New England painting portraits and murals on the walls of inns and houses. Porter was also a prolific inventor. He patented an improved life preserver, an automatic grain-weighing machine, a blower fan, churns, a punch press, clocks, and steam engines. Porter also recognized the inventive zeitgeist and, in 1845, founded *Scientific American,* a weekly publication for mechanics and manufacturers that claimed to be "the only paper in America devoted to the interest of those classes." The paper covered patents, inventions, and scientific advancements, and it quickly became a successful national publication. This was at a time when there were fewer than three hundred daily newspapers, local or national, in the entire country.[14]

The following decades brought a surge in patenting activity. In 1885 more than four hundred patents were granted in the United States per million residents, a rate of patenting that was more or less maintained until the Great Depression before declining.[15] These inventors were supported not only by *Scientific American* but also by a network of patent agents and lawyers.[16] Critically, there was a very active trade in patents. By the 1890s, 29 percent of newly issued patents had been assigned to a party unrelated to the inventor.[17] That is, the patent rights had been sold; there was a robust market for patents.

Economic historians Naomi Lamoreaux, Kenneth Sokoloff, and Zorina Khan see the market for patents as central to the rapid economic growth achieved by the United States in the nineteenth century.[18] Patents were cheaper to obtain and were more actively traded than in other countries such as the United Kingdom. The robust market for patents promoted the diffusion of new inventions. Often inventors were individual mechanics or farmers who lacked the resources to manufacture and fully commercialize their inventions. Also, high transportation costs meant that even those who did have manufacturing resources could not necessarily provide their inventions to the entire nation. The diffusion brought about by the patent market meant that the inventions became available to those who might realize the greatest rewards from them. That is, the market facilitated gains from trade. And this, in turn, created stronger incentives to develop and commercialize new ideas. Technology markets provided strong support for independent creation of new technologies and hence their diffusion.

But this robust activity did not last. In broad terms, during the late nineteenth and early twentieth centuries, the locus of patenting activity shifted from independent inventors who sold or licensed their patents via a market to inventors within firms—that is, firm research and development. As a result, the diffusion of technology through the market for patents declined.

This shift happened gradually.[19] Independent inventors became more closely tied to firms. Toward the end of the nineteenth century, specialist inventors sold a larger and larger share of their patents to major firms that acquired many patents.[20] Many of the most productive inventors became proprietors, commercializing their inventions themselves rather than selling them.[21] It also took some time before large manufacturers could establish the right kind of organizations to conduct R&D internally. For instance, it took time before inventors would routinely assign patents over to their employers as a condition of employment. Gradually, firms such as General Electric, DuPont, and AT&T developed organizations where employees were motivated to invent as part of their regular employment.

Several factors drove this shift. For one thing, declining transportation costs meant consolidation of national markets. Where before patents were licensed to a series of regional manufacturers, now they tended to be licensed to national manufacturers. There were far fewer national manufacturers, meaning fewer licenses, and these manufacturers had greater bargaining power. The law also changed to better allow employers to acquire the inventions of their employees.[22] And firms adapted their organizations to establish internal R&D. But a key factor in the shift was the rising complexity of technology. Lamoreaux and Sokoloff explain:

Perhaps more important [than employer adaptation], as the complexity of technology increased by the end of the nineteenth and
especially by the early twentieth century, it became more and more
difficult for inventors to maintain their independence. Even though
the growth of the market for technology had made it easier for pat-
entees to sell off their property rights at an early date and to form
corporations to exploit their inventions, they still faced a great deal
of financial uncertainty especially in those sectors of the economy
where the costs of invention, in terms of both human and physical
capital, were likely to be greatest.[23]

Consider, for example, the evolution of the Draper family, a dynasty of
inventors of textile equipment.[24] Ira Draper patented an "automatic loom
temple" in 1816 and patented an improved version in 1829. This invention
was for a simple device that could be added to a power loom to keep the
edges of the cloth straight as it emerged from the loom. The Draper family
licensed the patent and also sold a manufactured version for two dollars.
These actions insured that the technology was widely diffused. At the same
time, there were few obstacles preventing other inventors from introducing
alternative loom temple devices, and many of these were widely sold as well.

Throughout the nineteenth century, the Draper family developed, licensed,
and sold a series of such inventions that could be added to existing weaving
and spinning equipment. These devices tended to be of increasing complexity until 1895, when George Draper and Sons introduced the automated
Northrop loom. For many decades, independent inventors had tried to solve
the problem of automatically replenishing the weft yarn (the yarn threads
going from side to side of the emerging cloth) in power looms. The yarn
was stored on bobbins that shuttled back and forth in the looms, but when
the bobbins ran out of yarn, weavers had to remove the old bobbin and
insert a new, full one. As George Otis Draper, one of the three family members running the company in the 1880s, framed it, "The records show scores
of brilliant minds that labored to this end without avail. The result of such
experiments in the past has either been despair, or bankruptcy. One of the
most prominent English inventors in this line is now an inmate of a poor
house near London. Certain persistent men have at times made single looms
run with their devices, but they never stood the test of continuous use and

no public introduction ever resulted."[25] But George Draper and Sons, relying on its in-house R&D capabilities, succeeded where these individual inventors had failed, and this model of technology development came to dominate the market for looms and for other textile equipment.

In 1888, William F. Draper Jr. saw an attempt by an inventor in Providence, Rhode Island, to develop such an "automatic" loom. The Drapers judged that particular design to be impractical, but after researching available technologies, the company budgeted $10,000 to develop an alternative in 1888.

George Otis Draper recounted the development of this breakthrough technology to the National Association of Cotton Manufacturers in 1895. Two employees, Alonzo Rhoades and James Northrop, had different ideas for how to automatically replace the bobbins. These were tested in 1889, beginning a seven-year period of experimentation. Draper lists nineteen trials of different looms and then tells us, "This record could be enlarged a hundred times without exhausting the facts. Certain parts of the mechanism have been re-invented scores of times, our collection of sample shuttles alone numbering over eighty. The culmination of all this experimenting represents the inventive skill of many minds." He guesses that more than six hundred inventions were involved and notes that the inventors were "supplemented by draughtsmen, workmen, legal counsel, and the resources of a large and varied machine plant."[26] In addition, the bobbin changer interacted with other loom features, requiring development of additional inventions such as an improved warp stop motion in order to make the new loom commercially practical. In the end, rather than just a few patents to protect this new loom, the Draper Company amassed over two thousand patents, both developed in-house and purchased on the market.[27]

Complexity limited the role of independent inventors and of the patent market in several ways. Complexity meant that the amount of work required to develop the technology was beyond the means of most independent inventors. It was a rare individual inventor who could afford a seven-year investment employing many people, a machine shop, and test facilities for a technology that might well fail. And it was a rare banker who would finance such a risky $10,000 undertaking.

But it wasn't just the sheer number of inventions and improvements that had to be made that posed a challenge. It was that the various features being developed *interacted* with each other. These interactions are what make the technology truly complex. And these interactions were difficult for outside inventors to handle, ultimately making arm's-length market transactions an inefficient way to develop the technology. First, developing complex technologies typically involves significant coordination costs. People working on the different components needed to receive regular feedback from each other, making adaptations that, in turn, affected other components. That is much easier to accomplish when these people work in proximity, especially at a time when communication to remote inventors was slow and costly.

Second, arranging contracts with a large number of external inventors would have been difficult and inefficient. Contracting and bargaining over a complex product is far more challenging than doing so for a simple independent component such as the loom temple. It was impossible to determine in advance whether any inventor's component might be used in the ultimate invention. Alonzo Rhoades's shuttle changer was dropped; James Northrop's design was used. It would have been difficult to know in advance what share of the profits were owed to any particular inventor. And inventors with critical components could hold out, demanding excessive payments. While the Drapers did acquire some independently developed patents—in many cases to prevent a rival invention from coming on the market—the overwhelming economic value of these inventions was captured by the Draper Company.

Furthermore, and perhaps most important, outside inventors would have lacked access to critical knowledge about the technology as it was developing. Draper Company mechanics and inventors would have learned essential details of the technology from the hundreds of experiments they conducted. Much of this knowledge would not have been codified or standardized or written down; much would have remained tacit. Yet such knowledge was likely critical to refining the technology. The complexity of the problem limited the usefulness of modular design. While many outside inventors had designed shuttles, only those insiders who understood the experiments performed could design new shuttles that worked with the rest of the automatic mechanism. Extensive hands-on experience with the technology was likely essential to perfecting it and inventing the necessary improvements, yet this knowledge lay within the Draper organization and was not easily accessed by outside inventors, especially remote ones.

To summarize, the complexity of the automatic loom affected diffusion in three ways: (1) development and coordination costs put the research out of reach of most independent inventors, limiting the market (scale); (2) participation in the development process involved significant tacit knowledge learned from experience—this required hands-on involvement in the development (organization); and (3) the uncertainty, the tacit and private nature of knowledge, and the potentially large number of parties involved limited the ability of parties to bargain efficiently to conclude arm's-length transactions (market transactions).

In effect, the rising complexity of loom technology widened the gap between patents and technology. The market for patents worked well when technologies could be developed by individual inventors, when the transfer of a patent corresponded closely with the transfer of a complete technology, and when the inventions could be developed independently without much know-how or experience-based knowledge of the complete technology. But the market for technology is not the same as a market for patents.[28] When the technology became more complex, the market for patents was no longer the best way to organize the development of major new technologies, and the work of independent inventors gradually shifted to corporate R&D.

Independent inventors could no longer easily develop alternative technologies; this more complex technology required resources beyond the reach of independents. As a result, diffusion of the required technical knowledge declined. The Draper Company established and maintained a dominant market position for decades.[29] Complexity limited the extent of independent creation, allowing technology leaders to dominate their markets. Although the Drapers had much competition for loom temples in the early decades of the nineteenth century, they had little real competition for automatic loom technology. Independent inventors did not become extinct, but their importance to innovation in this field and in many others was drastically diminished.

Unprecedented Complexity

Of course, markets for technology have not disappeared. Firms do indeed engage in substantial licensing of technology.[30] Economists Ashish Arora and Alfonso Gambardella see a resurgence of markets for technology in recent years, leading to a new "division of innovative labor" where university scientists can develop basic scientific knowledge and license it to firms that can then commercialize it.[31] They attribute this resurgence to: (1) a shift to science-based technology as opposed to experience-based innovation; (2) advances in computer technologies that make it possible to represent and manipulate ever more complex representations of physical phenomena; and (3) stronger intellectual property, especially patents.

Possible evidence of a resurgence in licensing markets can be seen in the growth of university technology transfer offices following the passage of the Bayh-Dole Act in 1980. This law encouraged universities to license their federally funded research to commercializing firms, including the large amount of medical research supported by the National Institutes of Health.

Could this resurgence in technology markets signal an accompanying resurgence in independent creation of technology, leading to more competition? Unfortunately, the experience of university tech transfer shows that complexity still presents significant restraints on independent creation of technology. Following Bayh-Dole, scores of universities set up technology transfer offices and established rules on faculty research to encourage the patenting and licensing of university research in the hope that this would generate new funds to support research. Yet assessments of the results have not been strongly encouraging.[32] University research has long been commercialized without technology transfer offices, often by faculty creating their own startup firms. There is not clear evidence that the Bayh-Dole Act increased commercialization beyond what had been achieved before. Indeed, although a small number of university tech transfer programs have been profitable, most of them—87 percent—operate in the red.[33] And they have had substantial difficulty finding licensees for many of their patents.[34] With a few prominent exceptions, Bayh-Dole has not led to a dramatic expansion of independent innovation.

The difficulties faced bringing many of these ideas to market are similar to the challenges facing the development of an automatic loom a century ago. Many of the ideas are little more than prototypes, needing a huge amount of investment, complementary developments, refinement, testing, and so on before a viable product can be brought to market. As with the loom, tacit knowledge of the researchers has been shown to be critical for success; a simple patent license is hardly sufficient.[35] In a paper reviewing developments over the past several decades, Ashish Arora has reassessed the division of labor between university and corporate labs overall (along with coauthors Sharon Belenzon, Andrea Patacconi, and Jungkyu Suh), concluding, "Knowledge produced by universities is not often in a form that can be readily digested and turned into new goods and services. Small firms and university technology transfer offices cannot fully substitute for corporate research, which had integrated multiple disciplines at the scale required to solve significant technical problems. Therefore, whereas the division of innovative labor may have raised the volume of science by universities, it has also slowed, at least for a period of time, the transformation of that knowledge into novel products and processes."[36]

The complexity of the entire innovation process appears to limit the market for technology much as it did at the end of the nineteenth century. Licensing still occurs, of course, but mainly of components. Because of the complexity involved, neither university researchers nor small biotech companies nor independent inventors are able to fully develop many modern technologies. And this limits the emergence of independent rival technologies.

But the challenge is even greater for the large proprietary software systems used by today's superstar firms. By some metrics, these systems are far more complex than, say, drug development; they involve far more data. Moreover, these systems are often specific to firm organizational structures. For example, Walmart's system is specifically linked to the way it organizes suppliers, store managers, and headquarter managers.

As a result, rivals face a steep obstacle to developing systems that can compete with those of the dominant firms. The automatic transmission was an innovation that diffused relatively rapidly in the 1940s and 1950s due to both market transactions and sharing of knowledge. Today, third parties still develop transmissions as well as transmission control modules, the computers that now control transmissions. Improvements in these components can diffuse rapidly. But what really matters is the whole, integrated technology, and this is where complexity bites. Although smaller automobile companies can license a transmission control module, they are at a loss when it comes to integrating all of the components of a modern automobile as well as Toyota does. And so, the threat Toyota feels from independently developed technology is diminished.

Do Superstar Firms Want to License Their Technology?

But even if superstar firms face a diminished threat from independent creation of technology, they might still choose to diffuse their technology *voluntarily,* either through sharing or through licensing. Recall, for instance, that General Motors licensed its automatic transmission technology to other firms, including direct rivals such as Ford's Lincoln division, which competed directly against GM's Cadillac. And, as noted above, firms will sometimes freely share new technology with rivals. This was true of the early textile mills and is true with open-source software today.

However, these decisions depend on a specific economic calculation. In superstar markets, dominant firms will not want to license or share their technology for a very simple reason: the primary benefit of these technologies is that they differentiate the leading firm from its rivals. Licensing rivals will destroy this benefit, making such a transaction undesirable.

Consider the apparent economic logic behind GM's decision to license the automatic transmission to Ford. The critical factor was that the automatic transmission increased the total size of the market, bringing in new customers and creating an opportunity for what economists call gains from trade. Obviously, letting Ford have the automatic transmission increased the degree of competition with Ford, tending to reduce GM's profit. Even though GM would have earned royalties from Ford, if the market had remained the same size, then those royalties would likely not have offset the loss of profits GM experienced. This is because with greater price competition the joint profits of GM and Ford would decrease. Even if GM captured all of Ford's profits from the automatic transmission, its total profits would decline.

However, the automatic transmission substantially *expanded* the market. With the automatic transmission, cars could now be sold to that substantial number of people who had difficulty learning to drive manual shift cars or who found manual shifting to be cumbersome. A larger market meant higher joint profits to divide between GM and Ford. Although licensing meant a smaller share of the pie for General Motors, GM still made out better because the pie was that much larger. Hence, GM licensed Ford.

But today's superstar firms are employing technologies that mainly give them a larger share of the pie and do little to increase the size of the market. The way these technologies are deployed is more "business stealing" than growth enhancing.[37] When Walmart opens a Supercenter, consumers in the region do purchase somewhat more groceries and merchandise. But most of the gains in Walmart's sales come from other retailers. When Toyota introduces a new car model, perhaps the total number of car purchases might increase, but most of Toyota's sales are coming from other manufacturers or from Toyota's other models. Software systems that manage complexity give firms advantages at differentiating their products for rivals, but they don't necessarily increase the size of the market substantially. And for this reason, superstar firms often have little incentive to license or share their technology with rival firms.

The combined effect of reduced licensing incentives and a reduced ability to replicate complex systems is to limit access to the new technologies. And limited access means that it is more difficult for rivals to challenge or leapfrog dominant firms. Other developments reinforce these tendencies. Changes in intellectual property law and in employment law have tended to reduce the mobility of talented technologists and managers, making it more difficult for challengers to hire the talent they need to compete. And quality competition can lead to slower growth of innovative firms. I explore these developments in later chapters.

The Challenge of Limited Access

Is it really a problem if dominant firms have grown larger and more persistently dominant? Why should this trend be troubling? After all, these firms have grown more dominant by delivering greater value to consumers. They provide greater selection in stores, products with more features, and more highly targeted credit, insurance, and services. Using new software systems, the top firms mass customize products and services to meet individual consumer needs to an unprecedented degree. Moreover, in the process, they have created many jobs, and as we shall see, they pay higher salaries.

The troubling aspect of the superstar economy is that, so far, access to these new technologies has been limited, there is a technology gap, and diffusion has slowed. While keeping the technology proprietary may be best for the profits of superstar firms, it is not best for society. Consumers would be better off if more retailers had Walmart's logistics, inventory, and shipping capabilities so that they, too, could offer greater selection, faster response to changes in demand, and lower costs. And consumers would be better off if other automobile manufacturers could produce cars with Toyota-level quality and features. Moreover, diffusion would bring not only a direct benefit to consumers but also the long-term benefits of greater competition to spur ongoing innovation. Instead, limited access to the technology visits upon us a host of ills.

There is, indeed, a downside to the way the superstar economy has developed. Limited access means that innovative new firms face headwinds to growth, slowing aggregate productivity growth; it means that only select workers can gain critical new skills and, with these skills, higher pay, thus raising income inequality; it means that government regulators can be evaded or deceived.

Yet the information technology behind mass customization does not inherently imply limited access. It is true that these are large systems and will require large organizations to run them. It is also true that these systems are complex and are thus difficult to replicate. However, there are policies that can encourage greater access, and there are actions that firms can take to allow greater access. Indeed, some firms have found it very profitable to unbundle their technologies. The policy challenge is to preserve the social benefits of mass customization while opening access to the technology. Policy can affect the degree to which firms using the advanced technologies of mass customization are primarily engaged in winning a greater share of the economic pie as opposed to the extent to which they expand the size of the pie to the greater benefit of society as a whole.

5

The Automation Paradox

"Let me start by saying a few things that seem obvious," declared Geoffrey Hinton in 2016. "I think if you work as a radiologist, you're like the coyote that's already over the edge of the cliff but hasn't yet looked down, so doesn't realize there's no ground underneath him. People should stop training radiologists now. It's just completely obvious that within five years, deep learning is going to do better than radiologists because it's going to get a lot more experience."[1] Hinton, a computer scientist at the University of Toronto and Google, is a pioneer of new techniques in machine learning, including deep learning, one technique of so-called artificial intelligence (AI) technology. He joins a long line of eminent observers predicting—incorrectly—that dramatic job losses are about to occur because machines have become more capable than humans at some work tasks. Luminaries ranging from Karl Marx to John Maynard Keynes as well as many lesser lights have been making such warnings since the Industrial Revolution. As new AI systems have demonstrated abilities to read X-rays, drive cars, and handle customer service requests, news media have flooded us with warnings about the imminent end of work. Consultants have issued more than eighteen recent reports predicting job losses from automation.[2] More than a dozen recent economics papers have sought to identify the theory and empirical impact of automation.[3]

Yet to a great degree, all of this attention is focused on the wrong issue. New technologies *are* transforming the economy. But they are not so much replacing humans with machines as they are *enhancing* human labor, allowing workers to do more, provide better quality, and do new things. The impacts of AI and new information technology on other aspects of society are likely to be far more important than employment impacts during the next several decades.

Because such fears of mass unemployment are widespread, I take a brief detour in this chapter to explore the impact of automation. Automation will affect many jobs over the next several decades, as it has over past decades and centuries. But automation will not result in major job losses anytime soon because it is also creating new jobs. Jobs are shifting, not disappearing. These job shifts are still a significant social problem because they require workers to gain new skills, in many cases changing occupations and employers. Yet new technology is transforming the economy in other ways, leading to the increased dominance of large firms, contributing to growing inequality, and slowing productivity growth.

What these prophets of doom fail to see—and what they have consistently failed to see for the past two hundred years—is that demand matters. The impact of technology on society is not purely a supply-side matter. As described in chapter 3, the scope of demand means that industries become dominated by a few large firms when firms can compete by leveraging complexity. And the depth of demand means that industries often increase employment when automation reduces the amount of labor required to produce a unit of output. Human desire saves our jobs in the face of automation. But human desire is also leading us to a very different economy.

Replace Labor or Enhance Labor?

At the time of this writing, nearly five years after Hinton's prediction, no radiologist jobs have been lost. In fact, there is a worldwide shortage of radiologists, despite widespread offshoring of X-ray analysis to India.[4] This is not to say that machine learning has not produced some impressive proof-of-concept studies. For example, one typical study trained an algorithm using chest X-ray images that had been labeled as to which had signs of pneumonia. This algorithm performed somewhat better than four radiologists at identifying cases of pneumonia.[5] There are many other such studies, and scores of startups are trying to apply machine learning to radiology.

But these demonstrations, while impressive, are a very long way from showing that these machines are about to completely replace radiologists. For one thing, many of these trials involve small samples (four radiologists!), many have not been replicated or published in peer-reviewed journals, nor have many demonstrations been done in actual clinical practice where the challenges might be far more difficult than in carefully controlled laboratory settings. Indeed, one recent paper reviewed 2,212 machine learning trials attempting to diagnose Covid-19 on X-rays. The review concluded, "None of the models identified are of potential clinical use due to methodological flaws and/or underlying biases."[6]

More important, radiologists need to scan X-rays for more than just pneumonia, and scanning X-rays, in any case, is only a small part of what radiologists do. As Gary Marcus and Max Little write,

> Radiology is not just about images. Deep-learning systems excel at classifying images but radiologists (and other doctors, such as pathologists) must integrate what they see in an image with other facts about patient history, currently prevalent illnesses, and the like. As Dr. Anand Prabhakar, an emergency radiologist at Massachusetts General Hospital told us, "Although radiologists are experts at imaging pattern recognition, a large fraction of the work involves understanding the pathophysiology of disease so images can be interpreted correctly. For example, pneumonia on a chest X-ray could also have the same appearance as a variety of conditions, including cancer. A typical radiologist will suggest a diagnosis based on the patient's clinical presentation obtained from the electronic medical record—such as fever, age, gender, smoking history, or bloodwork."[7]

Although we are not yet at the point where AI systems will be widely used in radiology practice, it does seem likely that clinically tested scanning algorithms will be employed in radiology over the coming years. But the identification of possible disease on X-rays is only one task among the many that radiologists do, and even this task may require additional input from radiologists. This means that AI machines will not replace radiologists; they will instead become a tool that *enhances* radiologists' capabilities, allowing them to make better diagnoses and faster treatment recommendations.

In fact, while technology frequently automates specific tasks, it rarely automates every task an occupation performs. I studied what happened to the 271 detailed occupations used in the 1950 Census by 2010.[8] Many occupations were eliminated for a variety of reasons. In many cases, demand for the occupational services declined (for example, boardinghouse keepers); in some cases, demand declined because of technological obsolescence (for instance, telegraph operators). This, however, is not the same as automation. In only one case—elevator operators—can the decline and disappearance of an occupation be largely attributed to automation. Nevertheless, this sixty-year period witnessed extensive automation, but it was almost entirely *partial* automation. The same will likely be true for AI automation over the next several decades. Few AI applications are targeted at automating all of the tasks that occupations perform because human jobs typically involve many different tasks, many of which are hardly automatable.[9] While a few jobs—perhaps certain types of truck drivers, for instance—may be at risk for replacement, AI and technology generally are much more about enhancing humans than about replacing them.

And this difference is critical to understanding the impact of new technologics. In chapter 1, I noted that the bar code scanner did reduce the labor required of cashiers by 18–19 percent, decreasing labor costs in stores by 4.5 percent. But the major transformative effect of the bar code scanner was not its impact on jobs for cashiers; the major impact arose from the enhanced capabilities that the bar code scanner and associated technology provided Walmart. These altered the nature of the services that Walmart provides with major implications for competition, industry, and society. Focusing on supposed job losses is focusing on the wrong issue.

The Automation Paradox

In fact, the bar code scanner did not eliminate jobs for cashiers, despite some initial expectations that it would. The adoption of the scanner in grocery stores started slowly after that first installation in 1974 but then accelerated in the 1980s. By 1985, 29 percent of supermarkets used scanners. Yet the number of full-time-equivalent cashiers continued to increase during the 1980s and 1990s.[10]

Nor is job growth in the face of automation unusual. The automated teller machine (ATM) was initially expected to reduce the number of bank teller jobs. Hundreds of thousands of ATMs were installed at U.S. banks from 1995 to 2005, yet the number of full-time-equivalent bank tellers increased. The same was true for paralegals as software for electronic document discovery in litigation—some of it AI powered—became widely used by U.S. law firms. Indeed, there is an automation paradox: when machines start doing the work of people, the need for people often increases.[11]

Of course, this is not always the case. When people think of automation, they often think about manufacturing, where automation is sometimes associated with drastic job losses. The U.S. cotton textile industry had over four hundred thousand production workers in the 1940s, but this figure has declined to fewer than twenty thousand today. Most of this decline can be attributed to automation. Globalization has hurt the industry over the past two decades, but for at least half a century industry employment declined with little threat of imports. Yet even in manufacturing, the automation paradox can be observed. For over a century *before* 1940, employment in the cotton textile industry grew alongside automation, even as automation was dramatically reshaping the industry.

The key to understanding the automation paradox is consumer demand. Automation reduced the amount of labor required to produce a yard of cloth. But in a competitive market, this led to lower prices. And lower prices increased demand for cloth. Indeed, during the early nineteenth century there was large pent-up demand. This was because cloth was very expensive—the typical adult had only one set of clothing. When the price fell, consumers purchased more cloth for additional clothing and for other purposes. In fact, they purchased a lot more cloth. Demand for cloth grew so much that total employment increased even though the labor required per yard fell. Automation induced a highly elastic demand response.

But by the mid-twentieth century, textile demand in the United States was satiated. People had closets full of clothing, upholstered furniture, draperies, and so on. Automation has continued to increase output per worker at about the same percentage rate, but the demand response has become inelastic. Demand growth no longer offsets the labor-saving effect of automation. And so, employment falls.

This pattern is seen not just in textiles but also in the primary steel and automotive industries, businesses that also experienced sustained rapid productivity growth. These industries also experienced an inverted U in employment, growing for many decades at first and then leveling off or declining. Moreover, there is some reason to believe that this inverted U pattern might apply more generally to other industries.[12]

Current Evidence

This analysis implies that the effect of automation on employment within industries varies over time and that, at any time, it varies from industry to industry. What about today's industries, and what about new information technologies, including AI?

One of the most comprehensive sources of data about automation comes from the Netherlands, where government statistical agencies have been collecting information about how much individual firms spend on automation services each year. These data are linked to administrative data on firms and on individual workers. There are few other sources of data on all types of automation at the firm level and few linked to the extensive firm and worker data needed to explore impacts. These data cover about five million workers annually from 2000 to 2016 at some 36,490 firms in all major private, nonfinancial sectors.

My coauthors, Maarten Goos, Anna Salomons, and Wiljan van den Berge, and I explored what these data can tell us about the impact of automation on workers.[13] First, it is important to note that automation is not just about robots or manufacturing industries; it affects most every sector, some more deeply than manufacturing.[14] Indeed, robots affect a very small portion of the workforce. In our sample, many more workers were affected by automation generally—about 9 percent of the incumbent workers (those with three or more years' job tenure) were employed at firms that made major investments in automation each year. We focused our analysis on those firms that made major investments in automation. It turns out that firms tended to make discrete, "lumpy" investments in automation; they tended to invest a lot at once rather than invest incrementally in small amounts each year. These major investment episodes helped us identify the effects of automation because we could compare how firms grew following the automation events compared to similar firms that did not make such investments at the same time.

The data are very clear: employment grows substantially faster at firms that make major investments in automation compared to firms that do not. This finding, which is confirmed in other studies, means that automation is not simply replacing workers at such a rate as to directly cause mass unemployment.

Nevertheless, it might still be the case that automation reduces employment for several reasons. First, firms that invest in automation tend to grow faster than nonautomating firms even before they make their major automation investments. This makes sense because firms might choose to automate as a way to manage faster growth. But this means that perhaps employment would have grown even faster at these firms if they had chosen not to automate. That is, automation might have eliminated *potential* jobs. Of course, it is difficult to know how many jobs would have been created in the counterfactual case where these firms did not invest. A number of studies, including the Dutch study, have attempted to estimate the impact of automation on firm employment controlling for confounding factors using different econometric techniques. Overall, they find that automation has a neutral or positive effect on employment at the automating firm.[15]

Second, while automating firms might increase employment, jobs might be lost at other firms. For instance, the firms in an industry that don't automate may have lower productivity than the firms that do automate. As a result, these firms might be less competitive and see declining sales and employment.[16] Also, changes within an industry may affect other industries. Several papers have looked at the impact of automation on aggregate or industry-level employment. With one exception, these papers find that technology does not lead to aggregate declines in employment.[17]

Finally, even if net employment does not change much, many jobs may be eliminated while new job openings are created. That is, the net number of jobs may not change, but there is more labor market churn. This means that even if automation does not create mass unemployment, it may still impose a significant burden on workers: they may be unemployed temporarily, and they may need to acquire new skills, change occupations or industries, or even relocate.

The Burden of Automation

The Dutch study estimates the magnitude of these transitional burdens. We studied the impact of automation on incumbent workers, those workers who were employed at their firm for three or more years before the automation event. Over the five years following automation, these workers lost, on average, about 11 percent of one year's earnings or, in absolute terms, €3,800.

These losses arose mainly from spells of nonemployment. The daily wage rate did not change for these workers, regardless of whether they stayed at their firm or moved. But automation did cause workers to leave their firms. About 2 percent more of the incumbent workers left by comparison to the control group, either because they were laid off or because they chose to leave. Over five years, the cumulative separation probability was less than 13 percent. All told, workers at automating firms lost eighteen days of work on average (for both leavers and stayers) over five years.

Further, these losses were only partially offset by benefits from the Dutch social safety net. Overall, incumbent workers recouped some 13 percent of their losses from unemployment benefits, disability benefits, and welfare payments. This finding is comparable to that in other worker displacement events, where typically only a small part of the negative impact is compensated by social security.[18] Workers affected by an automation event are more likely to switch industries than workers in firms that automate later. Besides industry switches, we did not find economically sizable or statistically significant changes in terms of workers' average or median firm wage, firm size, or firm automation expenditure. Affected workers were also somewhat more likely to take early retirement and to enter self-employment.

Who is affected? As above, in each year of our sample, about 9 percent of the incumbent workers were at firms that experienced an automation event. While not every worker at each automating firm was affected, the number of workers at those firms was large. These firms were in all sectors studied, and although large firms tended to spend more on automation per worker than did smaller firms on average, many small firms did spend significantly.

We also looked at worker characteristics. We did not find significant differences in outcomes by gender. Nor did we find significant difference by wage after controlling for worker age. That is, contrary to a common perception, it is not low-wage workers who are primarily affected by automation. When we compared workers by wage to other workers in the same firms, we found, if anything, that higher-wage workers experienced larger relative income losses, although the difference is not statistically significant. Last, we did find that older workers are more severely affected. Workers fifty years of age and older experienced larger income losses, mainly due to longer periods of nonemployment. Older workers appeared to have a harder time finding new work.

Thus, automation does indeed have a significant negative impact on workers—not by permanently eliminating jobs but by burdening workers with significant costs of switching to new jobs. People have been focusing on the wrong issue when looking at effects of automation on workers. It is not mainly about mass unemployment; it is about job transitions.

How big is this burden? We can gain some sense by comparing these automation events to mass layoff events. Economists have studied what happens to workers after firms close or lay off many workers following bankruptcy, changing demand conditions, technological obsolescence, and other reasons. Automation events tend to affect fewer workers at the affected firms by comparison to those events, and workers leave more gradually after automation events. While the mass layoff literature studies layoffs of 30 percent of the workforce or more, the automation events account for only a 2 percent increase in incumbent employee separations during the first year followed by a continuing trickle of separations. Also, mass layoffs have been found to permanently reduce wage rates; we found no such effect for workers subject to major automation events. A rough calculation suggests that about 1 percent of incumbent workers leave their employers as the result of major automation events each year. In contrast, about 4 percent of workers in both the United States and the Netherlands are displaced annually in mass layoffs because of their employers' adverse economic conditions.[19]

Thus, while automation imposes significant losses on some workers, the impact seems somewhat smaller than the impact of mass layoffs and plant closures that occur from ongoing economic turbulence.

The Wrong Question

But it is a mistake to focus on automation. Many people seem to make a steadfast and automatic assumption that technology is mainly about eliminating labor. Perhaps this assumption derives from our long fascination with automated creatures. In Greek mythology, the god Hephaestus created automatons to do his work. In Jewish medieval lore, autonomous golems were created out of mud. In the nineteenth century, Mary Shelley's Frankenstein brought a creature to life. Perhaps we are fascinated by such stories because they cause us to think about what makes us different from machines. Or maybe our fascination stems from fears about how our inventions might work against us.

It is also true that the promoters of AI play to our fears. Geoff Hinton is hardly the first AI researcher to hype the technology. The pioneers of AI also made predictions in the 1950s and 1960s that seem a tad too optimistic. In 1957, future Nobel laureate Herbert Simon predicted that within ten years a computer would be the world chess champion (off by forty years) and would "discover and prove an important mathematical theorem" (not yet). After having coined the term "artificial intelligence," John McCarthy founded the Stanford AI Project in 1963 with the goal of "building a fully intelligent machine within a decade." In 1967, Marvin Minsky, another pioneer, posited that "within a generation . . . few compartments of intellect will remain outside the machine's realm—the problem of 'artificial intelligence' will be substantially solved." Hype is good for attracting research money and talented engineers, and the best hype targets our fears.[20]

But economists, too, have tended to focus on the effects of labor-saving automation rather than on other aspects of new technologies such as AI.[21] Nothing illustrates this more clearly than the apparent focus in the economics literature on robots. While robots are dramatic examples of labor-saving automation, investment in robots is *tiny* compared to other investments in technology. The U.S. Census reports that expenditures on all robotic equipment came to $6.5 billion in 2018.[22] That same year, private investment in information processing equipment and software was $778.6 billion.[23] Moreover, robots are mainly used in just a few manufacturing industries such as the automobile industry.

What is the effect of these broader technology investments on employment? The Dutch study also looked at what happens when firms make big investments in computers using the same methodology that we used in evaluating the impact of automation expenditures.[24] We found that major computer investments did not lead to increases in workers leaving firms or increases in nonemployment spells for incumbent workers. With Cesare Righi, I explored what happens when U.S. firms make major investments in developing their own software, the focus of this book.[25] Employment of non-IT workers grew about 7 percent after the year that the investment took place, but firm revenues grew even more at 11 percent.

These large investments in proprietary systems are having an effect on the economy, but it is not about replacing workers with robots. These systems help firms increase their sales and market shares; they help increase demand for workers. If we are to understand the transformative effects of this major switch in technology investments, we should not focus just on labor-saving effects or exotic robotic technologies.

Future Automation

But perhaps that is all about to change soon. Prophets of doom warn that "this time is different." They argue that in the past blue-collar jobs were replaced by white-collar jobs, but this time white-collar workers are affected. They argue that the coming changes will affect a broader swath of the economy and that these changes will come faster than the economy can adjust.

This time is, indeed, different. Yet these differences do not mean that the coming changes will bring mass unemployment over the next couple of decades. Yes, white-collar jobs are affected, but the evidence above suggests that new white-collar jobs are also being created. Yes, a broad swath of the economy is affected, but this was true, too, in the past, as when agriculture was mechanized.

Moreover, evidence suggests that the AI technologies deployed in the near future will tend to enhance humans more than replace them. A survey asked AI startups what benefits they deliver to customers.[26] Almost all respondents strongly agreed that their products enhanced the capabilities of their customers to make predictions or decisions, to manage and understand data, and to create new and improved products and services; only around half of the respondents cited reducing labor costs or automating routine tasks as benefits. And as with the cases of radiologists or bank tellers, even technology that automates labor can enhance worker capabilities and increase employment.

It is also possible that the pace of change will accelerate. But that does not imply permanent mass unemployment either. The reason, again, is demand. The above evidence about automation and employment implies that demand tends to be elastic on average in those occupations and industries affected by automation today. That is, the labor-saving effect of automation is offset by the accompanying increase in demand, leading to job growth. If the pace of automation increases and demand remains elastic, then this just means that the pace of job growth will also increase. This may mean a faster rate of churn and more rapid need for workers to transition to new jobs, but it does not mean mass unemployment or a major permanent loss of jobs.

And we have every reason to expect that if demand is elastic in those industries affected by automation today, it will remain elastic for the next couple of decades. The historical evidence clearly shows that the nature of demand only changes slowly. If consumers have large pent-up demand for clothing, they will still have substantial demand for additional clothing once they acquire a bit more in a few years. Indeed, it took over a century and a twentyfold increase in cloth consumption per capita before demand for cotton and synthetic cloth became satiated. To the extent that demand today for health care, entertainment, services, and finance is highly elastic, we have good reason to think that it will continue to be highly elastic for the next ten or twenty years at least. And that means automation will not generally bring job losses in these industries.

Of course, if we look fifty or a hundred years into the future, the prognosis is much less certain for a couple of reasons. First, in that time frame demand for the services that are highly elastic today might well become satiated. Also, technology might be able to completely automate more jobs. Yet even in this time frame, it is not clear that work will disappear. But much depends on the essential nature of demand.

To understand the economic outcomes, we need to speculate about essential human desires. Is much of what we desire in the service sector

based on human-to-human interaction? While humans are known to an-
thropomorphize robots and treat them as humans, perhaps there is an
element in us that demands actual social interaction that machines cannot
replace. Also, there may be some elements of demand that do not become
satiated. Can we ever have too much health care that improves both the
length and quality of life? Do we have a basic need for what economists
call status goods, goods that distinguish us from our neighbors or communicate a distinct identity? If so, then demand for these goods might not
satiate either.

Any such speculation about the nature of demand a century hence should
be done with considerable humility. Some very smart people in the past
have made predictions about automation and employment, and they have
consistently underestimated the depth of human demand. For example,
in 1930, Keynes, anticipating continued productivity growth, predicted
that in one hundred years his grandchildren would enjoy a fifteen-hour
workweek.[27] Now that we are close to that hundred-year mark, the average
workweek for OECD nations is thirty-four hours. Yet Keynes was right
about productivity growth. By 1977 a worker in the United States produced
the same output in fifteen hours as a worker in 1930 produced in a week
on average. What Keynes did not grasp was the depth of human wants and
desires—that is, the depth of consumer demand. We *choose* not to work
fifteen-hour weeks because we find meaning in work or because we demand
more goods and services that technology has made cheaper and better.[28]
A similar underestimation of demand lies behind many other failed predictions of automation-induced mass unemployment.

Demand thus powerfully mediates the impact of technology on society.
It is the depth of demand that softens the impact of automation. But it is
the scope of demand—the differences in our individual preferences and
willingness to pay—that the new generation of large software systems taps
into, enabling firms to differentiate from their rivals by addressing a broader
scope of consumer needs and to become dominant in their industries. By
meeting disparate demands, these software systems deliver substantial
social benefits. But because access to these technologies is limited, the use
of these systems also generates significant social problems.

6

The Productivity Gap

Headwinds

In 2005, two speech recognition startups, ScanSoft and Nuance Communications, merged, creating a powerhouse designed to attack what they saw, correctly, as a burgeoning opportunity. "Speech software is transforming the way people use digital devices and access information systems," said Paul Ricci, CEO of the new Nuance Communications, in the press release announcing the merger.[1] Nuance recognized early on that voice would become a central means of communication between people and computers, as we now see with Apple's Siri, Amazon's Alexa, and Google Assistant. Nuance began in 1994 as a spinoff from SRI, a Stanford laboratory that had developed speech recognition technology for the U.S. government.

Following the merger, Nuance grew rapidly for almost a decade—27 percent per annum growth in sales on average—until suddenly, around 2014, it stopped growing. Revenues in 2019 were roughly the same as revenues in 2013. Nuance ran into strong headwinds from dominant computer firms, Amazon, Google, and Apple. I spoke with Dan Faulkner, former senior vice president and general manager of Nuance, to understand what happened. Dan began his career on the engineering side, studying linguistics at the University of Manchester and speech and language processing at the University of Edinburgh. He came to the United States in 2001 to work for SpeechWorks, an MIT spinoff, that was soon acquired by ScanSoft. When Dan joined, the company had fifty employees; when he left, they had fourteen thousand. ScanSoft and, later, Nuance assembled a large portion of what was then a rare talent—data scientists, software developers, managers, and professional service people who had deep skills around speech and language technology. They did this through direct hiring, but also Nuance acquired talented startup companies such as SpeechWorks and successfully integrated them into their operations.[2] Nuance acquired more than fifty companies after 2005.

In the 1990s and early 2000s, speech recognition was constrained by the limited processing power of computers in use then. This meant that the systems of that time recognized only limited vocabularies. Nevertheless, there were important commercial applications that could be handled with small vocabularies, such as the transcription of medical records with specialized vocabularies or telephone customer support centers. For example, large banks received millions of phone calls a day, and most of these calls were for limited tasks that could be automated, such as checking a bank balance. Older telephone answering systems allowed bank customers to navigate a series of menus using touch-tone phone signals. With speech recognition, customers could simply speak their request into the telephone. If it was a simple request, the system could provide the answer without the involvement of a human agent; if not, then the system would route the caller to the appropriate human agent. Combined, these systems saved the banks a lot of money, and at the same time, they improved customer service. Based on these narrow applications, Nuance grew solidly following the 2005 merger.

Then, in the late 2000s, things changed. Nuance developed "large vocabulary continuous speech recognition." According to Dan, "Suddenly it became, you can say anything on any topic and we can accurately transcribe it. That was the thing that unlocked the [health care] business." They also used this technology in a new app for the iPhone called Dragon Dictation. "What we had uniquely solved was the ability to do accurate real-time dictation on to a glass phone that had a terrible keyboard all the people were complaining about. And it was amazing. It was really accurate. It was fast. It didn't care about your accent, and we were the only people who could solve that problem." Apple introduced the iPhone 3GS at its 2009 Worldwide Developers Conference, and the company featured the

Dragon Dictation app in its display. Once Apple validated the product, Samsung and all the other phone manufacturers wanted it. So, too, did Google, Amazon, and Microsoft. Nuance grew rapidly, by signing up all these major customers as well as millions of individual customers who purchased the iPhone app. The app became the number one business productivity application in the iTunes store.[3] Two years later, Apple introduced Siri, which was based on Nuance technology. Nuance revenues grew to $1.7 billion in 2013.

But this growth was short-lived. With the success of Nuance, the Big Tech firms realized that voice was poised to become a prime channel for humans to interact with computers and cloud services. Voice recognition was no longer just about dictation but about searching for information, shopping, selection of music or video entertainment, controlling appliances, and much more. Compared to keyboards or computer mice, voice recognition was hands-free, much faster, didn't require typing skills, and is a much more natural way for humans to communicate.

So, the Big Tech firms started plowing big investments and talent into this opportunity. Amazon, for example, has more than ten thousand engineers working on Alexa products, more than ten times the number of core R&D employees Nuance employed at its peak.[4] Amazon's R&D expenditures on voice-related products probably exceeds Nuance's revenues. And Big Tech has successfully raided Nuance's talent pool, bringing top people into their folds. Google, Apple, Microsoft, and Baidu are also investing heavily and recruiting aggressively.

The big opportunity that motivates these large investments goes far beyond dictation. Big Tech firms are using voice to handle a large variety of interactions, and their existing product and customer bases give them a distinct advantage over Nuance. Amazon's Alexa products were initially designed to handle many tasks from music to shopping, but Amazon also created an ecosystem where third-party developers could create additional skills. Today there are more than one hundred thousand such skills, and the voice engine handles each of them.[5] Also, Amazon has licensed the Alexa far-field technology to appliance manufacturers to control dishwashers, clothes washers and dryers, and vacuum cleaners. Apple's iPhone and Google's Android phones now use their own voice products to handle a wide range of tasks. Although Apple purchased the Nuance engine to power Siri, the company has since developed its own systems. While Dragon Dictation was widely used on Android phones, Google moved aggressively in 2014 to require handset manufacturers to include either all of Google's applications or none on their phones. Manufacturers that wanted to customize their offerings were now required to provide a full suite of their own alternatives, something few manufacturers could do.[6] This meant that Dragon products had to hand control over to Google applications using the microphone, excluding them from dealing with an array of tasks. In many cases, the manufacturers no longer preinstalled Dragon.

As a result, Nuance's products handled a much narrower range of tasks or interactions than the voice systems of the large tech firms. This was critical because these systems improve with use. That is, voice recognition uses machine learning; the more data from more different tasks that the systems encounter, the better they can improve their quality on those tasks. And the range of applications used by the Big Tech firms and the large numbers of users gives them a huge data advantage. There are three hundred million Alexa devices installed; Google handles 5.6 billion searches each day on average, and half of Google users report using voice for search.[7]

The headwinds that Nuance encountered blew directly from the superstar tech firms. Those firms precluded Nuance from accessing their phone platforms. Those firms made large investments to improve the quality of their voice technology, and they captured the data sources needed to build the best voice systems for general applications that handle a broad range of interactions (greater complexity). They began competing on the quality of the voice recognition systems on their phone platforms, and Nuance could no longer play that game. In 2018, Nuance announced that it was discontinuing support for many of its direct-to-consumer products to focus on vertical markets such as health care. In vertical applications such as health care, Nuance can still access the necessary data to develop the deep vocabulary needed to perform well, and Nuance's application-specific technological advantage is substantial. The move to a niche market strategy has improved profits and has been well received by investors, driving Nuance stock to an all-time high.

But Nuance has effectively exited the general market for consumer voice recognition. With enormous investments, the superstar tech firms leveraged their other businesses to build the best-quality consumer voice recognition and thus wrest control of that market from Nuance. This broad market is now a natural oligopoly. Although Nuance can thrive as a niche player, it is unlikely ever to grow so fast again as it did during the decade after its merger with ScanSoft. The niche strategy paid off. In April 2021, Microsoft announced that it was buying Nuance for $16 billion to expand its offerings in health care markets.[8]

This suppression of Nuance's growth is the flip side of declining disruption. As we saw in chapter 3, large investments by dominant firms can slow the growth of smaller rivals. The rise of superstar markets has changed industry dynamics. Let's now look at why small-firm growth rates matter, how they have changed, and what that means for productivity.

Productivity has become a major concern for economists because the growth rate of productivity has slowed dramatically since about 2005. The annual labor productivity growth rate for the nonfarm business sector fell from 2.7 percent per year from 2000 to 2007 to 1.4 percent per year since.[9] Labor productivity is the amount of output per worker, and it is important because this measure reflects how much income society generates per worker.[10] While not all of that income goes to workers, it represents the size of the proverbial pie. The bigger the pie, the better off we are on average. Over the past two centuries, productivity has grown robustly, and that growth has powered broad increases in the wealth of ordinary people. Now that growth has slowed, however, the economic prospects for many people are not improving.

Some people, such as Robert Gordon, author of *The Rise and Fall of American Growth,* argue that the slowdown has arisen because information technology no longer brings substantial productivity benefits.[11] That seems hard to square with the decisions of large firms to invest heavily in proprietary software systems. I argue instead that superstar industry dynamics, not a slowdown in innovation, can account for much of the decline in productivity growth. Moreover, I suggest that the superstar economy undermines the way economists measure productivity.

But first it is helpful to look briefly at a couple more examples. When a billion-dollar company like Nuance runs into strong headwinds, what happens to smaller companies and startups? Where do they get the needed data? They get it from their customers; they pay third parties for it; and they scrape the web, an activity that might land them in court.[12] Also, some startups use new techniques that allow them, to some extent, to synthesize data. But Dan Faulkner, the former Nuance executive, notes that this means that "the data disadvantage demands innovation at the periphery (how to address data acquisition and value) before the core business problem can be addressed."[13] Furthermore, acquiring data brings with it a significant regulatory burden. Firms selling in the European Union and firms whose customers sell in the EU must verify that their data handling and storage meet the requirements of the General Data Protection Regulation (GDPR). Other firms must verify that they conform to the U.S. National Institute of Standards and Technology Cybersecurity Framework. These regulations place a significant burden on startups. In one survey of startup firms, 69 percent of respondents who sell in Europe answered that they had to create a position in order to meet GDPR requirements.[14]

One might think that few startups would choose to enter this market because they face a severe disadvantage relative to the Big Tech firms. Some people have identified so-called kill zones where Big Tech dominance means that startups won't enter and venture capitalists won't finance startups. In fact, however, the rate of startup entry and venture capital has increased in this field. If we look at Crunchbase, a database of firms that includes startups, we see that the share of software startups going into speech recognition and natural language processing has quadrupled since 2005 and that 55 percent of these startups have received venture capital investments.[15]

Why are startups and venture capitalists still active in this technology despite the headwinds? Some, like Nuance, choose vertical niches where they have a specialization advantage that the dominant firms are not likely to acquire. But others develop general technologies with an eye to being acquired by a dominant firm. The developers who had created Siri formed a startup named Viv in 2012 to build "a more extensible, powerful version of Siri" in an intelligent personal assistant.[16] Samsung acquired Viv in 2016. Voysis, founded in Dublin in 2012, developed an independent voice platform for retailers.[17] It was acquired by Apple in 2020. Semantic Machines was created in 2014 to develop "next generation conversational AI." Microsoft bought it in 2018.[18]

Facing strong headwinds in a technology field, startups still enter and innovate and venture capitalists still invest. But they will not grow as fast or as large as firms such as Nuance did. Those that enter niche markets necessarily have smaller growth prospects. Those that aim to get acquired will typically do so before they grow large. The rise of dominant firms tends to slow the growth of startup firms.

And yet, the dream of startups developing a new technology that allows them to lead an industry has not died. UiPath is a startup that has grown rapidly to become Europe's first so-called unicorn with a valuation of over $10 billion. The company did this in the enterprise software market—the market for software systems that large firms use to manage accounting, resource planning, customer relations, and more—a $500 billion market dominated by large players such as Microsoft, SAP, and Oracle. I spoke to Daniel Dines, the founder and CEO of UiPath, about how the company has grown rapidly in a market dominated by large firms. Dines views the world very much as a software engineer. Speaking with a soft Romanian accent, he relates, "Five years ago, we were ten to fifteen people in a small office in Bucharest, Romania. Now I am not a businessperson, I am not fluent, I am not articulate in English, as you can see, but we had the technology and the vision and the funding . . . to change completely the world." Today UiPath employs around three thousand people and has a large global community of thirty thousand developers and analysts.

UiPath's technology is known as robotic process automation (RPA), which poorly describes what these systems actually do—they emulate tasks that humans perform on other software programs, allowing these tasks to be done automatically and allowing systems to be integrated. For example, suppose a firm has a customer relationship management (CRM) system that tracks interactions between customers and the company sales force and customer support department. Suppose the firm also has an accounting system from another vendor. In order to get a comprehensive picture of a single customer, employees need to navigate menus to identify the customer's history on the CRM software, obtain the customer ID, and enter this number in the appropriate menus of the accounting software. These steps can all be emulated using UiPath tools so that a worker can simply enter the customer's name to produce a customized report with both CRM and accounting information.

Robotic process automation eliminates such repetitive tasks and, more important, it allows for the easy integration of disparate computer systems. Vendors of enterprise systems usually provide interfaces to their systems so that software developers can access data and produce similar reports; these interfaces are called application programming interfaces (APIs). However, UiPath provides simple graphical tools that automate the process and are faster and less costly than custom programming an API. Moreover, as the underlying software programs are updated and change, UiPath maintains the ability to interpret the user interfaces so that software updates do not incur significant reprogramming.

Because robotic process automation allows large firms to integrate their systems relatively easily, it has emerged as a critical component of the proprietary software systems built by superstar firms. UiPath's customers include Walmart, Toyota, Facebook, and Google. The RPA market has been growing at about 60 percent per year to $1.4 billion in 2019. Within this market, UiPath zoomed to the top firm ranked by sales in 2018 after growing revenues sixfold over 2017.[19]

This growth did not go unnoticed by the large vendors of enterprise software. Of the top three largest vendors, Oracle partners with UiPath, SAP bought a French RPA company in 2018 to provide its own alternative, and Microsoft also introduced its own product, based in part on software developed by UK startup Softomotive.[20]

I asked Dines whether he was likely to disrupt companies like SAP or whether they are likely to dominate in his market: "Well, we're not replacing them. To me, SAP is just infrastructure. . . . I'm not going to build a completely horizontal system. . . . They can move into my business if they fully embrace it. . . . Of course, everybody can move into our market; it doesn't mean they will be successful." In fact, he said, the emulation techniques UiPath employs have been used many times before. For example, Microsoft has long used emulation to test programs with graphical user interfaces. "But in the world of much richer interfaces, it's much more difficult to build." Moreover, as "infrastructure," the dominant enterprise software firms cannot leverage their data or their existing software to gain dominance in robotic process automation. Indeed, the defining feature of RPA is that it works with the installed base of the large vendors. This means that the large vendors have no particular technical or data advantage and UiPath has a substantial head start in terms of technical expertise.[21]

I also asked Dines why his company had not been acquired. He suggested two reasons. First, fast growth makes valuation very difficult so that investors were not likely to value the company highly enough. While occasionally acquirers will pony up very large valuations, such as Facebook's offers for WhatsApp and Instagram, that did not happen. Second, UiPath has raised over $1 billion in venture capital, an astounding amount that has only been possible because recent returns on other financial instruments are near zero; that financing allowed UiPath to put off the need to "exit."[22]

UiPath demonstrates that it is still possible for startups to grow rapidly despite competition from industry-dominant rivals. Yet UiPath's circumstances are exceptional: a product that is difficult to imitate, limits to the extent that dominant firms can leverage their data or technology, extraordinary venture capital valuations, and a founder who retains control and is not interested in cashing out too soon. The overall picture that arises from these examples is that the rising dominance of large firms may suppress the growth of smaller firms, particularly innovative startups.

Measuring the Headwinds

This anecdotal evidence of headwinds is supported by more general quantitative evidence of a slowdown in the growth of startups. In the case of venture-backed startups, the time required to receive funding has lengthened substantially. The median time from the founding of a startup to the time it receives seed round funding grew from 0.9 years in 2006 to 2.5 years in 2020.[23] The median time to late-stage venture funding over the same period rose from 6.8 years to 8.1 years. Also, the time from first financing to exit rose. For firms that were acquired, the average time from first financing to acquisition tripled from a little over 2 years in 2000 to 6.3 years in 2018.[24] For firms that went public, the comparable times rose similarly. Researchers find that after 2005, startups in industries using cloud technology were less likely to receive follow-on financing and more likely to fail.[25] Another study identifies high-quality tech startups and finds that after 2000 they are less likely to grow sufficiently for a high-value acquisition or initial public offering (IPO).[26]

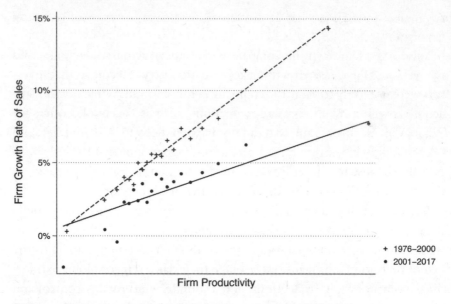

Figure 5. Firms grow more slowly in response to productivity
Source: Bessen and Denk, "From Productivity to Firm Growth."

But the clearest evidence is also the most basic: firms are growing more slowly in response to productivity. Innovation is sometimes hard to measure.[27] In many cases, productivity—the ratio of outputs to inputs—can be measured reasonably well, and hence many studies use this metric to gauge innovative success. I use what is called multifactor productivity, a measure that takes into account multiple inputs, including labor, tangible capital, and firm intangible investments.[28]

A key feature of Schumpeter's theory of creative destruction is that more productive firms—firms with better products or lower costs or better business models—will grow faster than less productive ones, eventually displacing less productive incumbent industry leaders. We can see this relationship in figure 5, where firms' rate of growth measured in sales increases proportionally to firm productivity.[29] But figure 5 also shows that this relationship changed sharply after the year 2000. The growth response to productivity dropped dramatically. On average, a firm with a given productivity could be expected to grow only half as fast after 2000 compared to the 1980s and 1990s. This decline is the counterpart to the decline in disruption discussed in chapter 2. When productive firms grow more slowly, they are less likely to leapfrog industry leaders and displace them. And many of the same factors are associated with the decline in the response to productivity. Much of the decline is accounted for by large firm investments in intangibles, by the growing concentration of industries, and by increased differences in productivity between firms.[30] The technology gap we saw in chapter 4 appears to be directly related to the slowdown in the growth rate of productive firms. Regardless of the causes, this figure provides unmistakable evidence of a decline in industry dynamism. But why should that matter?

Why Should We Care about Startups and Small Firms?

There are three major arguments about why the growth of startups and small firms might be important to our economic well-being, specifically for increasing innovation and productivity. One argument holds that small firms are more innovative than large ones and, therefore, that markets dominated by large firms will tend to be less innovative, all else equal. Indeed, there is a deep popular belief that small firms out-innovate their larger competitors.[31] Many people see creative destruction as a process where innovative small firms grow to disrupt large incumbent firms.

But Schumpeter himself challenged this view long ago. He argued that at least temporary market power was needed to incent firms to innovate.[32] Moreover, large firms have the resources to conduct extensive research. In a highly competitive market, firms cannot make significant profits and therefore have little motivation to invest in R&D.

Schumpeter's hypothesis and the controversial question of whether large or small firms are better innovators has spurred a large empirical literature. Innovation economist Wesley Cohen reviews fifty years of this literature to come to the general conclusion that firms of both sizes are important to innovation.[33] Both R&D and innovation increase with firm size, although "the number of innovations tends to increase less than proportionately than firm size, and the share of R&D effort dedicated to more incremental and process innovation tends to increase with firm size."[34] In other words, both small and large firms innovate, but small firms tend to do more product innovation and large firms tend to do more process and incremental innovation.[35]

If we look at the speech recognition market, there is no doubt that Nuance and Semantic Machines innovate and there is also no doubt that Amazon and Google are making major innovations. Indeed, the level of resources that Amazon is plowing into Alexa is far beyond the reach of small startups.

Some people argue further that the *acquisition* of small firms suppresses innovation. There is, in fact, some evidence of so-called killer acquisitions—that is, in some cases a large firm will acquire a small firm in order to shutter it and kill off potential competition.[36] But this evidence is quite limited. It pertains, so far, only to the pharmaceutical industry, where patents are well defined. This is important because it may be difficult to suppress a line of research without highly specific patents.[37] And it affects relatively few pharmaceutical acquisitions (5–7 percent). Furthermore, there are many examples where acquisitions helped acquiring firms increase innovation, including small and medium-sized companies. Indeed, Nuance developed its capabilities substantially through the acquisition of more than fifty companies.

In summary, both large and small firms are important for innovation, and the evidence does not support the conclusion that a greater role for large firms automatically means less innovation.

Another argument holds that competition from small firms drives large firms to be more innovative. The economist John Hicks famously asserted, "The best of all monopoly profits is a quiet life."[38] Competition disturbs that quiet life, forcing dominant firms to innovate.

There is, in fact, a lot of research on whether competition spurs innovation. Antitrust economist Carl Shapiro reviews this literature, concluding, "There is a very substantial body of empirical evidence supporting the general proposition that 'more competition,' meaning greater contestability of sales, spurs firms to be more efficient and to invest more in R&D."[39] For example, productivity economist Chad Syverson, studying the concrete industry, finds that productivity is higher when the producers are clustered more densely and so compete for customers more intensely.[40] There seem to be two effects here: more local competition spurs concrete producers to improve their techniques, and the low-productivity producers drop out.

But although competition spurs productivity improvement and innovation, this literature does not show that the competition has to come specifically from *small firms*. That argument was put forth by Joe Bain, a pioneer of the economics of industrial organization, in 1956.[41] He argued that some industries had entry barriers, such as economies of scale, that prevented small firms from coming into the industry. In his view, that meant less competition and thus less innovation and productivity improvement. This line of analysis was called the structure-conduct-performance paradigm and became an important guide to antitrust regulation for several decades. But in the 1980s, economists began questioning its empirical foundations.[42] They noticed that the causality could go the other way: firms that compete more effectively because they are better innovators might grow larger and drive smaller, less efficient producers out of the market.[43] In this case, industries dominated by large firms were sometimes more productive and more innovative. What mattered was the *contestability* of the market; a market dominated by a few large firms might nevertheless experience intense competition between them.[44] For example, the general speech recognition market is dominated by Amazon, Google, Apple, and Baidu, yet there is little doubt that these firms compete fiercely, spending large R&D investments in order to gain an edge. So, although competition is an important spur to innovation, this does not imply that innovation is greater when small firms dominate an industry.

A third, related argument holds that high-growth, high-productivity firms are the key to aggregate productivity growth. This argument fares better. It draws on an evolutionary view of industries, introduced by economists Richard Nelson and Sidney Winter, and related work on industry life cycles by economists Michael Gort and Steven Klepper.[45] In this view, more productive firms tend to grow because they can offer lower prices or better quality. At the same time, less productive firms cannot compete as well, so they shrink or go out of business. This Darwinian process serves to raise aggregate productivity. Competition is an important part of this process: competition is what weeds out the low-productivity firms. In the evolutionary account of productivity growth, highly productive young firms can play an essential role, but now it is growth rates that matter, not the distribution of firm sizes within an industry.

From this point of view, the changing relationship between productivity and firm growth seen in figure 5 is troubling. A group of researchers working with U.S. Census microdata on individual firms and establishments have shown the empirical importance of this change in a series of papers.[46]

Aggregate productivity growth can be decomposed into two parts: existing firms can become more productive (within-firm productivity growth), and more productive firms can grow faster while less productive firms shrink or exit (reallocation). When the researchers looked in detail at the actual growth patterns of U.S. firms, they found that the rate of reallocation slowed down sharply around the year 2000—corresponding to the decline seen in figure 5—and that this slowdown accounts for a substantial drop in the aggregate productivity growth rate. Critically, they found that this effect largely arises because startup firms are growing less rapidly on average and fewer of them grow very fast. In evolving industries, the growth of productive young firms is essential to raising aggregate productivity. This implies that suppression of young firm growth by dominant firms slows aggregate productivity growth. There is, indeed, reason to be concerned about industry dynamics in superstar capitalism.

In short, industry dynamism and the robustness of the startup economy do indeed matter. High-growth startup firms are critical to the evolution of productivity growth, their growth has slowed since 2000, and this deceleration accounts for much of the productivity slowdown of the past two decades. Large firm investments in intangibles generally and in software systems particularly are strongly associated with the slowdown in productivity. These headwinds to growth do indeed matter for aggregate productivity. Other factors may also contribute to the decline in productivity growth, but declining industry dynamism from superstar firms is a major factor.

The Myth of Declining Entrepreneurship

The research based on U.S. Census microdata attributes the slowdown in productivity growth to the slower growth of high-productivity firms. But many people believe that the slowdown arises instead from declining innovation, that firms are innovating less, and that for this reason their productivity grows less (within-firm rather than reallocation). The census researchers provide evidence that challenges this view. They find that we are seeing an even greater range in firm-level productivity after 2000, suggesting there is no slowdown in productivity-enhancing innovations. There are more firms with relatively higher productivity, presumably reflecting greater innovation.

Nevertheless, there appears to be a widely held belief that there has been a decline in innovation because of a sharp drop in the entry of new high-tech startups. For instance, congressional investigators have held hearings on antitrust and Big Tech (see chapter 9). They concluded that startup creation has declined and that Big Tech is to blame:

> In recent decades, however, there has been a sharp decline in new business formation as well as early-stage startup funding. The number of new technology firms in the digital economy has declined, while the entrepreneurship rate—the share of startups and young firms in the industry as a whole—has also fallen significantly in this market. Unsurprisingly, there has also been a sharp reduction in early-stage funding for technology startups. . . .
>
> There is mounting evidence that the dominance of online platforms has materially weakened innovation and entrepreneurship in the U.S. economy. Some venture capitalists, for example, report that they avoid funding entrepreneurs and other companies that compete directly with dominant firms in the digital economy. Often referred to as an innovation "kill zone," this trend may insulate powerful incumbent firms from competitive pressure simply because venture capitalists do not view new entrants as good investments.[47]

This view of declining new business formation and declining early stage financing for startups, however, is simply wrong. Figure 6 shows the number of young firms, aged five years or less, in thousands for the United States derived from comprehensive census figures.[48] The solid line shows the number of young high-tech firms (left axis), and the dashed gray line shows the total number of new firms in all sectors (right axis).[49] It is quite clear that new business formation rates have remained roughly constant for forty years with minor cyclical variation. However, new businesses include new restaurants, new retail shops, and many other companies that one would not expect to be based on innovation. The line for new tech firms shows that entry was greatest during the dot-com bubble in the late 1990s, but that entry rates have declined only slightly since that peak and have remained at double the level of the early 1980s before the bubble. It is hard to see how congressional researchers could conclude that there has been "a sharp decline in new business formation."

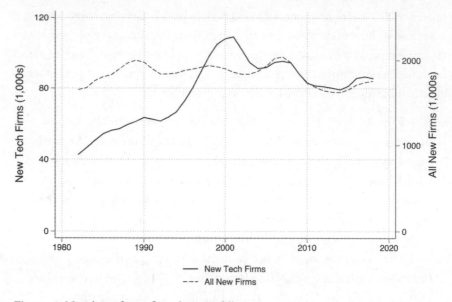

Figure 6. Number of new firms has not fallen
Source: U.S. Census Bureau, "BDS Data Tables."

Nor has venture capital funding for early stage firms declined. Figure 7 shows two data sets for total venture capital (VC) early stage investments for the United States.[50] The PitchBook data are more complete; they show a quadrupling of early stage investment since 2006. The CB Insights data don't capture as many deals, but they go back to 1995, which is helpful for long-term comparison. While early stage funding in this series peaked with the dot-com bubble, early stage VC has been growing robustly since the dot-com crash and is roughly eight times as high as it was in 1995. In addition, the number of early stage deals has risen strongly in both data sets.[51] Rather than declining, the market is awash with venture funding, not only for early stage deals, but also for angel and seed stage deals and especially for later stage deals. It is this flood of money that has allowed megadeals such as the $1 billion-dollar UiPath investments.

It is true that the share of young tech firms in the total population of firms has declined substantially since the dot-com bubble, but even this share is significantly higher than it was during the 1980s and early 1990s. Somewhat misleadingly, this ratio has been labeled the entrepreneurship rate, but it is really a measure of firm age. Given that the actual rate of

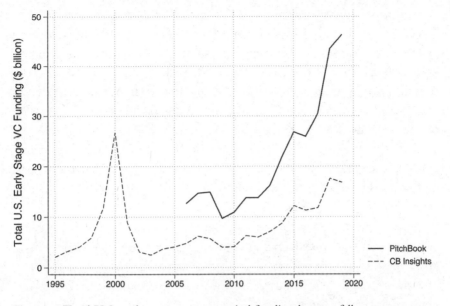

Figure 7. Total U.S. early stage venture capital funding has not fallen

entry has not declined, the drop in this ratio simply means that entrants are surviving longer. But this is not necessarily a bad thing, and it certainly does not, by itself, reflect on the innovativeness of the economy. Indeed, this trend may simply be a consequence of the greater availability of low-cost funds that can sustain firms that run into temporary difficulties.

There is also some evidence that Big Tech acquisitions in specific market segments may reduce venture capital investment in those market segments, creating what one venture capitalist called a kill zone. For example, one study looked at nine acquisitions by Google and Facebook (combined, these companies have made over three hundred acquisitions); it finds a reduction in VC investment in the related market segments.[52] On the other hand, another study finds that R&D tends to be higher in industries with greater merger and acquisition activity.[53] Indeed, acquisition seems to spur firm entry and VC investment in speech recognition. In any case, whatever effect Big Tech acquisitions may have, venture funding has nevertheless strongly increased.

Some people argue that although the rate of startups has not declined, the quality of startups may have diminished. Maybe we are seeing fewer innovative startups or marketing firms masquerading as tech startups such as WeWork. Economists Jorge Guzman and Scott Stern have developed a quality-adjusted index of entrepreneurship.[54] They derive this measure by identifying a series of firm characteristics that are correlated with the likelihood that the firm will be successful—that is, it will be acquired at a high value or will have an IPO on public markets. For example, one factor they include is whether the firm has filed for a patent. They find that although this measure peaked during the dot-com bubble, it has remained high since, at roughly double the level of the early 1990s. In other words, quality-adjusted entrepreneurship has followed the same pattern as unadjusted tech firm entry rates.

The basic story, then, is that productivity growth has slowed, not because fewer productive firms are being created, but because productive firms, especially startups, are not growing as fast relative to others. The problem is headwinds, and these headwinds blow from the software system investments of dominant firms.

Mismeasuring Productivity

Paul Krugman has famously said, "Productivity isn't everything, but in the long run, it is almost everything."[55] Economists and the business press are fixated on productivity, often measured as output per worker, and on output, measured as gross domestic product (GDP). As economist Diane Coyle relates in *GDP: A Brief but Affectionate History,* statistical agencies developed standard techniques for measuring GDP in the years after World War II to gauge the economic recovery.[56] Today, these measures help us understand how the economy is performing.

But Coyle identifies three well-known reasons that GDP fails to measure economic activity (let alone economic welfare) properly: (1) the shift to services and intangibles; (2) the growing complexity of the economy; and (3) the depletion of resources (sustainability). It turns out that the first two problems are greatly exacerbated by the shift to superstar capitalism. She writes, "The economy consists less and less of material items. It is relatively straightforward to measure economic output when you can count the number of cars or refrigerators or nails or microwave meals being shipped from factories. But how do you measure the output of nurses, accountants, garden designers, musicians, software developers, health care assistants, and so on? The only way is to count how many of them there are and how many 'customers' they provide with a service, but this entirely overlooks the *quality* of the service, which is of great importance."[57]

When firms compete on quality, providing rapid quality improvements, this task becomes even more difficult. One way that statistical agencies try to measure quality is to relate the price of the product or service to its underlying characteristics. Recall that General Motors competed with Ford by offering more car models with varying qualities. During the 1930s, automotive economist Andrew Court sought to create a quality-adjusted measure of automobile output.[58] He used a statistical technique (regression) to relate the model price to the weight, length, and horsepower of the car so that he could compute a quality index based on these three parameters. This "hedonic" pricing technique was later introduced into mainstream economics by Zvi Griliches, and statistical agencies use this technique today for measuring the quality of rapidly changing goods such as computers.[59]

But there are two general problems with this approach in the superstar economy. First, when automobiles have millions of lines of software code, an enormous number of features affect the quality of the car; they affect things like the handling and drivability. It becomes impossible to measure all of the underlying parameters and relate them to price. Second, when firms differentiate on quality, prices no longer simply correspond to the absolute quality of the product or service. Instead, prices also reflect relative differences. The price of a Toyota model compared to a GM model in the same class reflects the relative superiority of Toyota's quality and so it does not directly measure the level of quality.

A second difficulty that Coyle highlights is the dramatic growth in the variety of new products or versions of products.[60] The range and variety of product offerings has been going up according to a whole range of statistics, from car models to supermarket goods to movies and books and music to credit card offerings. Not only are there many more car models today, but auto manufacturers now allow consumers to customize their own model in so-called mass customization. One estimate puts the growth in product variety at 1 percent per year and notes that it has been accelerating at least since the 1990s. Yet statistical authorities have a hard time accounting for this increase. Coyle argues that "GDP underrecords growth by failing to capture fully the increase in the range of products in the economy."[61]

When firms compete on features, they introduce more new products or new versions of products and services, they increase product quality in complex ways, and their prices are not simple reflections of quality. For these reasons, superstar capitalism undermines GDP and productivity measures as metrics of economic activity.

On the other hand, Chad Syverson recognizes that there are well-understood measurement problems with GDP, but he argues there is no evidence that these have been accelerating or that they are related to information technology.[62] He notes that productivity growth has slowed across all developed countries but that the extent of the slowdown is unrelated to country investments in IT or in broadband. Yet those measures do not capture the effect of superstar firm investments. When Walmart moves into the Chilean market, it may well slow the growth of domestic Chilean retailers, but that impact on Chilean productivity may have more to do with the employment of software developers in Bentonville, Arkansas, than with information technology and communication equipment investments in Spain. Although speculative, it does seem likely that the continued investments by dominant firms in proprietary software systems will increasingly affect not only productivity growth but also the measurement of that growth.

A final confounder for productivity concerns the use of technology to differentiate firms. In these cases, the technology might improve the profits of the firm using the technology but decrease the business of its rivals. Profitable technology does not necessarily imply that aggregate productivity improves and the turn to product-differentiating technology might not be productivity enhancing.

Headwinds and the Technology Gap

Dominant firms remain undisrupted longer because they have access to key technologies that are not available to rivals, technologies that have not diffused. Conversely, this technology gap limits the ability of innovative smaller firms to grow. The fate of Nuance Communications was sealed in 2014 when Google compelled Android phone manufacturers to include all of Google's applications on their phones or none. This meant effectively that Google applications had first crack at voice interactions, forcing Nuance into a subsidiary role on the platform. Previously, Apple had effectively excluded Nuance from most voice interactions on the iPhone by taking Siri development inhouse. Together, these moves largely denied Nuance access to general-purpose interactions with phone users and the huge amount of data that generates. On the other hand, UiPath was able to continue growing precisely because its access was not limited. No dominant enterprise software firm could restrict access to UiPath because UiPath cleverly uses the interface those vendors provide for humans to interact with their systems.

Writ large, the technology gap we saw in chapter 4 is directly related to the slower growth rate of productive firms observed in this chapter, and that decline in firm growth rates is, in turn, directly related to the slowdown in aggregate productivity growth. Yet it is important to note that this outcome is not the inevitable result of new technologies; it depends very much on the choices made by firms and the policies set by governments. For example, antitrust authorities might well have prevented Google from reducing Nuance's access to Android users.

Limited access to key technologies affects more than aggregate productivity growth; it also has strong implications for labor markets. Because worker skills are often learned on the job with hands-on experience, many workers are unable to improve their skills when access is limited. Moreover, because many skills are more valuable when they are used on the most advanced technology, there are growing differences between dominant firms and the rest in what they are willing to pay; there is a war for talent.

7

Divided Society

During the 1990s, economists became increasingly aware that U.S. income inequality had been growing at least since 1980. By a variety of different metrics, the pay gaps between higher-paid and lower-paid workers have been increasing. A large literature developed exploring the nature and possible causes of this trend. One major factor was a growing gap between the pay of college-educated workers and those who had only a high school degree.[1] While the relative pay of college graduates had been declining during the 1970s, their pay relative to high school grads grew robustly during the 1980s and 1990s. Many economists identified technology, specifically computer technology, as the culprit in this change. The idea is that the wide adoption of low-cost computers beginning in the 1980s increased the value of college graduates' skills. College-educated workers in managerial and professional occupations could do more, better, and faster with computers, so their value to employers increased, as did their incomes. That is, computers complement college-educated workers. This idea became known as the skill-biased technical change hypothesis.[2]

Notably, in this model, the growing differences in pay between workers is driven by the individual characteristics of these workers, chiefly their education. Computer technology increased the payoff to education, magnifying differences between workers, what some economists have called the "race between education and technology."[3] In this account, inequality could be reduced by increasing the supply of college graduates. This is a very meritocratic story. Workers are rewarded depending on their individual effort and investments they have made in education. Unequal outcomes may be more socially palatable if they arise from such differences in effort and investment.

But, in fact, the reason incomes have become more unequal is not just because of greater payoffs to education for all individuals. Current research finds that most of the growth in income inequality in recent decades arises from the combination of individual characteristics such as education with the characteristics of the *firms* they work for. The differences in pay have grown mainly between firms and not so much between individual workers within firms. These findings were made after researchers were first able to use massive new databases that track both individual workers and their employers over time. One study found this result for West Germany, and another found it for the United States using Internal Revenue Service data for the entire U.S. labor market from 1978 to 2013.[4] Differences in the characteristics of individual workers are still important in determining wages, but these differences appear to be mediated by differences between firms.

Proprietary software systems play a major role in driving these pay differences between firms. Information technology, moreover, is related not only to differences in what firms pay but also to growing social divisions: it segregates us at our workplaces and where we live. These economic inequities and social divisions undermine the meritocratic rationalization for economic inequality and contribute to growing economic, social, and political polarization, resentment of elites, and deep populist discontent. Let's take a deeper look.

The Meritocratic Lie

Why should we care about income inequality?[5] One argument holds that inequality slows economic growth, reducing the long-term wealth of society as a whole. While there is evidence that economic inequality does slow national economic growth under some circumstances, such as in poor nations, the evidence is less clear for developed nations.[6]

Another major concern is fairness. If some people earn more because of unfair advantage, inequality is seen as unfair and detrimental to the cohesion of society. The robber barons of the Gilded Age were viewed as

having acquired their wealth unfairly, and they became an object of populist rage. Yet the ideology of meritocracy helps explain and rationalize
economic inequality. If some people earn more because they work harder
or because they have invested in more education, then that is seen as fair.
The meritocratic justification for inequality holds that a society is fair as
long as people have at least equality of economic opportunity. Indeed,
from this perspective, income inequality is a good thing if it reflects the
rewards to different levels of effort and investment. A society with strong
incentives to work and to invest will be a society with strongly unequal
outcomes. Moreover, meritocratic rewards can counter injustices: when
opportunity is truly equal, rewards based on performance are blind to
racial or gender differences.

But there is a downside to meritocracy, highlighted by Michael Sandel
in *The Tyranny of Merit*. Sandel argues that meritocratic ideology is more
than just an economic arrangement. "The meritocratic ideal places great
weight on the notion of personal responsibility." It affirms "a certain idea
of freedom. This is the idea that our destiny is in our hands, that our
success does not depend on forces beyond our control, that it's up to us.
We are not victims of circumstance but masters of our fate, free to rise as
far as our effort and talents and dreams will take us. . . . We get what we
deserve."[7]

The flaw with this view is that in our society, while better performance
might be rewarded, economic success also reflects luck, socially supported
public goods, family resources, race, gender, and other factors unrelated
to performance. For example, people growing up in wealthier neighbor-
hoods do better, all else equal.[8] To ignore these sources and consider income differences as deserved creates insidious distinctions that undermine
social cohesion, giving rise to populist resentment. Meritocracy "diminishes
our capacity to see ourselves as sharing a common fate. It leaves little room
for the solidarity that can arise when we reflect on the contingency of our
talents and fortunes."[9] For example, Sandel provides evidence that Trump
voters resented the "meritocratic elites, experts, and professional classes,
who had celebrated market-driven globalization, reaped the benefits,
consigned working people to the discipline of foreign competition, and
who seemed to identify more with global elites than with their fellow
citizens."[10]

The extent to which economic success depends on factors other than individual hard work gives the lie to the meritocratic ideal. And the large investments in proprietary software systems exacerbate this disparity. Because only some firms use the new technologies, only some workers can gain skills related to these technologies. As I argue elsewhere, a substantial part of the skills needed to use new technologies must be learned from experience.[11] This gives rise to a skills gap for employers and unequal opportunity for workers. These differences in skills are directly related to differences in income. Increasingly, your pay depends not just on how hard you work or how much education you have but on whom you work for. And firm hiring patterns are increasing social segregation: you are more likely to work with other people with similar education and occupations, and you are more likely to live near people with similar backgrounds. These trends undermine meritocratic ideology, and they have strong implications for the politics of resentment. To explore these trends, it is helpful to begin with skills.

The Skills Gap

Each year ManpowerGroup conducts a large survey of employers, asking them, among other things, if they face "talent shortages."[12] In 2019, 54 percent of employers reported difficulty hiring and retaining skilled workers, up from just 30 percent a decade earlier. A host of other surveys similarly report a so-called skills gap.

But the idea of a skills gap has been widely criticized. Labor economist Peter Cappelli asks whether these studies are just a sign of "employer whining."[13] Paul Krugman calls the skills gap a "zombie idea . . . that should have been killed by evidence, but refuses to die."[14] Matthew Yglesias calls it a "lie" in *Vox*.[15] The *New York Times* editorial board asserts that it is "mostly a corporate fiction, based in part on self-interest and a misreading of government data." According to the *Times*, the survey responses are an effort by executives to get "the government to take on more of the costs of training workers."[16]

Really? A worldwide scheme by thousands of business managers to manipulate public opinion seems far-fetched. Perhaps the simpler explanation is the better one: many employers might actually have difficulty hiring skilled workers. To be fair, some people have suggested, without much evidence, that the skills gap might be a cause of unemployment.[17] Regardless of whether that proposition is true, employers might still have legitimate difficulties hiring workers with critical skills.

One reason for the controversy is that there appears to be some confusion about what skills employers need and how they are supplied. Some critics of the skills gap argue that if employers have difficulty hiring talent, they just need to pay higher wages. The *Times* editors tell us, "If a business really needed workers, it would pay up." This argument might make sense if there were lots of nonemployed people with the needed skills who could be induced to go to work for higher pay. That might be the case, for instance, if the critical skills were just possession of a degree from a four-year college; there are many college grads who are not in the labor force. Unfortunately, far too many people equate skill with a four-year college education. But the skills needed to use new technologies today require experience with the technologies and associated business models. Yet because few workers can get that experience, those skills really are scarce. Simply offering a higher wage isn't going to magically create a new supply of workers who have those skills. On the one hand, critical skills must be learned by applying the technology in the new business models that superstar firms are using. On the other, many of the skill requirements are hybrid—they combine different areas of expertise and are thus not likely to be taught as such in the classroom.

Consider the way Walmart's technology decentralizes decision-making. Store managers need skills to access and interpret data. And they need merchandising skills, including some understanding of the local market, to make purchasing decisions. In a wide range of jobs, hybrid skills are needed. Burning Glass, a company that collects data from help-wanted ads, reports:

> In marketing and public relations, a new set of jobs requiring
> data analytics skills (marketing manager, digital marketing manager)
> require a combination of right brain thinking (creative design)
> with left brain thinking (analytics and data analysis) to succeed.
> Today's advertising managers are creative designers and analysts
> rolled into one.

In the area of computer science and data analytics, the opposite has occurred. Once considered highly technical jobs, now these jobs require writing skills, problem-solving skills, creative and research skills, and skills in teamwork and collaboration. So just like the marketing manager who is now an analyst, the software engineer or data scientist is now a business person, designer, and team worker.[18]

Data science and analytics occupations are key jobs involved in the superstar IT systems. These occupations comprise a burgeoning new category of over two million jobs, many requiring hybrid skills and experience-based skills.[19] For example, analytics managers must have knowledge of a specific functional domain—such as human resources or marketing—and they also must possess analytical skills, project management skills, and financial planning and budgeting skills. Preparing workers for these roles is problematic, since these skills cut across a diverse mix of functional areas. Marketing analytics managers, for example, require analytics skills such as SQL (a tool for accessing databases), Big Data, and predictive modeling along with firm-specific expertise in marketing, product management, and market strategy.

And employers frequently report difficulty filling these jobs. An annual survey of chief information officers found that 46 percent reported difficulty hiring and retaining workers in the category of Big Data and analytics jobs; surveyed employers report the greatest difficulty filling this job category.[20] And a skills gap appears as well by more objective measures. Data science and analytics jobs take longer to fill. While the average position takes forty days to fill, openings for director of analytics/data take seventy-three days to fill.[21] Furthermore, careful analysis shows that demand strongly exceeds supply in data science and analytics jobs.[22] Moreover, this mismatch occurs even though employers *do* pay more—these positions earn about $9,000 more per year for jobs with comparable educational requirements.

Clearly, the challenge of providing the skills that employers need involves much more than just having schools churn out more STEM (science, technology, engineering, and mathematics) workers. On the one hand, STEM workers need critical management, team, and social skills. Education economists David Deming and Kadeem Noray find that while STEM graduates initially earn higher pay than other graduates, their skills become obsolete more quickly and that those who fare best in the long run migrate

Table 1. IT-intensive firms demand higher skill for non-IT jobs in help-wanted ads

	Mean	Difference between high-IT firms and low-IT firms
Number of skills listed	11.0	2.1
Share listing IT skills	21.9%	20.1%
Share listing AI skills	0.1%	0.2%
Share listing soft skills	66.7%	6.8%
Experience (years)	2.9	1.0
Education (years)	12.5	1.5

into management or other jobs.[23] In other work, Deming also highlights the general growth in the importance of social skills, which he suggests is occurring in part because information technology changes work organization, making work tasks more variable and requiring team production.[24]

On the other hand, information technology is also changing the skill requirements of non-STEM jobs. We can see how new IT drives the demand for skills by looking at online help-wanted ads. In this chapter I derive a variety of statistics from a large database of help-wanted ads collected by Burning Glass Technologies.[25] Table 1 shows the skill requirements listed in job ads for all non-IT jobs. The first column reports the mean levels of these requirements. On average, help-wanted ads requested eleven specific skills, 22 percent of the ads required at least one IT skill (excluding Microsoft Office skills), 0.1 percent requested a specific AI skill, and 67 percent requested soft skills.[26] On average, job ads required a minimum of 2.9 years of experience and 12.5 years of education.

But jobs at IT-intensive firms required substantially higher levels of these skills. The second column in the table reports the difference in skill requirements between job postings from IT-intensive firms (top quartile) compared to postings for comparable jobs at low-IT firms (bottom quartile).[27] The second column shows that for every skill measure, IT-intensive firms demanded higher skills than comparable jobs at non-IT-intensive firms: more specific skills, more IT skills for non-IT jobs, AI, and soft skills, a year more experience on average, and a year and a half more education on average. When firms invest heavily in proprietary IT, they demand higher skills in a variety of dimensions across many non-IT occupations. And contrary to some expectations, IT-intensive firms require workers with greater social skills; teamwork becomes more highly valued in organizations deploying the new technologies. Information technology–intensive firms particularly demand hybrid skills that combine IT capabilities with non-IT capabilities in non-IT occupations.

Because hybrid skills are more difficult to acquire—they combine expertise in multiple areas not typically found in school curricula—the supply of workers with these skills has fallen behind the rapidly rising demand for such workers. The need to acquire new skills after leaving school is one reason behind the growth of online courses offered by Coursera, Udemy, Khan Academy, and, increasingly, universities. But despite these alternatives, the skills gap has continued to grow because critical skills require experience with the technology. Because only select firms invest in the new technologies, workers have limited access to learn new skills by working with these technologies on the job. Indeed, one study finds that workers will sacrifice in order to gain this valuable experience.[28] Using data from an online job board that captures job applicants' target pay, they find that workers are willing to accept lower pay in order to gain experience at an employer that has invested in new technology. Specifically, they compare employers that have invested in Hadoop—a core Big Data technology—to employers that have not. The workers are willing to make an investment by taking lower pay, and the researchers find evidence that they recoup this investment with higher pay later on, after they have acquired the new skills.

Thus, the lack of diffusion of today's proprietary information technology limits the development of workforce skills on the job. At the same time, new business models based on the new technology demand new, hybrid skills that are harder to acquire. Combined, these factors make it more difficult for employers to hire and retain workers with these skills; they create a larger skills gap. This gap slows the growth of new, productive companies, as discussed in the last chapter. Effectively, the talent wars allow dominant firms to reinforce the advantages they derive by restricting access to the technology.

But limited access to new skills has an additional effect: it exacerbates income inequality. In my 2015 book, *Learning by Doing*, I argued that the spread of new, technology-related skills through the workforce was essential for the broad sharing of the economic benefits of new technology in the past. Today, limited access to skills limits the growth of shared wealth.

Firms and Wages

As above, differences between firms have begun to play an increasingly important role creating differences in pay. Could technology differences between firms play a critical part in driving the growth in firm wage differences? There has long been evidence that computer technology is related to pay differences between establishments.[29] And we have just seen that firms investing in proprietary information systems demand greater skills in their new hires.

In fact, information technology is a big factor in pay differences between firms. We can see the magnitude of firm wage effects by looking at the salaries posted in help-wanted ads.[30] While advertised salaries are not the same as salaries actually earned, advertised salaries provide a straightforward way to analyze the differences in pay between firms. Firms that invest a lot in proprietary information technology (in the top quartile ranked by the share of IT jobs in total hiring) offer to pay 36.1 percent more in help-wanted ads than do firms in the bottom quartile of IT intensity on average.[31] This strikingly large premium is a gross difference in means that reflects differences in both what firms pay and the composition of their workforces. It is helpful to decompose these firm wage differences into two parts. First, there are firm wage effects: some firms pay more than others for workers of comparable skill and talent. Second, high-paying firms may tend to hire better-quality workers than others. This is called the sorting of workers across firms. Let us look first at the link between proprietary information technology and firm wage effects.

Firm Wage Effects

A long-standing puzzle in labor economics is that different firms pay significantly different wages for highly comparable workers in the same occupations.[32] Often, the largest firms pay more. For example, after controlling for observed and unobserved worker characteristics, secretaries at firms with more than a thousand employees were found to earn 7 percent more than equivalent secretaries at firms with one hundred or fewer workers. Janitors at these firms earn 10 percent more, truck drivers 6 percent more.[33]

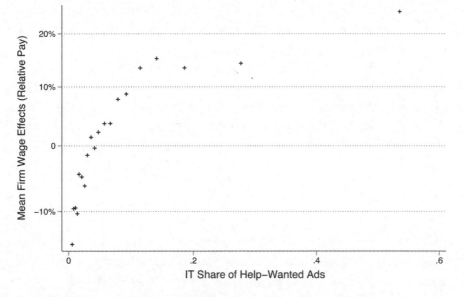

Figure 8. IT-intensive firms pay more for comparable workers on average
Source: Bessen, Denk, and Meng, "Firm Differences: Skill Sorting and Software."

Why should some firms pay more for apparently equivalent workers? This is indeed a puzzle for the orthodox economics of perfect competition. In that world, labor is a commodity that trades at a uniform price for a given set of characteristics. But labor markets differ from that ideal world for a variety of reasons. Economists have advanced several theories of imperfect competition where firms pay more or less for comparable workers, and considerable evidence supports some of these theories.[34] A common feature of all of these models is that more profitable firms pay their workers more. A rich body of evidence finds a robust relationship between firm profitability measured in a variety of ways with firm pay levels.[35]

Of course, proprietary information technology is one source of firm profit, so it makes sense to explore the extent to which IT-intensive firms pay higher wages for comparable workers. We can calculate firm wage effects by comparing the salaries offered in help-wanted ads for different firms controlling for a variety of job characteristics.[36] These firm wage effects are significantly associated with firm IT intensity, as seen in figure 8.[37] The mean firm wage effect rises sharply with the firm's IT share of help-wanted ads, leveling off at higher IT intensities. To put this in more concrete terms, firms in the top quartile by IT intensity offer salaries that are 17.4 percent higher than salaries for comparable jobs at firms in the lowest quartile, a substantial difference.

This 17 percent gap is a difference in the level of pay offered by firms for jobs with comparable requirements. But we saw in chapter 2 (see fig. 2) that firm investments in information technology rose eightfold since the 1990s. This implies, more or less, that growing IT intensity accounts for a substantial increase in pay differences between firms.

Sorting by Worker Quality

Pay differs between firms not only because some firms pay more than others for equivalent jobs but also because some firms hire better-quality workers than others. Jae Song and colleagues find that firms that tend to pay more also tend to hire workers who earn more because they have better skills. They attribute most of the growth of income inequality in recent decades to an increase in this "sorting" component.[38]

Above we saw that IT intensity is strongly correlated with skills required in help-wanted ads. Since IT intensity is also correlated with firm wage effects, we might expect that IT intensity accounts for some portion of the sorting of more skilled workers into higher-paying firms. We find that IT accounts for much of the sorting by skill. First, the skill measures reported in table 1 are significantly correlated with firm wage effects with the exception of soft skills.[39] But these correlations are substantially accounted for (46–92 percent) by the correlation between IT intensity and skills.[40] In other words, the increase in sorting of skilled workers to high-paying firms is substantially accounted for by increases in IT intensity.

Occupation provides another dimension of worker quality and sorting across firms. IT-intensive firms differ both in the occupations they tend to hire and in how much they pay workers in different occupations. Table 2 shows differences across occupations in help-wanted advertising.[41] The first two columns show that IT-intensive firms hire substantially more managers, professionals, and administrative support workers and fewer workers in other occupations compared to low-IT firms. Because outsourcing might distort occupational job shares for different industries, I exclude likely outsourced jobs from this table. Column 3 shows how much more IT-intensive firms

Table 2. Top quartile IT-intensive firms hire more and pay more in select occupations

	Occupation share of jobs		Salary premiums
	Low-IT firms	High-IT firms	
Managers	8.5%	19.7%	22%
Professionals	10.2%	35.1%	20%
Health workers	17.1%	6.3%	–3%
Business services	5.1%	2.3%	12%
Sales	25.9%	10.1%	5%
Administrative support	8.0%	15.1%	10%
Construction/ production	9.0%	8.6%	11%
Transportation/ material moving	16.1%	2.8%	–34%

pay for different occupations—the salary premium—after controlling for detailed occupation, industry, education, experience, state, and year. Managers and professionals earn substantially more at high-IT firms whereas truck drivers and other transportation workers earn substantially less.

The pay premiums for managers and professionals suggest that proprietary IT systems tend to complement these workers, consistent with the skill-biased technical change hypothesis. The story about truckers is a bit more complicated. It turns out that IT facilitates outsourcing for truck drivers, diminishing their wages.[42]

In any case, this analysis shows that IT-intensive firms hire more workers in highly skilled occupations and at higher pay. Combined with the differences in hiring by skills and the substantial firm wage effects associated with IT, there is little doubt that firm spending on proprietary IT is strongly associated with income inequality. This is, of course, not the only factor affecting inequality, but it is a major one.

Social Division

Information technology appears to contribute to undermining the meritocratic justification. When workers at IT-intensive firms earn 17 percent more on average than workers at low-IT firms in jobs with equivalent requirements regarding education and experience, then it is hard to ascribe those differences as deserved. But there is an additional way that superstar firms undermine social cohesion: they increase economic segregation.

In the 1990s, future Nobel Laureate economists Michael Kremer and Eric Maskin noted growing segregation of workers by skill: "Economic activity has shifted from firms such as General Motors, which use both high- and low-skill workers, to firms such as Microsoft and McDonald's, whose workforces are much more homogeneous."[43] This finding appeared substantial, robust to different ways of measuring skill, and appeared among multiple developed countries.

Superstar firms contribute to this trend. These firms hire proportionally more managers and professionals, making it more likely that workers in these occupations will work together and less likely that they will work with production workers or truck drivers or salespeople. Also, these firms hire more workers with specific skills, including skills related to the new technology. Because these IT-intensive firms tend to dominate their markets, I find a growing division between workers who work at dominant firms and others. Using LinkedIn data, I tracked workers' job changes, specifically looking at workers who were hired into firms that were in the top four in their markets. After controlling for a variety of factors, these workers were 5–6 percent more likely to come from another top-four firm.[44] Using data from Execucomp, I find that executives hired at top-four firms were 13 percent more likely to come from other top-four firms.[45] These estimates imply a significant, although not overwhelming, stratification of the workforce.

Proprietary information technology is also contributing to geographical divisions. Superstar firms tend to hire disproportionately in large cities. While 22 percent of the hiring by low-IT firms occurs in the ten largest metropolitan areas, 32 percent of the hiring of the high-IT firms does.[46] If we rank cities by the size of their IT workforces, then low-IT firms do 21 percent of their hiring in the top ten cities, but 36 percent of the hiring by high-IT firms takes place in those cities.[47] Information technology thus contributes to the development of a highly paid, highly educated, highly skilled urban elite, mostly coastal. This finding corresponds with research by Fabian Eckert, Sharat Ganapati, and Conor Walsh, who show that a large part of the rise in income inequality can be accounted for by knowledge-intensive occupations that are traded and that these jobs are highly concentrated in the largest cities.[48]

In summary, proprietary information technology is exacerbating economic and social divisions. It is widening the gaps between the pay of workers at different firms, in different occupations, and with different skills. It is leading to greater segregation of skill groups across firms and cities. Superstar capitalism is, of course, not the only factor affecting income inequality. The decline of unions and worker bargaining power plays a role. So, too, does the changing role of education in the economy. But current research finds that your pay depends not just on your education and how hard you work but also on who your employer is. And the rise of superstar capitalism explains why differences between firms are growing. Moreover, it is not just that inequality has increased; it is that inequality based on firm differences further undermines the meritocratic ideal. It increasingly appears that the economic winners are not necessarily deserving, and that shift adds fuel to politics of resentment against elites and populism. Of course, proprietary software systems are hardly the only thing fomenting social polarization. Globalization has played a role as, perhaps, have social media. But growing and unfair economic inequality and segregation surely add fuel to the fire.

8

Regulating Complexity

Clean Diesel

The career of Martin Winterkorn began to unravel when a couple of graduate students drove from Los Angeles to Seattle and back in the spring of 2014.[1] Winterkorn was the top executive of Volkswagen. The students were conducting a low-budget study run by Dan Carder at West Virginia University to show that diesel carmakers were capable of meeting more rigorous limits on emissions of nitrogen oxides. The car they drove was a VW Passat. This model was equipped with an advanced catalytic reduction technology intended to reduce nitrogen oxide releases, so the research team expected to find low levels of the pollutant.

The Passat was part of Volkswagen's fleet of so-called clean diesel car models, which the automaker aggressively touted as being environmentally superior to gasoline-powered vehicles. Indeed, diesel engines produce less carbon dioxide than equivalently performing gasoline engines. Because of this, European policy makers, working to meet their Kyoto Protocol commitments, initiated a "dash for diesel," encouraging Europeans to purchase diesel automobiles by reducing taxes on diesel fuel and with other incentives.[2] It didn't hurt that the diesel engine was a native European technology championed by German automobile manufacturers. But diesel engines also emit nitrogen oxides and higher levels of particulate matter, both of which are harmful pollutants. Nitrogen oxides are known to cause emphysema, bronchitis, and other respiratory disease.

The research team's Passat was fitted out with a jury-rigged portable emissions meter. Most emissions testing, including that conducted by regulatory authorities, is performed in laboratories using standard test protocols. A portable measurement system allowed the researchers to measure emissions under real-world driving conditions. The researchers faced a challenge to fit the laboratory into a car. The available equipment had a short battery life, so Carder's team bolted portable gasoline-powered electric generators to the backs of the test cars. This setup was noisy and prone to breakdown. Once they had to repair it at night in a shopping center parking lot in Portland, Oregon. But they were able to consistently measure the nitrogen oxides. To their surprise, the measured levels were *twenty times* higher than what had been measured in the stationary test facility and well above federal Environmental Protection Agency (EPA) limits.

The researchers were puzzled, guessing that the difference was caused by design flaws or technical defects. One of the graduate students, Marc Besch, presented their findings at an industry conference in San Diego in early 2014. In the audience were officials from the California Air Resources Board (CARB), the state agency responsible for emission standards. CARB researchers became suspicious. They began conducting their own tests and also contacted the EPA, responsible for national emission standards. The CARB researchers quickly found that emissions were much higher when the vehicle was operating under highway-like conditions. Presented with these findings, Volkswagen replied that the increased emissions from these vehicles could be attributed to various technical issues and unexpected in-use conditions. The regulators persisted in pushing Volkswagen for a solution. In December 2014, Volkswagen issued a recall supposedly addressing these technical issues. The EPA's violation letter to Volkswagen describes what happened next:

> CARB, in coordination with the EPA, conducted follow up testing of these vehicles both in the laboratory and during normal road operation to confirm the efficacy of the recall. When the testing showed only a limited benefit to the recall, CARB broadened the testing to pinpoint the exact technical nature of the vehicles' poor performance, and to investigate why the vehicles' onboard diagnostic system was

not detecting the increased emissions. None of the potential technical issues suggested by VW explained the higher test results consistently confirmed during CARB's testing. It became clear that CARB
and the EPA would not approve certificates of conformity for VW's
2016 model year diesel vehicles until VW could adequately explain
the anomalous emissions and ensure the agencies that the 2016
model year vehicles would not have similar issues. Only then did VW
admit it had designed and installed a defeat device in these vehicles in
the form of a sophisticated software algorithm that detected when a
vehicle was undergoing emissions testing.[3]

A defeat device is any mechanism used to trick a testing procedure.
Researchers later found that the Volkswagen defeat device was buried in
the thousands of lines of computer code of the engine control unit (ECU).
The ECU is a computer that receives information from a wide range of
sensors about the vehicle; it uses this information to manage the various
components of the engine, making tradeoffs between fuel consumption,
emissions, and the torque and acceleration the engine delivers. The best
driving performance of the car generally produces excess emissions, while
the best emissions performance has reduced drivability. The Volkswagen
defeat device worked by sensing when the automobile appeared to be
undergoing an emissions test. When the ignition was turned on, the ECU
acted as if the vehicle was being tested and it adjusted various controls,
such as the fuel injection timing or the recirculation of exhaust gases, to
minimize emissions.[4] As the vehicle operated, the surreptitious ECU code
performed ten checks to see if it had gone out of testing mode. For instance,
it checked how long and how far the car had been driven—the EPA test
lasts thirty-one minutes and covers 11.04 miles. In some models, it checked
whether the wheels had been turned more than twenty degrees. When the
ECU code detected that the vehicle was not undergoing a test, it changed
parameters to increase torque and acceleration, improving the driving
performance of the car but also increasing nitrogen oxide emissions.

This was hardly the first defeat device. For example, in 1995 General
Motors had to recall 470,000 Cadillacs because these cars enriched the
fuel-air mixture when the air conditioning or heating system was turned
on. Since emissions tests were conducted with the air conditioner and

heater turned off, this feature acted as a defeat device. It was not designed purely as a defeat device—the Cadillacs would stall when the air or heating was turned on without the richer fuel mixture—but it nevertheless circumvented the emission controls. Yet the Volkswagen defeat device is a whole other thing. According to Kirill Levchenko, a computer scientist at the University of California–San Diego, it is "arguably the most complex in automotive history."[5]

The Volkswagen device was much harder to discover. While the Cadillac defeat device could be detected relatively easily—the emissions went up when the air conditioning went on—the Volkswagen fudge was far subtler. Indeed, the West Virginia University researchers did not even suspect intentional obfuscation. And while CARB and the EPA did suspect a defeat device, they could not prove that one was at work. Doing so required identifying the computer code that implemented the deception, a small needle of code buried in a haystack of computer programs. Moreover, under U.S. copyright law, it is *illegal* for anyone but the manufacturers to access the code in their cars. Under section 1201 of the Digital Millennium Copyright Act, automobile companies can take legal action against anyone, including the owner of the automobile, who gets around the access restrictions protecting the firmware in each car no matter how legitimate their reason. The Electronic Frontier Foundation had to petition the librarian of Congress to gain legal access for researchers in this case, despite objections from automobile manufacturers.[6] And even with access to the firmware code—the machine-level instructions controlling the cars' devices—researchers had difficulty interpreting the code without documentation. Fortunately, the hobbyist community had accumulated sufficient leaked documents to assist in understanding the code and identifying the offending routines. In the end, once a lawsuit was initiated, subpoenas uncovered emails proving Volkswagen's knowing culpability.

But also, this new defeat device emerged at a far greater scale than earlier ones. Because the change to the ECU software was relatively easy to implement—one estimate suggests that fewer than ten engineers were involved—it could be readily extended across product lines.[7] Whereas fewer than half a million Cadillacs were involved in the 1995 recall, more than eleven million Volkswagens were affected worldwide. Moreover, it soon emerged that other manufacturers had installed similar code, many of them using ECUs supplied by Bosch, which was VW's supplier. And they all had been doing this for many years. Allegations of emissions cheating have been raised against Volvo, Renault, Jeep, Hyundai, Citroën, Nissan, Mercedes-Benz, Porsche, Audi, and Fiat.[8]

Once the EPA sent its notice of violation, things unraveled quickly for Volkswagen and for Martin Winterkorn, its chief executive. Winterkorn resigned five days later, saying, "I am shocked by the events of the past few days. Above all, I am stunned that misconduct on such a scale was possible in the Volkswagen Group." Nevertheless, he maintained, "I am not aware of any wrong doing on my part."[9] Winterkorn was charged with fraud and conspiracy in the United States on May 3, 2018; he was indicted in Germany in 2019. As of this date, thirteen VW employees have been indicted; two have pled guilty in the United States and have been sentenced to prison terms. For the automaker, the scandal cost VW $33.3 billion in fines, penalties, financial settlements, and buyback costs.[10] As the scandal has touched a growing number of countries and manufacturers, it has also had industry and political repercussions. One casualty may be the European championing of diesel technology. The case has certainly been hurt by revelations that EU and member state regulators had known that diesel emissions were far above legal limits for over a decade, yet they failed to act.[11] Countries and cities around the world are cracking down on the use of diesel and acting to reduce emissions. Paris, Madrid, Mexico City, and Athens have said that they plan to ban diesel vehicles from cities by 2025.[12] And of course, the real victims are the large number of people who have lost their health or their lives.

But this is not just a story about a few bad actors or corrupt regulators. There is a systemic problem here. As software has allowed automobile manufacturers to compete on complexity, it has become harder and harder to regulate these complex systems. Regulators can employ more sophisticated testing protocols, and they have begun to do so. But if manufacturers will be chastened for a while with regard to emissions testing, there are many other areas where complex software puts regulators at a disadvantage. And even in emissions testing, it is perhaps just a matter of time before some manufacturer deploys more sophisticated deceptions. This is an arms race, and without access to the software code and the resources to interpret it, regulators are overmatched.

Software-enabled complexity has changed not only the behavior of firms but the ability of governments to regulate them. A number of authors, including Nassim Nicholas Taleb in *Antifragile* and Chris Clearfield and András Tilcsik in *Meltdown,* have written about the general challenge of controlling complex systems.[13] But complex software affects regulation in very specific ways related to the use of information. And firm information has become central to the enterprise of government regulation. Because of this, specific changes in laws and policies are needed to counter the problem proprietary software poses for regulation.

In the Volkswagen case, complex software defeated regulators who were intending to measure an outcome: emissions of nitrogen oxides. The software obfuscated that measurement. But there are other ways that complex software can frustrate regulators, and given the broad implementation of complex software systems across the economy, there are many other industries where this occurs, sometimes with dramatic implications.

The Boeing 737 MAX

With the Boeing 737 MAX aircraft, software frustrated a regulator attempting to evaluate specific performance compliance.[14] In 2011, Boeing undertook to update its aging 737 airliner with more powerful engines and new functions in order to keep a large customer, American Airlines, from defecting to Boeing's competitor, Airbus. In order to accommodate larger engines, Boeing moved their position forward. This repositioning, however, changed the aerodynamic behavior of the aircraft, particularly on a maneuver known as the windup turn. This is a steep banked spiral that brings the aircraft to the point of stalling. Although rarely used in flight, the windup turn is a safety test required by the Federal Aviation Administration (FAA). Normally, when an aircraft approaches a stall, the pilot feels force on the control stick and takes this as a sign to lower the nose of the plane to avoid stalling. However, with the new engine configuration, the 737 MAX actually loosened the control stick when approaching a stall.

This alone would not have been a safety problem. But, according to FAA rules, it would have required additional training for pilots on simulators, something that was both expensive and slow. Instead, Boeing chose to install a software fix. Engineers added a sensor to the plane to detect a steep ascent angle. When the angle became too steep, risking a stall, the software automatically adjusted the tail stabilizers to push the nose of the plane down. With this fix, the aircraft passed the FAA safety test. Because Boeing considered this to be a minor adjustment unlikely to be encountered in normal flying conditions, the company excluded mention of it in the pilot's manual. It also failed to install a second, redundant sensor in case the first sensor failed. And Boeing did not fully inform the FAA of these changes.

The result was disastrous. On October 29, 2018, a flight with 181 passengers on board took off from Jakarta. About three minutes into the flight the angle sensor apparently malfunctioned and the software automatically sent the plane into a decline even though it was at low altitude and not approaching a stall. The pilots struggled frantically to bring the nose up, repeatedly trying to counteract the automatic adjustment. After nine minutes of the pilots' panicked attempts to right the plane, it crashed into the sea. The software fix had hidden this problem from regulators; it also, apparently, hid it from Boeing managers, who quickly placed the blame on poorly trained pilots. The 737 MAX planes were permitted to keep flying until a similar failure crashed another plane in Ethiopia the following March, killing 157 people. Only then, and after substantial political pressure from around the world, was the 737 MAX fleet grounded.[15] And only after additional examination did the real source of the disaster emerge.

Subprime Mortgages

Complex software misled regulators in a different way in the 2008 global financial crisis. Software models and software-enabled financial instruments obscured the financial condition of major banks and the magnitude of systemic risk. On July 19, 2007, as a declining housing market was sending many subprime mortgages into default, Ben Bernanke, chairman of the Federal Reserve Bank, testified before the Senate that he saw no more than $100 billion in losses in the subprime mortgage market. He was far off the mark. By November 2009, the International Monetary Fund estimated that top banks in the United States and Europe had already lost over $1 trillion in toxic assets and bad loans, and they predicted that number would rise to $2.8 trillion. The collapse of the subprime mortgage bubble was a major factor behind the Great Recession. How could financial regulators have been so far in the dark?

These assets were not simple mortgage loans but complicated financial instruments based on mortgage loans. Mortgages are loans to homeowners secured with the value of the house as collateral. Mortgages can have a fixed rate or variable rate interest. They can be second mortgages—that is, mortgages secured by the value of the house above the value of an original mortgage. Many mortgage loans are effectively guaranteed in case of homeowner default by government agencies (Freddie Mac, Fannie Mae, and Ginnie Mae). Some loans fail to meet the credit requirements to qualify for this government insurance. These are called subprime loans; they have a higher risk of default on average, and for that reason, they typically carry higher interest rates, sometimes substantially higher, making them attractive to investors who are willing to bear that risk.

Wall Street devised a variety of financial vehicles based on simple mortgages. First, they created mortgage bonds, which are pools of mortgages. The advantage of pooling mortgages is that it might reduce risk. While a single subprime mortgage might have a high risk of default, only a portion of a pool of mortgages might be expected to default under typical conditions. This was true as long as there were not some events—say, a general collapse in house prices—that might cause most of the pool to default at once. The portion of expected defaults could be factored into the interest rate for the mortgage bond, and the bond would then have less risk than the individual mortgage under typical conditions.

Software was essential to create these instruments—for example, to figure out the composite interest rates and how to handle defaults of individual bonds. Software was even more critical to the process of evaluating their riskiness. Investors in mortgage bonds did not have access to the details of the underlying mortgages. Instead, they relied on bond rating agencies such as Moody's and Standard & Poor's to affix a label to each instrument reflecting its risk. These agencies build proprietary software models to come up with a risk rating based on average characteristics of each pool of mortgages, such as the average credit scores of the mortgagees or the share of loans that were fixed rate versus floating rate.[16] There were several problems with these bond ratings, however. The rating agencies did not study the individual mortgages or conditions in local markets; they looked only at the average characteristics of the pool. This meant they had a harder time detecting conditions likely to lead to default, including falling home prices and fraud. Also, this meant that the rating system could be gamed—Wall Street firms packaged loans together that would get a higher rating than the real level of risk. And finally, these models made optimistic assumptions that housing prices would not fall. Indeed, many subprime loans were at risk of default as soon as housing prices fell or interest rates went up, which happened in 2006. In short, the software models used to assign risk ratings obscured the real level of risk.

With Moody's and Standard & Poor's putting favorable ratings on pools of loans, it became possible for the loan originators to sell all sorts of dubious loans. There was a flood of money going into questionable subprime mortgages. The author Michael Lewis tells of a Mexican strawberry picker earning $14,000 annually who was given a no-money-down loan to buy a $724,000 house in California. Many negative-amortizing loans were made—the borrower could pay little or no interest and simply accumulate greater debt. Very common were loans that initially charged a low teaser rate that then bumped up after three years. All of these implied greater risks of default when suddenly the borrower could no longer make monthly payments or if home values fell below debt levels, prompting borrowers to walk away. But the ratings agencies papered over the real risk.

Moreover, this obfuscation was compounded by various widely traded financial instruments based on mortgage bonds. Individual mortgage bonds were pooled into composite securities, collateralized debt obligations (CDOs), that spread risk further and allowed large investors to acquire these substantial assets. In addition, holders of these financial instruments could ostensibly lower their risk by purchasing credit default swaps. These were effectively bets that the instrument—a mortgage bond or CDO—would not default. If it did default, you received the initial value of the bond or CDO. Although these swaps acted like insurance, they differed in that you did not have to actually own the bond or CDO in order to buy a swap (place a bet). The same financial instruments could be insured many times over, and credit default swaps on subprime mortgage bonds became a $1 trillion market.[17] These huge investments were all made under the mistaken belief that rating agency models were providing an accurate assessment of risk. Further, all of these assets made their way onto bank balance sheets and the banks used their own proprietary software models to evaluate risk and to provide required reports to bank regulators. Bank regulators use these data and models to evaluate how much risk exposure banks have under different hypothetical scenarios. When bank risk is too high, regulators require banks to increase their capital relative to loans, providing assets to protect against loan failure. This is a key mechanism central bank regulators use to manage systemic risk. But when the data and models are faulty, capital requirements can be too low and the financial system can become dangerously fragile.

And this is what happened. When housing prices stopped rising, a cascade of defaulting financial instruments followed. Not only were the Federal Reserve and bank regulators surprised; so, too, were many banks and Wall Street firms that had apparently failed to remember that these instruments were intended for the suckers only. Bear Stearns, Lehman Brothers, and Merrill Lynch all faced collapse as did AIG, which had sold credit default swaps on mortgage bonds and CDOs. The defaults threw millions of borrowers into financial distress and bankruptcy, and the collapse of the banking system created a severe recession.

Software is implicit in some of the biggest regulatory failures of recent years. This is no accident. The kind of information managed by software has become increasingly central to the practice of regulation over recent decades, and regulators have become more reliant on this sort of information. It is important to understand how and why the nature of regulation changed.

The Information Revolution in Regulation

In the United States, the federal regulatory state emerged in part in reaction to new, large-scale technologies that helped capitalists to become dramatically more powerful.[18] Large railroads, meatpackers, steel mills, and petroleum refineries affected farmers, labor, consumers, and small businesses in new and unprecedented ways, provoking a political backlash. From the populist movement of the late nineteenth century, through the Progressive Era and the New Deal, the federal government was increasingly empowered to counteract social ills brought about by the new era.

The first federal regulatory agency exerting major new powers regulating the private sector was the Bureau of Animal Industry established in the U.S. Department of Agriculture in 1884.[19] This agency had extensive powers to quarantine and destroy livestock, burn buildings, and arrest violators within states in order to control cattle diseases that were spread rapidly across the country thanks to the railroads and large meatpacking centers. The railroads also became a target of farmers, who were often subject to local rail monopolies. Their political pressure helped bring about the Interstate Commerce Act, regulating rail prices, in 1887 and the Sherman Antitrust Act of 1890, as discussed in the next chapter. The subsequent decades brought new federal powers to regulate labor, food and drug safety, other consumer protections, and much more. The government emerged as a counterbalance to new, powerful corporations, and the federal government, in particular, acquired new and extensive powers. Perhaps the most intrusive economic powers were granted under the short-lived National Recovery Act of 1933 to set industry wages and prices. The Supreme Court, however, found this to be unconstitutional.

From the beginning, new regulators faced a dilemma: while private companies did not always act in the best interests of society, regulators lacked the information to fully guide how private companies *should* behave. Adam Smith argued that private parties, acting in their own self-interest, would produce efficiently, thereby furthering the social good. The corporate abuses of the Gilded Age made clear that this logic was incomplete. For example, the profit-seeking owners of a steel mill might be motivated to find the most efficient way to produce steel, but that method might also pollute the air and water near the mill. Since the owners might not bear the costs of pollution, they did not take it into account in determining how to run the steel mill. Economist Arthur Cecil Pigou identified this problem in 1920, calling it an externality.[20] The problem for regulators is that their goal is to both reduce pollution and provide society with low-cost steel. There is typically a tradeoff between two such objectives. While they can identify the problem of pollution, they lack the knowledge to run a steel mill so as to optimize this tradeoff.

This is an example of Hayek's dilemma of economic organization, discussed in chapter 1. Government regulators, like centralized socialist economic planners, lack needed information that diverse plant managers have. Moreover, the managers have reason not to truthfully reveal what they know because it affects their profits. That is, this is a problem of private or asymmetric information.

Following Hayek's insight, economists have developed a rich literature on the economics of information. This has transformed the analysis of regulation as well as the means by which regulations are implemented. And these ideas have had significant influence. Yet it does mean that regulation has become more dependent on measurement of outcomes and communication of formal metrics, exposing regulators to greater risk from the misuse of software in some cases. It is helpful to sketch out several important ways to deal with private information that have been developed for regulators.

Technocracy

The original and most straightforward way for regulators to acquire knowledge of the firms they are regulating is to hire people who are experts on the industry. This was the case, for instance, with the Interstate Commerce Commission (ICC), which regulates rail prices.[21] The first commissioner was Thomas Cooley, a lawyer who had represented the railroads for many years.[22] Experts staff a wide range of regulatory agencies, from the Food and Drug Administration to the Environmental Protection Agency to the Federal Reserve.

Of course, it has long been recognized that reliance on industry experts may instill regulators with a pro-industry bias—that is, regulators may become "captured."[23] This may occur as so-called cultural capture, in which regulators acquire a perspective that reflects the concerns and worldview of industry. Or it may involve less exalted forms of capture in which regulators may expect compensation for siding with industry—for instance, by expecting to receive lucrative employment in industry once they leave the regulatory agency. These and other possibilities were recognized early on, for example, with the Interstate Commerce Commission. Milton Friedman quotes a letter from Richard J. Olney, U.S. attorney general under Grover Cleveland, to Charles E. Perkins, president of the Chicago, Burlington and Quincy Railroad, a few years after the ICC was established:

The Commission . . . is, or can be made, of great use to the railroads. It satisfies the popular clamor for a Government supervision of railroads, at the same time that that supervision is almost entirely nominal. Further, the older such a commission gets to be, the more inclined it will be found to take the business and railroad view of things. It thus becomes a sort of barrier between the railroad corporations and the people and a sort of protection against hasty and crude legislation hostile to railroad interests. . . . The part of wisdom is not to destroy the Commission, but to utilize it.[24]

Mechanism Design

Beginning with Pigou, economists have designed policies that are much less reliant on experts. Rather than mandating specific actions for firms to take or directly setting prices, these policies aim to change the incentives of firms so that firms' profit maximizing behavior will take social goals into account. Returning to the example of the polluting steel mill, Pigou proposed taxing the mill for the amount of pollution it emits. In this way, the owners of the steel mill would be induced to adjust production to a method that emits less; they might also be motivated to develop new techniques that produce steel efficiently at low levels of emissions. Carbon taxes aimed at reducing the emissions of greenhouse gases are another example of this kind of Pigovian tax. The idea is that activities that emit greenhouse gases, such as driving a car, will become more expensive, and so people will choose to do them more judiciously. But the key insight here regarding information is that policy makers do not need to know the techniques used in running steel mills nor all of the manifold activities that generate greenhouse gases.

Economists have taken this simple idea and enhanced it, applying it to many different regulatory situations. Leonid Hurwicz, Eric Maskin, and Roger Myerson developed a generalized approach for designing policies of this sort labeled "mechanism design."[25] They won the Nobel Prize in Economics for this contribution. So, too, did Jean Tirole who, along with Jean-Jacques Laffont, developed an approach for regulating the rates that public utilities charge or the prices of government procurement contracts that have been traditionally awarded on a cost-plus basis without regulators needing to know the actual cost structures of the utility or contractor.[26] An example of mechanism design is the auctions used to allocate electromagnetic spectrum by the Federal Communications Commission (another application built on the work of other Nobel laureates). Economists used the tools of mechanism design to determine subtle features of the auctions.[27] Another innovative policy approach in a similar vein is cap-and-trade policies in which regulators set a maximum cap on the pollution firms can emit.[28] They then allocate permits to emit given quantities, the sum of those permits equaling the cap. Firms can then trade these permits with one another, bidding up the values in order to get the quantity they desire. In this way, the effective pollution tax is determined by the market in pollution permits.

Mandated Disclosure

Another set of policies concerns the private information firms provide consumers and workers rather than the information they provide directly to regulators. Firms might not reveal to consumers important aspects of the quality of their products, and they might not reveal to workers important aspects of the quality of jobs they offer. To make good decisions, car buyers need to know fuel mileage of different models; borrowers need to know what their actual payments will be; workers need to know health and safety risks. But firms might fail to provide consumers and workers with the information needed to make a fair transaction. Worse, firms might provide misleading information. Furthermore, firms might play to the cognitive limitations of consumers and workers. It has long been recognized that individuals do not always act in their own self-interest because they might not understand the full implications of their actions or they may have cognitive biases that lead them to make harmful or risky choices. Modern behavioral economics has demonstrated important cognitive biases.

For the past half century, a favored policy response to these problems has been mandated disclosure. Mandated disclosure policies require firms to spell out in standardized forms and clear language exactly what consumers are committing to, what they should expect to receive, and what the warranties and guarantees are. These disclosures are the fine print we ubiquitously encounter when we borrow money, buy travel tickets, get medical treatments, sign up for health insurance, and even visit websites.

Disclosure has often been paired with deregulation. The idea is that by providing consumers with the information they need to make sensible decisions, regulators can free firms from restrictive regulation. Consumers, not government, can decide what is in their own best interest. For example, financial disclosure forms have been imposed at the same time that lending restrictions have been relaxed. In the United States by the middle of the twentieth century, most states had usury laws that capped the maximum interest rates that could be charged and imposed other restrictions to protect borrowers. For instance, many mortgage loans required significant down payments and minimum income levels, and the loans were restricted to fixed interest rates and fixed terms. These paternalistic policies reduced home ownership and excluded many legitimate borrowers who could safely borrow without subjecting themselves to unfair risk or unaffordable interest payments.

Beginning with the Truth in Lending Act of 1968, disclosure laws required lenders to provide clear, standardized information about interest rates and total payments required by a loan.[29] Shortly thereafter, federal laws began preempting state usury laws, allowing mortgage lenders to collect higher interest than before, to issue adjustable-rate mortgages and negative amortization mortgages, and to remove income and down payment requirements. Consumer credit grew rapidly and contributed to rising home ownership, but it also imposed steep cognitive requirements on borrowers, requirements that many subprime mortgagees could not meet, and, as we have seen, it may have increased borrowers' risk of default and bankruptcy.

Mandated disclosure can also be enhanced. Cass Sunstein and Richard Thaler argue that disclosure policies can be supplemented with "nudges" or defaults.[30] For instance, in addition to receiving information about different retirement savings plans, workers can be automatically signed up for one appropriate plan that they are free to override if they choose.

The Challenge of Complexity

Over the past half century, regulation has become more dependent on the formal communication of information. At the same time, software has made technologies and products more complex. This combination is rife with opportunities to subvert or evade regulation. Consider some of the challenges to regulation created by complexity:

Regulatory Capture

As noted, when regulators rely on industry experts, they risk becoming biased toward industry. The more complex the matter of regulation, the greater the reliance on industry experts, and the greater the risk of capture. Political scientist Nolan McCarty argues that complexity makes regulatory agencies and legislators reliant on industry experts, shifting regulation closer to industry preferences.[31]

The effect of complexity on regulatory capture is seen clearly in the history of the Boeing 737 MAX regulation. Because the complexity of modern aircraft has been difficult for FAA regulators, they have long relied on designated engineering representatives who are based at the manufacturers. These people directly observe the development of new aircraft, they can monitor all of the highly detailed features, and they certify these features as being safe as the development proceeds. In the past, these engineering representatives were typically employed by the aircraft manufacturer, but they reported directly to the FAA. Alex MacGillis describes a critical shift: "In 2005, embracing the deregulatory agenda promoted by the Bush Administration and the Republicans in Congress, the F.A.A. changed to a model called Organization Designation Authorization. Manufacturers would now select and supervise the safety monitors. If the monitors saw something amiss, they would raise the issue with their managers rather than with the F.A.A. By sparing manufacturers the necessity of awaiting word from the F.A.A., proponents of the change argued, the aviation industry could save twenty-five billion dollars in the next decade."[32]

In the regulatory approval process for the Boeing 737 MAX, more and more of the certification decisions were handed over to Boeing managers until, by the end, Boeing was virtually certifying the safety of the plane itself.[33] Yet emails uncovered in subsequent investigations reveal that Boeing employees knew about the problems with the fix Boeing had created in order to pass the windup curve test; they reported these problems to management, but Boeing managers chose not to alert the FAA.[34] Moreover, Boeing management described the fix as a minor modification of an existing system and had it deleted from the pilot's manual so that the FAA would not impose new training requirements for pilots. While Boeing clearly had culpable managers, the bigger lesson here is that the complexity of the aircraft made the FAA reliant on Boeing for critical information, making it extremely hard for the FAA to exercise independent judgment.

Measurement

Regulations managed under a mechanism design approach rely on measurement of outcomes. In some cases, government agencies can take these measurements themselves—for instance, measuring air pollution emissions from large industrial plants (point sources). But in other cases, regulators must rely on standardized tests, as with vehicle emissions, or on company-reported information. To the extent that the measured outcomes are managed by software, opportunities for obfuscation arise. Possibilities arise in many areas of regulation, including tax compliance, medical billing, fair pay and labor standards regulation, public utility billing, discrimination in housing and employment, high frequency stock trading, and airline overbooking. For example, software systems are used to effect cross-border transfer pricing schemes that evade tax compliance.[35] A burgeoning field of study is the role of bias and discrimination in software systems used in policing, judicial decisions, hiring, online advertising, and more.[36] To the extent that regulations are intended to be nondiscriminatory, algorithmic bias represents another form of regulatory subversion.

A parallel set of problems affects mandated disclosure. Just as Volkswagen cheated on emissions tests, so it cheated on tests used to determine the fuel economy ratings disclosed to consumers.[37]

It is hard to know the extent to which regulators are misled in so many areas. But it is safe to say that as more and more complex economic activity is managed by software, regulatory compliance will be increasingly manipulated and obscured.

Risk Assessment

A similar set of opportunities for distortion arises regarding the assessment of risk. Regulators assess the risk levels of banks, stock traders, insurance companies, and other financial institutions. Consumers rely on disclosures of risk regarding the safety of vehicles and consumer products. Compared to physically observable outcomes, such as nitrogen oxide emissions, risk is harder for regulators to directly observe and measure. Instead, regulators and consumers are even more dependent on private firms and their statistical models.

Furthermore, risk may become sharply more difficult to assess as complex software systems manage more products. This is because complex systems often have very different risk profiles. Consider, for example, vehicle safety. Insurance companies and safety regulators estimate the likelihood that a particular automobile model will experience an accident by reviewing data on many vehicles over time. They calculate the number of accidents per mile driven. Under some assumptions, this estimate is a good prediction of *future* accident rates, and hence it serves as a measure of vehicle safety. One critical assumption is that the causes of the accidents are independent—that is, the likelihood that a car crashes because the driver had poor visibility is independent of the likelihood that the brakes fail, which is independent of the probability that the tires skid. The law of large numbers tells us that large-sample estimates of risk from independent causes will be accurate predictors of future risk. Independent causation is a reasonable assumption for simple mechanical systems.

But this is not necessarily a good assumption for complex systems such as self-driving vehicles controlled by machine learning software. First, it is devilishly difficult to determine what the causes of failure are in these systems. For example, the crash of a Tesla running on autopilot that killed Joshua Brown in 2016 may have been caused when the software misinterpreted a trailer truck crossing the road as an overhead sign and, for that reason, did not apply the brakes.[38] But also, these obscure causes may not be independent; they may interact. When this happens, the law of large numbers might not apply. Seemingly rare events might happen much more frequently with interactions. Using past experience to estimate future risk might require observing accident rates over a very large number of miles driven; in the worst case, past experience might simply not be an accurate guide to future risk. Safety regulators, insurance companies, and consumers need much more extensive data and analysis to assess risk of complex software systems.

Disclosure

Legal scholars Omri Ben-Shahar and Carl Schneider contend that mandated disclosure "may be the most common and least successful regulatory technique in American law. It aspires to help people making unfamiliar and complex decisions while dealing with specialists by requiring the latter (disclosers) to give the former (disclosees) information so that disclosees choose sensibly and disclosers do not abuse their position."[39] There is little evidence that these policies work except in, perhaps, some limited ways.[40]

But complexity subverts mandated disclosure policies in several ways. First, complex disclosures, often enabled by software, become incomprehensible to typical consumers. For example, legal scholar Lauren Willis argues that truth-in-lending policies for home mortgages "functioned relatively well—or at least did little harm—in a world of fairly simple uniform loan products, the price and risk of which were hemmed in by usury limits and credit rationing. But the world has changed."[41] Today, borrowers of adjustable-rate mortgages need to understand disclosures involving "indexes, margins, discounts, caps on rates and payments, negative amortization, payment options, and recasting (recalculating) your loan."[42] It seems highly doubtful that disclosure of these terms usefully informed that Mexican strawberry picker who spoke no English but took out a $724,000 house loan. Willis provides evidence that subprime mortgagees are paying too much in interest compared to competitive alternatives and that they are purchasing overly risky loans compared to alternatives.

Furthermore, even if one understands the concepts described, one needs to be an expert to understand the legal implications and enforceability of the various terms. Regarding credit card disclosures, Elizabeth Warren tells us, "I teach contract law at Harvard, and I can't understand half of what it says."[43]

Beyond these problems, however, sophisticated software systems subvert mandated disclosure policies in a more sinister way. These policies assume that people presented with the basic terms of a loan, for example, can make a rational decision about the right level of risk and the right size of future payments for their own needs. But behavioral economists have now firmly established that many people have cognitive biases; people underestimate risks, and they misjudge the real costs of future payments. If the people with such biases were a small, random portion of borrowers, then that might not limit the usefulness of disclosure policies. But the borrowers who make these poor choices are not randomly selected; they are *targeted* by lenders that have sophisticated marketing programs for credit cards, home equity loans, and other kinds of credit. Using extensive data on financial transactions and artificial intelligence software systems, lenders are able to disproportionately reach and sell to just those people who will pay too much and shoulder too much risk. Mandated disclosure policies are simply no match for these sophisticated tools.

Compliance Costs

Last, a consequence of rising complexity is the rising cost of promulgating and maintaining regulations and the costs to private parties of compliance. The complexity of regulation has been rising generally. For instance, the number of words in the Code of Federal Regulations has tripled since 1970.[44] Some of that increase can likely be attributed to the growing complexity of the technologies that the federal government is regulating, although that is not the only reason.[45] In any case, the rising complexity suggests a growing cost to the government of regulation or, since administrative budgets have not been rising as fast, regulatory agencies that may well be becoming progressively more understaffed and, therefore, less able to provide proper enforcement.

But there is another consequence of regulatory complexity: rising costs that fall disproportionately on small firms, further boosting the dominance of large firms.[46] For instance, for small banks (less than $100 million in assets), regulatory compliance consumes 10 percent of expenses (excluding interest expense). For large banks, compliance accounts for only 5 percent of expenses.[47] Regulatory compliance costs are relatively more expensive for small banks because they have a large fixed component—that is, they exhibit scale economies. For example, truth in lending for mortgages is the second most costly compliance activity. Because truth-in-lending compliance requires setup costs for each type of financial instrument, large banks can spread that cost over many more customers. When software enables a proliferation of many different financial instruments, those fixed costs can rise. There is evidence that compliance costs have been rising as a share of bank noninterest expenses.[48]

The upshot is that greater regulation, even in the seemingly innocuous form of truth-in-lending requirements, may further increase the dominance of large firms. In banking, large firm dominance has been rising for decades.[49]

Open-Source Regulation

In sum, complexity undermines regulation in three ways. First, it allows for obfuscation or deception, as in the Volkswagen example. Complex software provides ample opportunities to deceive regulators. Second, it allows for the capture or corruption of regulators or of trusted intermediaries, as with the FAA supervision of Boeing or with the bond ratings agencies and subprime mortgages. In these cases, greater complexity meant greater reliance on industry sources leading to greater capture. Third, greater complexity means more information overload and greater regulatory cost burden. For example, truth-in-lending regulation presents mortgage borrowers with incomprehensible disclosures and places a relatively greater compliance burden on small banks.

It is beyond both the scope of this book and my reach to identify the best way to fix these specific problems. But I can suggest some general principles about how to regulate software from the experience of the open-source software movement. Concepts that are critical for developing complex software on a large scale are useful for thinking about how to regulate complex software.

Since the early days of computers, programmers have informally shared software code. In the 1970s and 1980s, various organizations began licensing rights to software code that could be used freely, including rights to change and distribute the code. This became known as open-source software, and it is widely used in a broad range of applications today. For example, much of the plumbing of the Internet occurs over open-source software. It is also prominent in artificial intelligence, the Internet of Things, autonomous driving, distributed ledgers, and cloud computing infrastructure.

Because open-source software is free, one might expect it to be of little use in commercial applications. The argument went that proprietary software would always be better because its developers had stronger incentives to improve the code. This, however, turned out not to be true in general. Today, most of the big software companies make large investments supporting open-source projects that they use, including Microsoft, which once vocally opposed open-source software. Although the open-source code is free, commercial vendors make money by providing it along with complementary hardware and software. For instance, IBM makes money on hardware that it sells with Linux, an open-source operating system. And the advantage to IBM is that the large number of programmers who work with Linux fix bugs and add features that improve its quality. Indeed, some evidence suggests that in general, the quality of open-source projects may often be better than that of comparable proprietary software.[50] The reason is the distributed nature of error detection and quality improvement. In the words of Eric Raymond, an early open-source advocate, "Given enough eyeballs, all bugs are shallow."[51]

From the point of view of regulators, deceptive or obfuscatory code is also a bug, and such bugs can be found and corrected by similar means. An open-source-like review structure would provide access to key aspects of the technology to regulators as well as select third parties.

Clearly, regulators need access to software code that is used to deliver the products and services they regulate. Inspection of the code can reveal attempts at obfuscation, and it is hard to identify such deception without access to the code. It is nuts that access to that code might not only be unavailable to regulators but actually illegal to obtain. At least one federal agency, the Consumer Financial Protection Bureau (CFPB), has powers to access the code of the financial institutions it regulates.[52] CFPB examiners have used this power and they have uncovered violations with it, but they have used it only occasionally.

Of course, software code by itself can be difficult to interpret. In the Volkswagen case, researchers identified the offending code only after they gained access to software documentation in addition to the firmware object code. So, as in open-source projects, regulators also need access to documentation.

But regulators might not have the knowledge or motivation to review and test code. This is why the "many eyeballs" aspect of the open-source software process is important. Today, third parties often play an important role complementing or sometimes replacing government regulators. For instance, insurance companies rate the safety of cars and charge premiums based, in part, on car safety; these actions provide important incentives to manufacturers to improve safety. Or, as above, financial regulators have outsourced the risk assessment of bonds to independent ratings agencies. Open-source-style regulation would grant a select community of third parties access to the code and/or data, including organizations such as these but also, possibly, a broader community, including hobbyists and those without a direct financial interest. Indeed, hobbyists played an important role in the Volkswagen revelations.

The selection and restrictions on such communities are important because open-source software raises a number of concerns. It might be self-defeating to grant hot rod enthusiasts access to automobile code if that allows them to soup up their cars at the expense of pollution emissions. Obviously, some restrictions on uses of the code need to be in place. Similarly, we might not want to share code among rivals. There has been a general concern about open-source software undercutting innovation incentives, but the experience with open source suggests that a well-designed process does not do this, especially when the revealed code is complementary to hardware or to proprietary software. Indeed, open-source access may provide opportunities for the community to suggest improvements in the code, as happens with open-source projects. Another concern is cybersecurity. If hackers can access source code, perhaps they can identify vulnerabilities. This has been an active area of controversy and research. However, despite a few well-known open-source security bugs, some research suggests that the security of open-source projects is no worse than that of proprietary software and might well be better because "many eyeballs" allow quicker identification and correction.[53]

In some cases, access to software code is not enough. Particularly for machine learning applications, access to data is essential. For example, self-driving vehicles depend on AI systems that are built on large amounts of data from vehicle sensors and cameras. Without comparable data, it is difficult if not impossible for regulators or insurance companies or other third parties to assess the safety of these vehicles. One possibility is to require autonomous vehicle manufacturers to share their data along with their code. While the U.S. Department of Transportation has set up a voluntary program for autonomous vehicle operators, this appears to be insufficient.[54] Another is for third parties or government to create their own data. These data are a public good and might well be efficiently provided by the government.

Finally, even without access to code and data, "many eyeballs" can be applied in some cases through the use of simulators. The problems of the Boeing 737 MAX were readily apparent to pilots operating simulators.[55]

Simulators that are also available for automobile powertrains could possibly reveal emissions problems.[56] Of course, simulator code can also be gamed.

Complex software undoubtedly poses challenges for regulation. But the problem, of course, is not just that the software is complex but that it is proprietary. Widely shared or open-source software would not be so open to abuse. Open-source regulation puts a new twist on Supreme Court Justice Louis Brandeis's statement that "sunlight is said to be the best of disinfectants."[57] Exposure of code and data to many eyeballs can go some way toward leveling the balance of power between corporations and regulators.

9

Platforms and Antitrust

The hearing was a curious spectacle. For nearly six hours on July 29, 2020, the CEOs of four top tech firms, Jeff Bezos of Amazon, Tim Cook of Apple, Mark Zuckerberg of Facebook, and Sundar Pichai of Google, were interrogated on video by members of the antitrust subcommittee of the U.S. House Judiciary Committee.

The *New York Times* headline described this event as Big Tech's "Big Tobacco Moment," comparing it to the 1994 hearing when the CEOs of the seven largest tobacco companies appeared before Congress to answer questions.[1] That hearing marked a turning point in the regulation of tobacco. For decades, the large tobacco companies and tobacco growers had formed a potent lobby, preventing effective regulation despite well-known dangers of tobacco addiction. At the 1994 hearings, the executives were questioned about whether tobacco was addictive and should therefore be regulated as such.[2] The tobacco chiefs all testified that they believed that tobacco was not addictive; several of them specifically denied that they manipulated the levels of nicotine in their products. Everyone knew they were lying, and evidence soon appeared proving that they had lied. Public outrage against tobacco surged, and tobacco's long, cozy relationship with politicians broke apart, opening the way for regulation and court cases.

While the Big Tech hearing might result in some legislation and perhaps emboldened the Justice Department to initiate an antitrust suit against Google, it does not seem likely that this hearing will mark such a drastic change in tech company fortunes. To be sure, just the fact that the hearing occurred signaled a change in politicians' attitudes toward Big Tech companies. Just a few years earlier, these companies had been lionized by politicians as exemplars of American success. Now the CEOs of these companies were aggressively grilled. Nor did the hearings lack substance or preparation. The committee had taken hundreds of hours of interviews and collected over a million documents, including some private emails of the CEOs.

But, in contrast to the tobacco hearings, there did not seem to be a single focus or policy issue likely tied to a deep vein of public outrage. One analyst counts twenty-eight separate policy issues raised in the hearings.[3] Some of the questioners confronted the CEOs with detailed evidence about company behavior. Jeff Bezos of Amazon was challenged about how it competed against and later acquired Diapers.com; Mark Zuckerberg was challenged about why Facebook bought Instagram. Other questions were farther afield. Republicans asserted that Big Tech firms had an anticonservative bias; a Democrat questioned how they had facilitated Russian misinformation during the 2016 election. Google and Facebook were criticized for taking ad revenues away from newspapers, hastening print media's decline. One representative asked Mark Zuckerberg why Facebook deleted Donald Trump Jr.'s tweets about hydroxychloroquine as a supposed treatment for Covid-19 (that was Twitter, actually). Another congressman asked Sundar Pichai, CEO of Google, why campaign emails to his father ended up in his father's spam folder.

Even though some of the questions raised substantive policy issues and some comments highlighted unfair, unethical, and possibly illegal behavior, few seemed likely to tap into deep public outrage. The public lacks the same sort of indignation regarding Big Tech as they had regarding Big Tobacco. People do have concerns about Big Tech companies, especially Facebook. A recent survey found that 72 percent of respondents felt that Facebook had too much power.[4] But 90–91 percent had a favorable view of Google and Amazon (81 percent for Apple and 71 percent for Facebook), and only 4–5 percent felt that Google, Amazon, and Apple have a negative impact on society (25 percent for Facebook). In contrast, at the time of the Big Tobacco hearings, Americans knew that tobacco was unhealthy and addictive; it had been three decades since the surgeon general issued a warning about cigarettes, and health warnings were mandated on cigarette packages. The tobacco hearings focused on a much more clearly identified issue of importance to many people. Moreover, the Big Tech hearings may have tilted public opinion toward Big Tech. Nearly half of eighteen- to thirty-four-year-olds felt more favorably toward Big Tech *after* the hearing, perhaps reflecting a reaction to the aggressive questioning tactics of the congressional representatives.[5]

This is not to dismiss concerns about dominant corporations. As I have argued, there is much to be concerned about. But the hearings revealed that neither congressional representatives nor the broader public have a very clear idea about exactly what is wrong with today's big companies and what remedies are needed. While the hearing brought numerous examples of possibly bad behavior by Big Tech (it was hard to tell conclusively because the CEOs were given little time to respond), the hearings failed to communicate a convincing picture overall. For one thing, the hearings may have chosen the wrong targets, companies that the public views rather favorably (with the exception of Facebook). Yet the problems of corporate dominance extend to all sectors of the economy, including more than a few large firms that do generate public outrage. Indeed, a number of companies are ranked in surveys as the "most hated companies in America," including some that dominate their industries.[6] The top three are Comcast (#1), Bank of America (#2), and Mylan (#3), the pharmaceutical company that gained a monopoly on the EpiPen emergency allergic reaction treatment and raised prices 500 percent.[7]

Why would the antitrust subcommittee, concerned about corporate dominance, instead go after companies that the public *likes*? These companies have rapidly increased their size and power. They have rapidly generated huge wealth, and billionaire CEOs make juicy targets. They have disrupted many existing businesses, such as newspapers, and many enemies means much ammunition. But perhaps the most fundamental reason the committee focused on Big Tech is a general recognition that technology affects competition in new and different ways that may call for new and different regulations. Indeed, Representative David Cicilline, chair of the subcommittee, hired as counsel a legal scholar and advocate, Lina Khan (now chair of the Federal Trade Commission), who has written about Amazon and how such digital platform technologies require new, invigorated antitrust regulation. Platform businesses use technology to bring together independent parties like sellers and consumers (Amazon) or consumers and advertisers (Google). Khan and related scholars argue that platform technologies provide new opportunities for predatory pricing and exclusionary conduct. Hence, the hearings brought up numerous detailed examples of improper mergers and unfairly treated competitors. These scholars call for breaking up the Big Tech companies or for regulating them as public utilities.

But the lack of public outrage directed against Big Tech revealed a tactical flaw. If Big Tech has destroyed competition leading to higher prices, lower quality, and less innovation, the public doesn't see it at this time. With the exception of Facebook, these companies are just too well liked to be targets of outrage, and the reason they are well liked is that many people appreciate the value they get from Big Tech companies. People like the services and products that Big Tech delivers, they like the prices, and they are apparently not too concerned about the impacts Big Tech is having on society. Much of the public, apparently, does not seem too worried that digital platform technologies might be undercutting competition and hurting consumers and society. For this reason, the hearings failed to tap into the kind of deep public outrage that brought change to the tobacco industry and that brought us the first antitrust laws a century ago.

Yet there *is* a real and new problem with big technology today: technology does affect competition, not only for platform businesses, but also companies in most sectors of the economy, including some of the most hated companies in America. The focus on platform businesses is misdirected. The congressional investigators cast their net too narrowly, they focused on the wrong aspects of technology, and their remedies may actually be detrimental.

Open digital platforms are not so much the problem as they are part of the *solution*. It is true that platform businesses pose new challenges to antitrust regulators, and for this reason there is need to improve or strengthen antitrust enforcement. But the bigger problem lies with the rest of the economy, where proprietary platform technology is allowing firms to dominate their industries, giving rise to greater inequality and slower innovation. And antitrust policy can play a role in improving competition in these industries. That role is not to break up platform businesses or turn them into public utilities but to encourage or compel more firms with proprietary technology to *become open platform businesses.* These firms need to open up, allowing partners and competitors partial access to the technology so that it may be more widely shared. Well-regulated platforms *increase* competition that can overcome some of the ills of industries dominated by IT superstars.

Technology and the Rise of Antitrust

Because antitrust law is confusing—some would say confused—it is helpful to look at the history of antitrust and the evolution of key principles. From the beginning, antitrust was intimately connected with new technology—in particular, new technology that exhibited economies of scale. The last quarter of the nineteenth century witnessed a wave of new large-scale technologies. In chapter 3 we saw how the Bessemer process revolutionized steel production, slashing the price of steel rails. With cheap rails and new railroad technology, railroads experienced an investment boom. Increasingly, with lower transportation costs, the market for farm produce grew and farmers turned to commercial agriculture. Other technologies similarly changed petroleum refining, sugar refining, meat production, farm machinery, and other industries with substantial scale economies.

New technologies used by a small number of large firms brought lower prices and new opportunities in many industries, but with that they also gave those large firms, called trusts, significant power over people's lives. Railroads gave farmers new opportunities in commercial agriculture, but they also meant that farmers became dependent on railroads. In many rural regions, only a single railroad was economically feasible, so local monopolies tended to emerge. Although railroads initially provided lower transportation costs, they also had the power to raise prices, which they used, squeezing the farmers.

The power and unfairness of the railroads became a major issue for the populist movement. The public's deep outrage led to the Interstate Commerce Act of 1887, which regulated railroad rates, and the Sherman Antitrust Act of 1890. This was the first federal legislation covering competition, but it faced significant difficulties in the courts. Indeed, during the first decade of the Sherman Act, there were no successful prosecutions of large companies. Instead, the Sherman Act was used against labor unions.

But during the first decade of the twentieth century, public outrage deepened further, fanned by so-called muckraking journalists who exposed corruption in government, unfair behavior of large corporations, and other social ills, such as lynching, sexual harassment, and the treatment of the mentally ill. The muckrakers exposed company use of child labor and the oppression of unions. Upton Sinclair's book *The Jungle* bared the unhealthy practices of meat packers and other food companies; Justice Brandeis wrote about how banks promoted the consolidation of industries in a few hands; Samuel Hopkins Adams revealed the false claims made by pharmaceutical companies; Ida Tarbell vividly painted the details of how Standard Oil extorted its way to become the largest oil refiner in the world.

President Theodore Roosevelt picked up on this broad discontent, making trust-busting part of his Square Deal. Under Roosevelt, the United States initiated a lawsuit against Standard Oil for Sherman Act violations, winning a victory in 1911 that led to the dissolution of the company. That victory marked the real start of antitrust enforcement in the United States. In 1914, recognizing the weakness of the Sherman Act, Congress passed the Clayton Antitrust Act, which significantly strengthened antitrust enforcement powers and detailed various forms of illegal conduct.

The Social Costs and Benefits of Bigness

Antitrust law is not exclusively about large firms. For instance, it prohibits collusion and price-fixing for firms of every size. Nevertheless, large firms are the central concern of antitrust policy, as the name indicates. And the motivating force, the outrage that propelled this new policy, was the growing *power* of big firms over the lives of ordinary people. The trusts had power in product markets, power in labor markets, and political power.

Yet this posed a practical challenge for antitrust law: firm size appears to be something of a double-edged sword. While large firms can and do use their power to profit unfairly, they also deliver significant social benefits.

Prices

It is standard economics that dominant firms can have market power, implying higher prices. This finding is supported by both theory and empirical research. For example, after U.S. Steel was created in 1901, comprising two-thirds of U.S. steelmaking capacity, it was able to maintain relatively stable prices until the Great Depression despite its costs falling by half.[8]

But large firms can also lead to lower prices if they are more efficient. For example, economies of scale allowed the early Bessemer steel mills to reduce prices drastically. In 1900, the price of steel in deflated dollars was less than a third of the price in 1868. Also, it is well established that more productive firms grow faster. That is, firms often *become* large by offering lower prices or greater quality. Hence, being a large firm might be a signal of lower costs, greater efficiency, and greater social benefit, and does not necessarily imply that the firm has engaged in predatory behavior to rivals.

Wages and Labor

When a large firm dominates a local labor market, it can pay lower wages. Recent research shows that wages are somewhat lower in markets dominated by a few large employers.[9] On the other hand, as we saw in chapter 7, large firms have long tended to pay significantly higher wages on average. Moreover, research shows that large firms also tend to provide better benefits and work amenities.[10]

Large firms are also more likely to be unionized, although that might be because large firms make better targets for union organizing. On the other hand, large firms and their owners have also been involved in some of the most violent suppression of strikes, such as John D. Rockefeller Jr.'s role in the Ludlow Massacre, a mass killing of striking coal miners and their families in Colorado in 1914.

Innovation

It has long been argued that monopolies have lower incentives to innovate. This was the argument Justice Brandeis made about U.S. Steel:

> Take the case of the Steel Trust. It inherited through the Carnegie Company the best organization and the most efficient steel makers in the world. It has had since its organization exceptionally able management. It has almost inexhaustible resources. It produces on so large a scale that practically no experimental expense would be unprofitable if it brought the slightest advance in the art. And yet

in only ten years after its organization, high American authority—
the Engineering News, declares:

"We are today something like five years behind Germany in iron
and steel metallurgy, and such innovations as are being introduced
by our iron and steel manufacturers are most of them merely following the lead set by foreigners years ago.

"We do not believe this is because American engineers are any
less ingenious or original than those of Europe, though they may
indeed be deficient in training and scientific education compared
with those of Germany. We believe the main cause is the wholesale
consolidation which has taken place in American industry. A huge
organization is too clumsy to take up the development of an original idea. With the market closely controlled and certain of profits
by following standard methods, those who control our trusts do
not want the bother of developing anything new."[11]

On the other hand, innovation scholar Joseph Schumpeter argued that
monopolies provide the most conducive structure for pursuing research and
development.[12] As we saw in chapter 6, large firms are not necessarily worse
at innovation. Even firms that are dominant in a market may be aggressive
innovators when their market is actively contested by rivals, large or small.

Political and Social Power

With great financial power comes greater political power. Large
firms have resources they spend to influence political and regulatory outcomes. For example, Standard Oil contributed $250,000 ($8 million in
today's dollars) to the Ohio Republican Party boss to defeat populist
presidential candidate William Jennings Bryan and to extract favors.[13] Legal
scholar Timothy Wu argues that corporate power substantially contributed
to the rise of fascism in the 1930s, although his historical analysis has been
challenged.[14]

On the other hand, large firms appear more responsive to public concerns
about social issues. While some corporate expressions of support for
popular social goals may be little more than public relations, some of them
seem real. Large corporations hire more diverse workforces, employing
more black and more female workers on average.[15] And they appear to

discriminate less as well. After controlling for measured and unobserved worker characteristics, an analysis finds that large firms pay women 13.0 percent less than comparable men and Blacks 1.9 percent less than comparable whites. But firms with fewer than a thousand employees pay women 19.7 percent less than comparable men and Black workers 6.7 percent less than comparable white workers.[16]

The naive although widely held view that "big = bad and small = good" is too simple.[17] While the power of large firms raises concerns, large firms by themselves are not necessarily evil. Yet there is something else to be concerned about, something that played a key part in motivating the outrage against trusts during the Progressive Era: large firms can leverage their size to take advantage of competitors, creating even greater market power with significant negative outcomes. Even if a firm becomes large by being more productive, it might abuse its power to limit future competition. Firms that begin attempting to "do no evil" might change their ways.

Leveraging Size

We saw this sort of leveraging in the discussion of the U.S. steel industry in chapter 3. Economies of scale meant that a dozen large mills could supply the domestic steel market in the 1870s and do so at dramatically lower prices. But the economies of scale also meant that only a handful of firms could enter the market, and with only a dozen firms in the market, it was feasible for them to undertake anticompetitive action to enhance profits and ensure greater stability. First, the mills formed a cartel in the 1870s, restricting output to maintain prices.[18] That cartel failed when Andrew Carnegie did not play along. Then financial engineering brought consolidation through mergers and acquisitions backed by the resources of J. P. Morgan. U.S. Steel emerged controlling two-thirds of the market in 1901. As noted, steel prices stabilized then.

Big firms could also leverage their size against competitors in more nefarious ways. Standard Oil epitomized such abuse of size. Ida Tarbell detailed how Standard Oil, which owned about 10 percent of the U.S. oil refining capacity in 1872, used various sorts of leverage to wrest control of over 90 percent of this market by 1879.[19] This process began in Cleveland, the leading center of the industry. Crude oil production blossomed in western Pennsylvania after Col. Edwin Drake's successful well in Titus-ville, in 1859. This crude oil was shipped to Cleveland, where it was refined, and then final products were shipped by rail or water (Lake Erie). As with steel, petroleum refining exhibited substantial economies of scale so that only relatively large operations were financially viable. But as the market grew, more firms could profitably enter. By 1872, there were about 250 refiners in the United States, 26 of them in Cleveland. Standard Oil was the largest.

This large size provided key leverage with the railroads. In 1872, a "South Improvement" corporation was chartered in Pennsylvania controlled by John D. Rockefeller, the largest shareholder in Standard Oil, with several other refiners as partners. Since they were large, although not a monopoly, the railroads were willing to cut them a deal. Members of the South Im-provement Company received substantial rebates on their shipping—40–50 percent on crude oil and 25–45 percent on refined product. In addition, the railroads were to pay South a percentage of the rail fees charged to non-South refiners. Tarbell described what happened next: "To the owners of [the other] refineries, Mr. Rockefeller now went one by one, and explained the South Improvement Company. 'You see,' he told them, 'this scheme is bound to work. It means an absolute control by us of the oil business. There is no chance for anyone outside. But we are going to give everybody a chance to come in. You are to turn over your refinery to my appraisers, and I will give you Standard Oil Company stock or cash, as you prefer, for the value we put upon it. I advise you to take the stock. It will be for your good.' "[20]

And Rockefeller assured the holdouts that they would be crushed. Within just three months, almost all took his advice, and Standard Oil grew from controlling 10 percent of U.S. refining capacity to controlling 20 percent. Outrage ensued—Pennsylvania canceled the corporate charter of South Improvement—but the damage had already been done.

Rockefeller also used his market power to acquire assets in vertically related industries. Charles L. Morehouse began producing lubricants in Cleveland using the tar remaining after the distillation of petroleum dur-ing the 1860s. He had developed a number of patents and trademarks and produced a range of lubricants for all varieties of machinery. After Rock-efeller gained control of the Cleveland refining industry, Morehouse went to Rockefeller, who encouraged him to expand his business as Standard Oil was not in this field. Rockefeller signed a contract to provide eighty-five barrels of tar a day, and Morehouse invested $41,000 in a new plant. But then in 1874, Rockefeller reduced the supply to twelve barrels a day and raised the price. That supply was insufficient to run the business profitably, so Morehouse pleaded with Rockefeller for more. Tarbell recounted: "Mr. Rockefeller was firm. All he could give Mr. Morehouse was twelve barrels a day. 'I saw readily what that meant,' said Mr. Morehouse, 'that meant squeeze you out—buy your works. They have got the works and are running them; I am without anything. They paid about $15,000 for what cost me $41,000.' "[21]

And there were other ways big firms leveraged their size to gain market share. Justice Brandeis remarked, "Experience has taught us likewise many of the specific methods or means by which the great trusts, utilizing their huge resources or particularly favored positions, commonly crush rivals: for instance, 'cut-throat' competition; discrimination against customers who would not deal exclusively with the combination; excluding competitors from access to essential raw material; espionage; doing business under false names; and as 'fake independents'; securing unfair advantage through railroad rebates; or acquiring, otherwise than through efficiency, such a control over the market as to dominate the trade."[22]

Conduct, not Size

The outrage over abuses of power by large firms helped motivate the creation of antitrust law, and from the beginning, the law distinguished between simply being a large firm, which was not illegal, and abuse of power by large firms that diminished competition, which was. According to the Sherman Antitrust Act, section 2, it is illegal to "monopolize, or attempt to monopolize, or combine or conspire with any other person or persons, to monopolize any part of the trade or commerce among the several States, or with foreign nations." Even Justice Brandeis, who held that "not a single industrial monopoly exists today which is the result of natural growth," focused antitrust inquiries on firm conduct, not simply firm size.[23]

But the difficult part was—and still is—determining which actions are illegal monopolization and which are merely effective competition. Some actions, such as colluding to fix prices, are identified explicitly in the Sherman and Clayton Acts as per se illegal. But in the Standard Oil case, the Supreme Court introduced a rule of reason—the facts of each case could be examined to judge whether the actions taken by the dominant firm unreasonably restrained trade.[24] As Brandeis wrote in the 1918 decision in *Chicago Board of Trade v. United States,* "The true test of legality is whether the restraint imposed is such as merely regulates and perhaps thereby promotes competition or whether it is such as may suppress or even destroy competition."[25] Note that the key determination is not whether the conduct hurts competitors—effective competition may very well hurt inefficient competitors—but whether it hurts *competition.*

The way the courts have interpreted this rule of reason has swung dramatically over time.[26] A major shift occurred during the 1930s and 1940s. Beginning with efforts by Thurman Arnold at the Justice Department and bolstered by the economic ideas of Joe S. Bain, firms with large market share were seen as inherently self-perpetuating and harmful to consumers.[27] The Justice Department sued Alcoa in 1938 for dominating the aluminum industry. Alcoa argued that it had not illegally excluded competitors, but when the case reached the U.S. Court of Appeals in 1945, Judge Learned Hand held, "We can think of no more effective exclusion than progressively to embrace each new opportunity as it opened, and to face every newcomer with new capacity already geared into a great organization, having the advantage of experience, trade connections and the elite of personnel."[28] That sounds like being an effective competitor.

During the 1970s and 1980s, the pendulum swung in the other direction in reaction. A new generation of empirical economists challenged the underpinnings of the Bain analysis showing that large firm size does not necessarily indicate a lack of competition.[29] And Robert Bork and other laissez-faire scholars of the Chicago School argued that antitrust analysis should dispense with considerations of firm market share and, instead, inquire whether firm conduct had harmed consumers. This focused on consumers, largely ignoring the effect of firm power on workers, politics, and society. And the rule of reason placed a significant evidentiary burden on plaintiffs—so much so that Judge Richard Posner quipped, "The content of the Rule of Reason is largely unknown; in practice, it is little more than a euphemism for nonliability."[30]

Today, there is debate about the strength and adequacy of antitrust enforcement. Some researchers argue that enforcement is too weak, resulting in rising industry concentration, although I argue that rising concentration is mainly the result of software investment.[31] Case studies in hospitals, health insurance, beer, and other industries find rigorous evidence that mergers created market power, raising prices.[32] Economist John Kwoka reviews the literature and concludes that merger enforcement is too weak overall, but researchers from the Federal Trade Commission contest his analysis.[33]

Making judgments about merger policy is difficult because the economic analysis involved is sophisticated and subject to interpretation. But in at least one area the performance of antitrust authorities in both the United States and Europe can be judged without such complications and found wanting: enforcement against repeat offenders for price fixing. Companies sometimes collude on setting prices; one firm sets a high price and the others do not undercut that price. To do this, they meet secretly or set up secret codes to signal their actions. Occasionally, they get caught, taken to court, convicted, and punished. And in some industries—chemicals, electronics, auto parts, and finance—dozens of large companies are caught doing this over and over again, in one division after another, some of the cartels lasting fifteen years or longer.[34] Corporate management tends to blame these infractions on so-called rogue division managers, but when we see it happening repeatedly—and we only observe the few who are unlucky enough to get caught—it speaks to anticompetitive behavior by top management and inadequate enforcement by antitrust authorities. While this is a long-standing problem, the bigger challenge to antitrust comes from new digital technology, and that is more recent.

How Do Digital Platforms Affect Competition?

It is widely recognized that digital technology has affected competition in some way, but it is less clear exactly which technologies are involved and how. Various expert panels have described the relevant phenomenon as "digital markets," "digital platforms," or "multi-sided platforms."[35] Because there is a confusing welter of terms, it is helpful to set out a simple taxonomy.

Table 3. Taxonomy of platforms

	One-sided	Multisided
Closed	CAD systems; AWS before 2006	Walmart system for suppliers and store managers
Open	Amazon direct sales; AWS after 2006	Amazon Marketplace; Google advertising; AWS after 2012

"Platforms" refer to modular base components of a technology that are used (combined with) multiple higher-level components or applications. For example, automobile manufacturers often use a common chassis and drive train in different models. Since 1908, General Motors has used a common platform across its Chevrolet, Buick, Pontiac, and Oldsmobile brands. Information technology is highly modular, often with many layers, and various interfaces are called platforms or application programming interfaces. For example, Intel-compatible personal computers are platforms for the Windows operating system, which is, in turn, a platform for various application programs such as spreadsheets and word processors. Websites are also platforms. Using standardized interfaces, they communicate to your web browser, delivering information content and responding to your browsing requests.

This last example makes clear that platforms facilitate human interaction; the technology interface supports a human interface. A web platform can facilitate information retrieval for a large number of people (weather.com), it can facilitate digital services (Google search), or it can facilitate commercial transactions (Amazon). Moreover, some platforms handle interactions between multiple groups of people. For example, Walmart's system using scanner data allows both suppliers and store managers to view detailed sales information at individual stores and to take actions to initiate new orders. Such a platform can be described as two-sided or multisided.

Last, there is an important economic distinction between closed and open platforms. Open platforms are accessible to the public; closed platforms are not. In between, of course, are platforms that are open to limited groups, but I will abstract away from that distinction to focus on how the economics differ with openness. The key idea is that open platforms facilitate transactions and competition. We can organize different types of platforms in a simple way (table 3).

In table 3, starting in the upper right and moving counterclockwise, the Walmart system described in the last paragraph is two-sided and private. Computer-aided design (CAD) systems assist engineers in designing products, allowing them to collaborate on complex designs. These systems can be seen as one-sided platforms that facilitate coordination among engineers. Amazon Web Services (AWS) began as an internal platform that provided data storage and computing services on an internal cloud for Amazon's different IT projects (this history is described in the next chapter). In 2006, Amazon opened up this platform to the general public, initiating the cloud computing service industry. When Amazon sells merchandise that it owns and inventories, its website is serving as a one-sided open platform. When independent merchants sell products to consumers on Amazon, the website functions as a two-sided open platform. This last category is sometimes referred to as digital markets. In 2012, AWS became a two-sided platform when it allowed third-party developers to produce apps that could be used by AWS customers.

Note that this taxonomy applies as well to noncommercial interactions and to implicit transactions. For example, a CAD system accessed by large numbers of engineers and managers for designing an airplane model is a closed one-sided platform. Google search provides a two-sided open platform where users enter search requests and are shown results along with advertisements. Advertisers and users make up the two sides of this implicit market; advertisers pay, but Google users obtain the service for free.

But these categories also apply to the nondigital world. Ancient bazaars and medieval trade fairs are literally two-sided markets. The platforms of the fairs provided warehouses, selling space, credit services, and even private judges to administer newly developed commercial law. Newspapers are also two-sided platforms, serving both readers and advertisers.

The question here, then, is how does digitization change the economics of these different types of platforms, and what does that imply for competition? But the impact on competition depends on the type of platform. I identify two sets of effects, one on closed systems (the top row of the chart) and one on multisided markets (the bottom right quadrant). For closed systems, the key technical change is that large, proprietary

IT systems have allowed these platforms to handle much greater complexity, providing key competitive advantages in differentiated markets. With open systems, by contrast, many of the socially undesirable features of proprietary technology are avoided. Many firms and workers may be able to access all or part of the technology, allowing them to benefit from its use and possibly to improve it. The transition from closed to open systems, such as the opening up of AWS, brings these benefits.

But it is the last group, the open multisided platforms, that have been the focus of much expert scrutiny, and the Big Tech firms hauled before Congress all have businesses that fall into this category. And the economics of these platforms complicates the already-confusing considerations of antitrust law. There are two main complications.

First, there is cross-subsidization. Owners of two-sided platforms can subsidize one side and tax the other. For instance, newspapers subsidize subscription fees, making up the losses presumably by charging advertisers more. There are a number of reasons this might make economic sense, but cross-subsidization makes it harder to identify predatory behavior. That is, newspapers charge subscribers less than the cost of the paper, but does this mean that they are illegally trying to monopolize the market? Perhaps a careful economic analysis can determine whether newspaper subscriptions are predatory, but the evidentiary burden to make such a determination might be costly and difficult and the Supreme Court has, in *Ohio v. American Express,* shifted this burden to the plaintiff, discouraging antitrust enforcement.[36]

A second complicating characteristic of multisided markets is that they can have network effects. A network effect occurs when the value of using a platform increases with the size of the network of users. For example, the more subscribers a newspaper has, the more valuable it is to advertisers.[37]

This kind of network effect acts much like an economy of scale, and it can lead to very aggressive growth dynamics. For instance, a newspaper might charge a lower subscription rate, perhaps even to the point of losing money, in order to win subscribers away from the competition. With more subscribers, it can raise ad rates, use them to subsidize deeper discounts for subscribers, and continue to grow. There are thus strong incentives to become dominant. In the past, these incentives led to newspaper wars in which intense competition for circulation spawned yellow journalism and fabricated news (maybe some things never change) that provided a pretext for the Spanish-American War. These incentives also, more peaceably, led to a great merger boom in newspapers. In 1920, five hundred cities had competing daily papers; by 1963 there were fewer than fifty such cities; by 2017, only ten.[38] Indeed, it was this consolidation—and what it meant for declining diversity of political views—that led to A. J. Liebling's quip about the freedom of the press being guaranteed only for those who own one.

The economics of networks differ in some ways from the economics of returns to scale. For one thing, the economic advantage of a dominant firm with network effects is dynamic. It builds slowly over many years as the number of users grows. The scale advantages of, say, a steel mill are gained quickly once the mill is built, but the competition between platforms for market share can go on for long periods of time. Also, the advantages of network economies might not be as permanent. Although the productive capacity of a large steel mill does not disappear quickly, users might rapidly switch to an alternative platform. They can do this if they are not tightly locked in to a dominant platform. Indeed, there is a long list of supposedly untouchable dominant firms in network markets that were displaced, including Yahoo! in search, MySpace in social media, and Nokia in mobile phones. While leading firms are frequently disrupted in emerging markets generally, these examples show that network effects do not guarantee continued dominance.

When network effects are combined with quality differentiation, markets can be more completely dominated. When consumers prefer the very best product, even if the quality difference is small, and the best product has the largest network, the dominant firm can conquer a large share of the market. It becomes a winner-take-most market. Economies of scale can also lead to winner-take-most situations if the market is not too large, but, as we saw in chapter 3, scale economies have limits—the returns to scale diminish at a certain point so that they no longer guarantee market dominance in large markets. Network effects also diminish, but sometimes at a very large size. We know that they diminish in some cases because big markets support multiple platforms in phone operating systems (iOS and Android) or computer platforms.[39]

In sum, the economics of multisided markets are, in fact, quite similar in character to the economics of markets with scale economies. There are important differences, but these are not truly radical differences. Nevertheless, multisided markets pose a difficult challenge for antitrust regulation because they are considerably more *complicated*. Because of cross-subsidization and long-term dynamics, it may often be difficult and costly to determine how certain actions affect competition. This makes regulation more difficult, and it also tends to be confusing for regulators, policy makers, the courts, and the public. Indeed, much of the public discussion of multisided markets seems to focus on issues of cross-subsidization and long-term dynamics while losing sight of the effect of these actions on competition.

Digital Platforms and Antitrust

Confusion about the intersection of digital platforms and antitrust pervaded the discussion leading to the congressional hearings, the arguments raised during the hearings, and the report the committee issued afterward.[40] For example, in her influential article "Amazon's Antitrust Paradox," Lina Khan argues that antitrust law needs to rethink predatory pricing in light of firms with network effects such as Amazon.[41] She notes that Amazon has sustained years of losses or minimal profits (although becoming more profitable recently), and she contends that they did this to set prices below cost in order to drive out competition. She argues that legal doctrine should be changed to presume that a dominant platform found to be pricing below cost is engaging in illegal predation.

To illustrate her thinking, Khan provides the example of Amazon's rivalry with Quidsi, the owner of the Diapers.com e-commerce website, an example also discussed at the congressional hearing. Amazon wanted to acquire Quidsi, which was rapidly growing and not interested in being bought out. Amazon started pricing diapers aggressively below cost, it set up a subscription program to leverage its large customer base against Quidsi, and it engaged in a number of other efforts to squeeze Quidsi. Quidsi relented and agreed to be acquired by Amazon in 2010, perhaps at a lower price than what it might have otherwise obtained. This sounds like a tale out of Ida Tarbell's history of Standard Oil. But there is one big difference that makes it difficult to evaluate the Quidsi example: John D. Rockefeller acquired 90 percent of the U.S. petroleum refining capacity, eliminating all significant competition. Did Amazon eliminate or even substantially reduce competition in the market for diapers? Amazon may have behaved reprehensibly and perhaps even illegally, but you can't have predatory pricing unless it leads to illegal monopolization. Even though a competitor might have been hurt, what matters is whether *competition* was hurt.

The retail market for diapers, both online and off, remains intensely competitive. Indeed, in 2017 Amazon and Walmart began an all-out price war over consumer-packaged goods, including diapers.[42] Only 22 percent of diapers are sold via e-commerce, so most of the competition was with brick-and-mortar stores. Generally, substantial evidence on pricing behavior shows that competition between offline and online retailers has intensified competition.[43] But even strictly online there is intense competition in diaper sales. For example, I checked prices online for one package of Pampers.[44] Amazon offered it for $48.00. But on the Amazon website there were fourteen other sellers of this package, one offering the Pampers for $47.99 with free shipping. In addition, there is intense competition from other websites, mainly because Google competes with Amazon in search— about half of all product searches begin on Google.[45] Searching via Google, I found many other sellers. Walmart.com matched Amazon's price, but Wish.com offered it at $46.21. Given the economics of multisided platforms, one cannot assume that aggressive pricing leads to the elimination of competition, especially when the platform itself is open to third-party rivals.[46]

Khan's article also raised questions about how the courts have viewed vertical integration, arguing that the market power of two-sided platforms gives firms like Amazon leverage over related markets. For example, the Institute for Local Self-Reliance argues that because Amazon is cross-subsidizing its shipping operations with fees from Marketplace sellers, it is about to dominate parcel shipping markets.[47] Consequently, it calls for Amazon to be prevented from vertically integrating into parcel shipping, echoing calls to break up Amazon from Elizabeth Warren and Donald Trump. But in fact, Amazon's parcel shipments comprise only a modest share of the courier and express delivery market, which is heavily dominated by UPS and FedEx.[48] In other words, Amazon's cross-subsidization significantly *increases* competition in a highly concentrated market. Nor does Amazon force its Marketplace sellers to use its shipping services; in the next chapter we'll look at how Amazon is actually facilitating other fulfill-ment services that its sellers can use.

Similarly, Amazon has been criticized for introducing its own private-label brands to compete with other sellers on its website, but here, too, Amazon's activities may actually increase competition. Competing against other sellers might appear to be a conflict of interest, but rightly or wrongly, retailers have long used private-label goods to compete against brands, often to a great degree.[49] On Amazon, the largest private-label categories are for high-volume commodity goods. Batteries is the number one cat-egory, and here, again, Amazon is introducing competition and lower prices into a highly concentrated market where the top two firms control 75 percent of the market.[50]

To be sure, both private-label goods and cross-subsidized shipping raise opportunities for Amazon to engage in anticompetitive practices such as restricting Marketplace sellers to using Amazon shipping services or putting rival sellers in a disadvantageous location on the website. Similarly, the dynamics of two-sided markets might invite predatory behavior to restrain trade. Complaints about bad behavior by the Big Tech firms were aired at the congressional hearing, and they do need to be investigated. Platforms in multisided markets do need to be scrutinized for anticompetitive conduct, and these examinations might be difficult because of the complicated eco-nomic environment. But the point here is that open two-sided markets can also create new competition even in highly concentrated markets. For this reason, it is a mistake to presume as a matter of principle that below-cost pricing is illegal predation or that two-sided platforms should be prevented from operating in vertical markets and broken up if they already are.

Moreover, the power of two-sided platforms can appear greater than it is, exaggerating the apparent ability of these firms to leverage their power in related markets. While Amazon has a dominant share in some market segments, such as bookselling, critics call Amazon a monopoly in general e-commerce. Yet careful calculation puts its share of the U.S. e-commerce market at about 35 percent and its share of the U.S. retail market at 6 per-cent, substantially smaller than Walmart, which is now also a serious e-commerce competitor.[51] Moreover, 35 percent is the market share of the Amazon website, but the majority of its website sales are made by other sellers. This means that the website's market share is somewhat insecure—

most of Amazon's Marketplace sellers also sell on other websites and their business can quickly shift.[52] Moreover, some of these alternatives, such as Walmart.com and Shopify, are rapidly growing. The fluidity of Amazon's market power can be seen in the rapid changes in share that occurred with the onset of the recent pandemic. As Amazon had difficulty meeting demand, its U.S. e-commerce market share by one estimate fell from 42 percent in January of 2020 to 34 percent in April.[53] While this does not portend a long-term drop in Amazon's dominance, it does highlight that Amazon's market power is of a very different and more conditional sort than that delivered by Standard Oil's 90 percent share of oil refining capacity.

These examples indicate how the combination of multisided platforms and antitrust creates confusion. At the same time, multisided platforms may very well increase the opportunities for anticompetitive abuse. Assuming we keep the principle that large size is not itself illegal, what can be done?

One thing is to increase funding for the Federal Trade Commission and the Antitrust Division of the Department of Justice. More complicated analysis calls for more expert analysts. The Big Tech firms need closer antitrust scrutiny, and resources are needed to perform that scrutiny. Perhaps training for judges could also help. Some people have called for the creation of a specialized agency or court to handle digital platform antitrust issues.[54] This might be a good idea, but it also raises the danger that such an agency might be prone to regulatory capture. It could become reliant on industry experts and become aligned with industry thinking. Indeed, that seems to have been the experience when Congress created a specialized court to hear patent appeals; that court has tended to favor expanding patent rights at the expense of other innovators.[55]

But the real problem with the focus on Big Tech's digital platforms is this: it distracts from much more serious problems, difficulties that might actually be solved with open platforms. Big Tech is simply not a very big part of the U.S. economy. The combined domestic sales of Amazon, Apple, Facebook, and Google are less than 2 percent of U.S. gross output. Yet we are seeing top firms becoming more dominant in industry after industry, with serious effects on innovation, productivity, and inequality. Breaking up a few Big Tech firms won't fix that problem; it's not even clear what it would accomplish. The online market for diapers is not that significant, nor is the use of private-label goods by online platforms. While stronger antitrust enforcement of mergers is surely warranted, that, too, is unlikely by itself to deal with the bigger problems raised by superstar capitalism.

Moreover, the problem is not digital platforms per se. Both digital and nondigital platforms are powerful tools for generating economic value. Digital platform companies would not have grown so powerful except that they have delivered large benefits to consumers and created jobs, many of them highly paid. It is true that open digital platforms raise particular challenges to antitrust enforcement. This calls for closer scrutiny and more resources for competition agencies. But these challenges of predatory pricing and cross-subsidization are nothing new; they apply equally to antitrust enforcement of newspapers, for example. The real challenge of platforms is that access to the platform and the associated knowledge are currently restricted; diffusion is limited. With greater access, there would be more competition, innovative startups would not face such strong headwinds, talent wars and skills gaps would diminish, and government regulators might be able to do their jobs. It is not the technology of plat-forms itself that is the problem; it is the way superstar firms use the tech-nology and provide access to it.

This implies that open platforms are better than closed platforms. It would be a mistake for antitrust policy to penalize successful open platforms unnecessarily; we want more Amazons, not fewer. In the next chapter we'll explore how policy can open things up.

10

The Next Unbundling

Large firms have used software-enabled systems to better meet disparate individual needs. They offer greater selection, more product features, and more tailored services. These capabilities have made these firms more dominant and powerful. Yet it is important to recognize that although these firms have made great progress, their ability to meet all disparate consumer needs is still far from complete. A typical Walmart store carries 120,000 items.[1] This is far more than most of its brick-and-mortar rivals, helping it dominate the retail industry. Yet this number is much, much smaller than the number of items carried by e-commerce sites. Walmart's own e-commerce site offers thirty-five million items for sale. Diffusion of technology and knowledge becomes important because, despite the newfound powers brought by software, superstar firms still cannot manage all possible products, they have no monopoly on innovative ideas, and they can't incorporate all possible product features. Other firms, employing other workers, are needed, and when they are barred from critical technical knowledge, society suffers greater inequality, slower pro-ductivity growth, and lost potential. The policy challenge is to find ways to promote greater diffusion.

It is significant that some leading firms choose to unbundle their technology—that is, to make parts of the systems accessible through an interface and/or to share or license portions of their software code, data, know-how, or hardware so that others can use or access key technologies. It turns out that unbundling can powerfully transform industries and can accelerate diffusion, ameliorating some of the negative effects of superstar capitalism on productivity and inequality.

IBM Opens Up

The modern packaged-software industry began on June 23, 1969— the day IBM unbundled. IBM had previously sold its software and its hardware together. There were no separate prices for the software; the customer bought a computer and associated software, including custom software that IBM engineers would write, as a package. Independent software companies found it hard to compete when IBM's software was, at least on the surface, free. This practice also made it difficult for other computer manufacturers to compete against IBM.

Initially, software for commercial computers was custom programmed by the hardware manufacturer, the customer, or someone the customer contracted with. By the end of the 1960s, there were thousands of custom software engineering service firms.[2] Some of these companies found opportunities to deliver a given software program to multiple customers.

In the late 1960s, the term "software package" emerged, describing the software object code that could run on the customer's machine, along with documentation, and often installation and training services.[3] A listing of software packages was first published in 1967, and it included about 100 program descriptions.[4]

But this was a difficult and fragmented business, and the market for software written for any one model was often very limited. Although software firms could reproduce the code they had written for one customer at relatively little cost, the hardware on which it was meant to run was not highly standardized. Each manufacturer and each model typically had its own operating system. Also, because the computers of that time were underpowered, software often had to be written to optimize performance based on the specific features of each particular model.

That changed when IBM introduced its 360 series in 1964.[5] IBM introduced software compatibility across all of the models in this series; software written for the smallest model would also run on the largest model and on every model in between. Customers could be confident that the software that had been written for one model would still work if they needed to upgrade to a different model. Also, software packages written for one model could run on another, increasing the pool of available software. Partly because of these advantages, the 360 series was enormously successful for IBM, capturing at least two-thirds of the market. This might have created a strong market for computer application programs, but because of IBM's bundling policy, it was difficult for independent software firms to take advantage of that opportunity.

Bundling also made it harder for other computer manufacturers to compete; they could not offer a similar range of software, and they lacked the custom engineering resources that IBM had. Led by Control Data Corporation, these firms began pressuring the Department of Justice in 1967 to file an antitrust suit against IBM on these grounds.[6] At the same time, executives within IBM's Data Processing Division began exploring whether unbundling might be a profitable strategy for the company. They conducted two studies, but the results were ambiguous, and they could not convince either their division or IBM top management that this direction was worthwhile.

Unbundling was back on the table a year later, as IBM's counsel Burke Marshall, who had formerly overseen antitrust litigation at the Justice Department, told CEO Thomas Watson Jr. that bundling represented classic tying, a clear antitrust violation.[7] Hoping to forestall a government antitrust lawsuit, IBM decided in December 1968 that it would unbundle, and it did so the following June, but not before the Department of Justice filed an antitrust suit in January 1969.[8] In the unbundling announcement, IBM established fixed rental prices for seventeen application programs and set charges for system engineering, custom coding, and training. IBM also reduced hardware prices by 3 percent to compensate for the formerly free software and services.

The initial reaction was negative. Many customers felt that the hardware price reduction was inadequate, and the move created "an angry customer community."[9] And while there was an initial flurry of entry into the packaged software market, the 1969–71 recession drove many of these undercapitalized companies out of business. Nevertheless, the packaged software industry began growing, slowly at first, and then ultimately far beyond the expectations of most people in the computer industry. This growth was helped by parallel growth in minicomputers and then, a decade later, by the personal computer. Between 1970 and 1980, domestic software revenues increased almost sixfold; between 1980 and 1988, they increased tenfold again.[10]

It turned out that unbundling resolved a fundamental information problem. Surely, the general growth of the computer industry, driven by rapidly falling prices for computers, expanded the market. But even with cheaper computer hardware, the software market faced a bottleneck. IBM's customers wanted to use computers to address a wide variety of problems, many of them shared by only a small number of other firms. These were problems related to local information, and for that reason, general software packages often failed to effectively solve them. IBM had not addressed these problems; indeed, IBM had offered only seventeen software packages in its unbundling announcement.

Unbundling fundamentally changed the economics of applications software. First, it meant competition for IBM's software and engineering services. A customer could choose between custom programming from IBM or a software package from an independent developer. But because the independent developer could amortize sales over many customers, it could offer far lower prices, and customers who could not afford custom programming could afford packaged software, further expanding the market. Of course, IBM could and did introduce more of its own software packages, but competition pressured IBM to lower the prices of software packages across the industry.

In addition, with more eyeballs addressing a specific problem, new and innovative solutions were more likely to be found, providing features beyond what could be expected from custom programming. Even though packaged software programs might not address all of a customer's specific needs as well as a custom project could, in many cases, customization could be done to augment a software package. Moreover, over time, software packages could add more and more features to address a broad range of specific needs. Software feature wars such as those described in chapter 2 dynamically propelled software packages to add capabilities to handle more and more of the specific needs of individual customers. While this did not eliminate custom programming, it meant that packaged software could address a much broader market.

Unbundling also became, over time, a blessing for IBM. It reduced the company's implicit share of the software market, but by lowering costs and increasing the variety of available software packages, it greatly expanded both the market for software and the market for computer hardware. The greater variety of software applications meant more sales of the complementary hardware, and IBM still maintained its position as a dominant supplier of software and engineering services, although the competition grew substantially. The reduced share of the pie was more than offset by the growth in the size of the pie.

Proprietary software has fostered the rising and persistent dominance of large firms; it has slowed diffusion of new technology, reducing productivity growth; it has restricted the opportunities for workers to gain new technology-related skills, contributing to growing economic inequality; and it has increased the power of large firms both relative to consumers and relative to government regulators. Broadly speaking, IBM's switch from proprietary software to unbundled hardware and software has facilitated the diffusion of technical knowledge. A broad base of innovators has continuously improved the software and expanded the market, raising the question of whether today's dominant firms can follow IBM and unbundle their software, restoring competition and productivity growth. Perhaps unbundling serves to resolve some of the problems caused by proprietary software systems.

Unbundling Past

Government policy is a key factor here. It seems that IBM's unbundling in 1969 was in large part a response to antitrust litigation, especially the government lawsuit, although this view is contested. Economist Franklin Fisher, who served as the chief paid expert witness for IBM in the U.S. antitrust case, argues that IBM would have unbundled on its own, thanks to the many independent software firms doing custom programming: "IBM's bundling in the relatively early days of the computer industry was a response to consumer demand, providing a guarantee that computers would function and solve users' problems. That was highly desirable in a period in which computers were great, unfamiliar, frightening beasts. When a community of users arose that did not need the bundle, bundling diminished, starting in 1968."[11]

There is an element of truth to this argument, but also an error. We know from the recollections of IBM executives such as Burton Grad and

Watts Humphrey that advocates for unbundling within IBM were not able to make a convincing business case for it in 1968.[12] And the angry reaction of IBM's customer community did not demonstrate overwhelming demand for this move. Also, we know that around the same time, IBM top executives concluded that they could not successfully defend an antitrust legal action against unbundling.[13] It is hard to conclude that IBM would have unbundled when it did without the sword of antitrust litigation hanging over the company.

However, Fisher is right that "when a community of users arose that did not need the bundle, bundling diminished." IBM's policy of bundling delayed the development of that community, especially as regards packaged software. It is quite possible that in the long run IBM would have unbundled without government prodding once the firm better understood the opportunity for growth through an expanded software market.

This dynamic is not unusual. Indeed, there is a typical pattern: major new technologies begin life as proprietary technologies, but firms unbundle once the opportunity for market expansion is clear. This was the case with early automated weaving technology. Only a few firms possessed this technology at first; the necessary skills were learned via hands-on experience at those few firms, and the components were not standardized, slowing the diffusion of technology. Because the knowledge was specialized and not widely available, textile mills built their own machines. But as the market grew and the technology and training became standardized, unbundling offered the possibility of a much larger market, albeit at a reduced market share. When that happened, the leading textile firms unbundled; they spun out their machine shops as independent textile equipment manufacturers.

While the business case for unbundling was ambiguous in 1968, eventually IBM might have recognized the opportunity and unbundled without government prodding. In 1968, however, few people realized the potential size of this market expansion. As IBM executive Burton Grad put it, "Certainly, in 1970, very few in the computer industry or the financial community could envision the opportunity for growth in packaged software or professional programming services that would occur over the next 30 years."[14] The role of the Department of Justice appears to have been to accelerate the process. As economic historian Steven Usselman concludes, the matter "was one of pace rather than direction."[15] Yet that change of pace was important. It is hard to imagine what the software industry and U.S. leadership of it would be like had unbundling taken a decade longer to occur.

The Art of Unbundling

Today, some leading firms are already unbundling. They are developing new types of organization and competing in ways that give them the benefits of large software systems without reducing access to the technology and diffusion. These efforts represent solid evidence of a possible path forward. However, whether the economy takes this path and how quickly it does so will depend very much on government policy, and unfortunately, current policy has been moving in the wrong direction, partly as a result of the undue political influence of dominant firms.

Let's first look at some pioneers.

One company that excels at unbundling more than any other is Amazon. Amazon went into business selling books online in 1995. It grew meteorically, exceeding $3 billion in revenues by 2002 and then entering a long period of consistent revenue growth of 25–30 percent per year. Jeff Bezos, Amazon's founder, did not initially intend to create a new form of organization: Amazon more or less stumbled into it. But the company has successively unbundled one business line after another, perfecting the art of this process.

Each time a prospective customer brings up the Amazon website, a complex series of interactions begins. If the customer selects a particular item to look at, the browser sends messages to one of Amazon's data centers to look up the information on that product in a database and display it on the browser. If the customer purchases an item, messages are sent to handle the payment and to initiate the shipping process. That all sounds simple enough on a small scale but is a major challenge for a company that handles 350 million items and sells nearly $300,000 per minute.[16]

The transaction volume can be highly variable, reaching peaks on major sales days, and data systems need to adjust. If the website slows, customers will go elsewhere. If the system is overwhelmed, transactions may fail or get logged incorrectly. Moreover, as a global seller, Amazon needs data centers distributed across the globe to keep response times low. These data centers need to be coordinated, shifting processing load from one to another as demand shifts. Furthermore, to secure against outages when components fail, the system needs to build in redundant processing. And with the system doubling in size every two or three years, these complex systems are effectively rebuilt periodically.

The challenge became even more difficult after Amazon signed deals with Target, Circuit City, Toys "R" Us, and other retailers to use the Amazon e-commerce engine to support their online stores.[17] To do this, Amazon developers built a platform—an applications programming interface (API)—so that developers at these merchants could access Amazon's e-commerce infrastructure.[18] The API provides an interface between application programs and the infrastructure that, say, stores and retrieves web pages. But executives soon realized that this approach would also be useful for meeting internal development challenges.

Developers on different teams were duplicating effort, each building databases, data storage, computing, and other basic capabilities for their disparate projects. When development teams began using standardized components with formal APIs, they could build and modify applications more quickly. At the same time, the teams managing the infrastructure were able to streamline and improve the applications. Combined, this meant that Amazon could scale and adapt its information technology efficiently and easily.

In 2003, executives meeting at Jeff Bezos's house concluded that these capabilities were a key competitive advantage of the company. Rival e-commerce companies could not match Amazon's proprietary information technology. Yet at the same meeting they began thinking that these capabilities had important uses outside the company. They imagined that this infrastructure could be a sort of operating system for the Internet that anyone could use to build applications. In the words of Andy Jassy, who led the effort, "We realized we could contribute all of those key components of that internet operating system, and with that we went to pursue this much broader mission, which is AWS [Amazon Web Services] today, which is really to allow any organization or company or any developer to run their technology applications on top of our technology infrastructure platform."[19]

Amazon officially unbundled AWS as a public service in March 2006. This meant that the company would abandon a proprietary advantage it had over its e-commerce rivals, but on the flip side, it meant that Amazon was able to provide new services to a large new market. Big customers like Netflix and Dropbox and many others, large and small, generated revenue of $35 billion in 2019. Amazon reports that hundreds of thousands of small and medium-sized businesses use AWS.[20]

Just as IBM created a new packaged software industry when it unbundled, so Amazon's unbundling fostered the creation of an entirely new cloud computing industry. It was joined in this industry by Microsoft, Google, and others offering cloud computing services that allowed even small startups to access top-notch computer processing, data storage, machine learning, and other IT infrastructure. The infrastructure technology needed to build frontier Big Data applications has now diffused widely and is easily and inexpensively accessible.

This unbundling has worked to reverse some of the effects of proprietary software systems. Startups using the cloud are more likely to survive, they grow faster, and they are more productive. Using detailed U.S. Census data, economists Wang Jin and Kristina McElheran have demonstrated that cloud computing has provided a significant advantage to young manufacturing firms.[21]

But although IT infrastructure is a core competence of Amazon, it is not Amazon's core business. Online retail is. And Amazon has also unbundled its key e-commerce technologies. In thinking about the significance of this decision, it is helpful to recall the example of Walmart's competitive advantage. Walmart built an organization around its unique logistics and inventory management technology. With this, Walmart stores could handle a far greater variety of products, they could keep hot-selling items in stock, and they could offer lower prices thanks to their lower costs of delivering the items to the stores. This turned out to be a potent proprietary advantage. Large competitors like Sears and Kmart could not compete; neither could many small retailers. Walmart wiped out a swath of small stores in towns across the nation.

Amazon has, similarly, developed a best-of-breed logistics capability, albeit one directed to delivering goods directly to consumers rather than to stores. But Amazon, in contrast to Walmart, has unbundled the components of its system so that even tiny sellers and producers can gain access to its advanced logistics. Competing fulfillment companies with their own logistics also can gain access to Amazon's sellers.

Amazon did not initially plan on opening up in this way. It more or less stumbled into this arrangement in a series of steps. The company began selling books but quickly expanded into electronics, software, video games, apparel, furniture, food, toys, and jewelry. Initially, it relied on third parties to fulfill (warehouse, pick, pack, and ship) the orders it received on its website. When, in 1997, Amazon began handling its own distribution with two warehouses, one in Seattle and one in New Castle, Delaware, it did not have advanced logistics capability and struggled to acquire it. While the general principles of logistics were well known, few companies had the deep technical knowledge to build a system like Walmart's. Amazon, in fact, hired a team of Walmart IT workers and consultants, including Richard Dalzell, Walmart's vice president of Information Systems.[22] Walmart sued Amazon for trade secret misappropriation to prevent those hires, but that suit was settled in 1999.[23]

Over time, this team substantially decreased how long it took for Amazon orders to be delivered. This was crucial to Amazon's growth. I spoke with a software engineer/operations research scientist who worked on fulfillment systems at Amazon in the early days. He told me, "Every time we dropped shipping speeds from five days to three days to two days, consumers bought more."[24] Shorter delivery times meant that more customers preferred to shop online rather than at brick-and-mortar retail stores.

The critical key to improving delivery speeds is being able to predict demand for each item available for sale. If someone in Pittsburgh orders a BabyBjörn baby carrier, it can be quickly delivered if it is in stock in the Pittsburgh warehouse. However, it is expensive to keep large inventories of items in warehouses, so retailers distribute goods to warehouses in proportion to the expected demand. The average speed of delivery depends on how well retailers estimate demand, and that, in turn, depends on the quality of the predictive analytics software they have, which in turn depends on both the knowledge of the software engineers and the amount of data they have to work with. In short, when high-quality software engineers have access to large amounts of data, they can shorten delivery times.

Amazon discovered that it could get more data by opening up its website to independent sellers. This discovery was more or less accidental. In the late 1990s, eBay dominated e-commerce. On the eBay website, independent sellers offer goods to sell at auction as well as at fixed prices. Jeff Bezos thought it was important to compete in that space. Amazon began with auction webpages, but after two failures, that effort changed into Amazon Marketplace. Marketplace unbundled Amazon's selling website, making it easier for small sellers to engage in e-commerce.

Here is Bezos's account from his 2014 letter to shareholders: "Marketplace's early days were not easy. First, we launched Amazon Auctions. I think seven people came, if you count my parents and siblings. Auctions transformed into zShops, which was basically a fixed price version of Auctions. Again, no customers. But then we morphed zShops into Marketplace. . . . The idea was to take our most valuable retail real estate—our product detail pages—and let third-party sellers compete against our own retail category managers. It was more convenient for customers, and within a year, it accounted for 5% of units."[25]

Initially, the Marketplace sellers did their own fulfillment; they did not benefit from Amazon's improved logistics capabilities. That changed in September 2006, when Amazon unbundled its fulfillment capabilities. Under the Fulfillment by Amazon program, independent Marketplace sellers store their goods in Amazon warehouses and have them picked, packed, and shipped by Amazon for a fee. If they meet inventory requirements, their goods can be shipped with one- or two-day delivery to Amazon Prime members. Prime is Amazon's popular program that provides free one- or two-day delivery to customers who pay an annual fee. Now tiny sellers can take advantage of logistics capabilities that rival or beat those of Walmart. The program is also open to companies that do not sell on the Amazon website. More than 450,000 small and medium-sized businesses use Fulfillment by Amazon.[26]

The use of this technology has widely diffused, bringing widespread productivity benefits. Today, there are millions of Marketplace sellers. Over 58 percent of Amazon's e-commerce sales in 2018 came from third-party sellers, not from Amazon itself.[27] Amazon earns fees from this business and collects data that improve Amazon's predictive analytics.

However, Fulfillment by Amazon did little to diffuse the technical knowledge required to build or improve advanced logistics systems. While independent merchants or independent fulfillment companies could hire software engineers and operations research specialists in logistics, they typically lacked the access to the high-volume data of a large e-commerce website. Worse, sellers on Amazon who did not choose to use Fulfillment by Amazon were put at a disadvantage to sellers who could advertise Prime free delivery. This disadvantage went away in 2015, when Amazon initiated Seller Fulfilled Prime. Now, independent sellers on Amazon's Marketplace qualify for Prime if their fulfillment operations meet certain performance standards. And dozens of independent companies have developed logistics operations that can meet the high standards of Amazon fulfillment, and they are working to meet Amazon's announced future goal of same-day delivery.

But how can these companies compete against Amazon fulfillment when Amazon has so much more data? I asked the former Amazon employee, who now works at one of these independent fulfillment operations. He explained that they have different data. While Amazon has data on all of the baby carriers sold on Marketplace from all different manufacturers, most of those manufacturers also sell on other websites, including Target, Walmart, eBay, Shopify, and their own sites. An independent fulfillment operation for BabyBjörn, however, sees the data across all of these sites for the BabyBjörn products in particular. In other words, BabyBjörn's fulfillment service may have better data than Amazon for predicting local demand for these particular products. And with better predictions, they can deliver faster.

Seller Fulfilled Prime unbundles the Marketplace from Amazon's fulfillment operation, allowing independent fulfillment companies to develop and improve top-of-the-line logistics capabilities. The technology itself is now diffusing. Thus, Amazon has unbundled both sides of its two-sided market. It has opened up its sales website so that independent sellers can participate as equal players whether they use Amazon's fulfillment or not. And it has opened up the fulfillment capabilities so that any seller can use Amazon's advanced services. The result has been the growth of a large, dynamic community of sellers and the emergence of a new generation of logistics and fulfillment providers.

The AWS unbundling and the unbundling of the different e-commerce businesses have some important differences. AWS was at first a one-sided platform, whereas the Marketplace created a two-sided platform.[28] Yet both platforms involved a similar tradeoff. In both cases, Amazon initially used a proprietary internal platform with strong capabilities that provided a competitive advantage. It had superior IT infrastructure, and it had a superior website (powered with that infrastructure) that allowed it to be an effective e-commerce company. Opening up its IT infrastructure with AWS and opening up its selling website with Marketplace allowed some rivals to use its proprietary advantages, diminishing Amazon's competitive advantage. But in both cases, unbundling also expanded the market, increasing the growth of Amazon's complementary services to more than offset these losses.

With the two-sided platform, the market expansion was especially large because of what economists call network effects and what Jeff Bezos calls the Amazon flywheel: "The success of this hybrid [Marketplace] model accelerated the Amazon flywheel. Customers were initially drawn by our fast-growing selection of Amazon-sold products at great prices with a great customer experience. By then allowing third parties to offer products side-by-side, we became more attractive to customers, which drew even more sellers. This also added to our economies of scale, which we passed along by lowering prices and eliminating shipping fees for qualifying orders."[29]

The importance of expanding the market explains why Amazon is willing to open its huge Marketplace to independent logistics companies on an equal footing, providing them the opportunity to improve their predictive algorithms. According to the former Amazon scientist, what the company gets out of offering Seller Fulfilled Prime is that "more merchants can ship things faster and they get more inventory that is time-enabled. . . . The Amazon retail business cares about how many SKUs [items] are on time. So, we are a great partner to them because we enable thousands of little merchants to offer Prime on Amazon. They also have a fulfillment business and they might think of it as like we are competing with them. We don't think that way because we all believe that the competition is the offline world."[30]

While unbundling means that independent fulfillment services get a piece of Amazon's business, more importantly, it means more merchants can deliver faster, bringing additional customers over from the brick-and-mortar world.

An Opening

The expansion of Amazon's e-commerce community and of its cloud customer base has been highly profitable. It has also propelled Amazon to dominance in e-commerce and cloud markets. But that dominance comes without some of the perverse effects of large proprietary software systems. There is increased competition and startup growth for Marketplace sellers, for independent logistics companies, and for startups using AWS. And, at least for the last group, we have solid evidence that productivity growth has increased. This does not mean that Amazon's market dominance is no longer a problem. The company could still use its market power to abuse rivals; antitrust authorities still need to be vigilant. But Amazon's powerful platforms are not inherently anticompetitive. Rather, because the platforms have been opened up, they provide a powerful means for increasing industry dynamism.

IBM and Amazon are not the only companies that have unbundled. Microsoft effectively unbundled its server capabilities, also by developing Azure, an open cloud platform that potentially cannibalizes its existing server business. Apple unbundled the iPhone so that independent developers could write apps, giving a huge boost to the smartphone market. Intuit has similarly opened up its QuickBooks accounting platform to third-party developers. Travelocity is the descendant of American Airlines' Sabre system for airline reservations, which was unbundled.

Business consultants and business school professors see firms increasingly converting products and services to open platforms, and they view this as a key strategic move that many companies can make.[31] Management professors Andrei Hagiu and Elizabeth Altman write, "Transforming an offering into a platform might enhance your company's competitive advantage and raise barriers to entry via network effects and higher switching costs. We're not suggesting that every company should try to emulate Airbnb, Alibaba, Facebook, or Uber. But many companies would benefit from adding elements of a platform business to their offerings."[32] One can imagine other sorts of unbundling. Walmart could enter the business of providing logistics and inventory management to smaller stores; large banks could open their credit card operations to provide services to other banks.

Not all industries and firms seem amenable to this kind of unbundling. For instance, although automobile and aircraft manufacturers use large internal platforms to design their products, it does not seem feasible today for these firms to unbundle by offering, say, design services to independent assemblers. Such an approach would seem difficult because the manufacture of these products involves close coordination with component suppliers that play a central role in developing new models. A platform does not provide the same relationships. However, perhaps unbundling might work for other manufactured products, especially as 3-D printing opens new possibilities. Moreover, even in the automobile industry, electric vehicles may provide some opportunities for open platforms because they are much simpler products.

Open platforms may be poised to change the economy. Where proprietary software systems have slowed the diffusion of new technology, unbundling may accelerate diffusion, bringing new industry dynamism and innovation, reversing the negative effects of proprietary software systems on productivity growth, income inequality, and geographical divergence. The trend to open platforms offers hope that the negative trends of the past two decades can be at least partially reversed.

However, it is also clear that even in industries where open platforms are desirable, dominant firms with large proprietary systems are not always interested in unbundling, and government regulators have done little to encourage them. Banking is one such industry. Banks with access to detailed customer transaction data can develop product offerings tailored to different prospective customers, and they can effectively target their marketing to them. Customer data have proved to be a key advantage for a handful of large banks in credit cards and other markets. One form of unbundling for this industry is Open Banking, allowing customers or their designated agents to access their own data via a standardized API. Open Banking promises not only to increase competition and spread the use of predictive analytic technology for credit but also to enable entirely new kinds of financial services. So-called fintech startup firms offer the prospect of providing innovative sources of credit, financial management, advice, and other financial services. Fintech firms Mint.com (now Intuit Mint) and NerdWallet, for instance, offer to provide consumers with an overview of all of their financial assets and liabilities in one place and to provide advice based on that overview. These are services that individual financial institutions cannot provide by themselves.

But these products require fintech firms to be able to access consumer data that is held at different financial institutions. And since financial institutions have been resistant to letting customers have the data from their own transactions, fintech firms have had to find a way around their lack of cooperation. They began by web-scraping. With a customer's agreement, they would access each of their accounts and collect data from what was displayed on the browser. Banks first attempted to block web-scraping in 2015, but a popular backlash prompted them to back down and even to provide APIs to limited customer data for select fintech firms.[33]

The result, however, is less than ideal. First, these arrangements do not necessarily provide fintech firms access to all of a customer's data. Second, some of these APIs are granted to only some fintech firms. Third, there is no standard open API, although some industry groups are attempting to develop such standards. This means that fintech firms have to make different, costly investments to interface with different financial institutions.[34]

The U.S. government has declined to compel financial institutions to provide third parties access to customer data even though regulators have the power to do so. The Dodd-Frank Wall Street Reform and Consumer Protection Act, passed in 2010, created the Consumer Financial Protection Bureau (CFPB) and gave it powers to compel financial institutions to provide data to consumers or their representatives as well as to promulgate standardized data formats.[35] However, the CFPB chose instead to promote voluntary guidelines for financial institutions. Only in July 2020, ten years after the passage of Dodd-Frank, did the CFPB finally announce plans to issue an advance notice of proposed rulemaking regarding consumer-authorized third-party access to financial records, an early step in the process to actually implement this aspect of the law.[36] In Europe and some Asian countries, regulators have played a more aggressive role. Notably, in January 2018, the European Union put into effect a directive that requires financial institutions to provide an API on a nondiscriminatory basis.

Encouraging Open Platforms

The comparison with Europe shows that regulators can make a critical difference when it comes to unbundling. This was also the case when IBM unbundled in 1969. Today, the economy and society suffer as the result of the growth in large proprietary software systems by dominant firms. Yet this state of affairs need not be permanent if the right policies are implemented.

Unfortunately, regulators too often fail at this job. In the case of finance, industry-specific regulation affects the dominance of large firms and their resistance to opening up. But there are also broader policy biases that cut across many industries—in particular, about the proper role of intellectual property (IP) regulation. Intellectual property maximalists assume that IP owners should be given control over every aspect of the use of their technology. This, it is assumed, is the way to ensure the maximum incentives to innovate. Yet the examples of IBM and Amazon show that carefully designed unbundling allows the technology creators to receive ample profit incentives while allowing other users to benefit from and further improve the technology. Innovation also faces a challenge of dispersed information: IP owners do not have knowledge of all the beneficial uses of the technology. Indeed, the IBM example demonstrates that private firms can have difficulty anticipating the profits that might arise from unbundling. Risk-averse companies might choose to maintain more certain profits from continued proprietary control rather than seek the uncertain but potentially much greater profits from unbundling. In traditional markets, this challenge can be overcome by licensing the technology. But in superstar markets, where technology is used to differentiate firms, IP owners have insufficient incentives to license or unbundle in other ways. This is why policy is needed to spur unbundling.

A number of policies might accelerate a turn to unbundling much as antitrust authorities accelerated IBM's decision fifty years ago. However, in recent years, policies have been changed in the wrong direction, thus encouraging firms to keep their software proprietary. Consider several policy changes that could reverse this trend:

Compulsory opening. Antitrust authorities and courts have long used compulsory licensing of patents and the divestiture of patents as a remedy for anticompetitive conduct, as a condition for a merger or acquisition, or where there is a pressing public need, such as the under-supply of a needed vaccine.[37] The aim was to counter market power by allowing the diffusion of these technologies. While these orders were used often in the 1950s and 1960s, they have been used less frequently in recent years.[38] The same approach, however, could be applied to proprietary software systems, licensing the code and associated intellectual property, possibly under an open-source license. In addition, orders and consent decrees could place key data in the public domain. In other cases, courts or antitrust regulators could order unbundling and the creation of an open API.

Open standards. Policy makers need rules to preserve open standards created by industry groups or individual firms. In a series of recent legal cases, private parties have been able to significantly raise the costs of using standards that were intentionally created to have low and nondiscriminatory licensing rates. Legal rules need to secure the openness of standards and protect them from unfair efforts at holdup and rent extraction.

Worker mobility. To the extent that workers learn new knowledge and skills related to new technology on the job, technology diffuses when they move to a new employer. But worker mobility—the frequency with which workers change jobs, change occupations, or move to another location—has declined substantially in recent decades.[39] To some extent, this decline can be attributed to new laws and to the use of noncompete agreements—that is, employment contracts that prevent workers from taking a job with a rival firm. Policies are needed to encourage worker mobility.

To understand how policies discourage open platforms in these areas and why that has happened, it is helpful to review these policies in the context of the broad history of intellectual property protection in the United States.

Owning Minds

The U.S. Constitution sets out a role for intellectual property: "To promote the progress of science and useful arts, by securing for limited times to authors and inventors the exclusive right to their respective writings and discoveries." This involves a tradeoff between providing an incentive for authors and inventors and limiting the term of the rights in order to maximize the diffusion of new technologies and the ability to improve them. Intellectual property policy involves a balance between individual incentives and diffusion.

Yet the long arc of history has shifted this balance in favor of private incentives at the expense of diffusion, and it has shifted the ownership of those incentive rights from individual inventors to firms. Now, at a time when large firms are slowing the diffusion of technology, the tension between incentives and diffusion appears distinctly out of balance. Restoring a better balance is key to encouraging those firms to open their platforms.

We can see that shift in patent law, in copyright, and in trade secret law. At the beginning of the nineteenth century, individuals owned the rights to their inventions, even to inventions that they developed on the job.[40] Employers had to negotiate to be able to use those inventions, to obtain so-called shop rights. Over time, courts shifted the law so that employers would have rights to use those inventions by default. Then by the early twentieth century, the courts went beyond usage rights to give employers ownership rights.

As we saw in chapter 4, that change was important for the creation of corporate R&D labs. Today, courts have gone even further, upholding employment contracts that give employers rights to inventions that employees make on their own time and in fields unrelated to their work. Consider the case of Evan Brown, a software developer for DSC Alcatel USA, who came up with an insight unrelated to his job while he was on vacation.[41] When Brown refused to share his idea with his employer, they fired him and took him to court. After losing the court battle, he was required to develop that idea for his former employer over a three-month period without pay. While this is an extreme and atypical case, it shows just how far the balance between individuals and employers shifted in favor of employers over the past two centuries. Yet when employee rights are restricted, they are less likely to play a role in diffusing new technology as they switch jobs or create spinoffs.

The scope of patent law has also moved in ways that limit the diffusion of software. In 1972, shortly after IBM unbundled the System/360, the Supreme Court issued the *Benson* decision, which placed strong limits on the patenting of software. Over the next two decades, the software industry grew dramatically, largely without patents. Much of this dynamic growth was powered by sequential innovation, in which new programs improved on earlier ones, expanding the quality of the software and the size of the market. Then, beginning in 1995, the U.S. Court of Appeals for the Federal Circuit issued rulings that encouraged the patenting of software ideas, including rather abstract concepts, as well as the patenting of methods of doing business.

Unfortunately, there is a fundamental difference between patenting a tangible invention and patenting a concept: it is often much harder to identify the boundaries of the property right for software patents. When property boundaries are poorly defined, parties are more likely to sue. The result of software patenting has been an explosion in patent litigation, much of it coming from patent trolls, parties who purchase or develop patents, not to introduce a new technology, but to extort payments through the threat of litigation.[42] This litigation has been found to reduce the diffusion of new technology and also to reduce the incentives of small firms to invest in R&D.[43] More generally, patents in software and related fields have been found to reduce sequential innovation. Using a clever research design looking at what happens when courts invalidate patents, patent economists Alberto Galasso and Mark Schankerman find that in software-related fields, patents reduce follow-on citations, especially by small firms.[44] Lower citations mean that fewer firms are building on the initial inventions.

Copyright has also gone through an expansion of scope, and the term of copyright has been dramatically extended. The original U.S. Copyright Act of 1790 covered only maps, charts, and books, in line with the aim of the Constitution to further science and the "useful arts." Copyright protection then was for fourteen years, renewable once. Legislation has successively expanded that term until today it is for the life of the author plus seventy years for most works. And copyright covers far more, including music, art, performances, piano player rolls, records, DVDs, radio and TV broadcasts, including provisions for cable and satellite TV, and, starting in 1976, software. Legal scholar Jessica Litman describes this process: "About one hundred years ago, Congress got into the habit of revising copyright law by encouraging representatives of the industries affected by copyright to hash out among themselves what changes needed to be made and then present Congress with the text of appropriate legislation."[45] Significantly, the interests of the general public largely went unrepresented, tending to lead to unbalanced laws. This is how we arrived at a state where it is illegal to access the software code in your car to detect whether the manufacturer has cheated on emissions or gas mileage tests.

Trade secrecy has also expanded its scope and tilted in favor of firms and against employees. Originally, trade secret law protected well-defined secrets that had been identified and labeled as secret. A violation required actual misappropriation of the secret information; it was not enough for a supposed defendant merely to possess the information. This was important because trade secret law did not want to discourage other parties from independently arriving at the knowledge contained in the secret. But U.S. trade secret law has been expanded in ways that stifle employee mobility through the Uniform Trade Secrets Act, adopted by most states, and, in 2016, by the federal Defend Trade Secrets Act. For one thing, the scope of secrets was broadened to cover such things as know-how, not just labeled documents. Also, many state courts interpreted the law to have an inevitable disclosure doctrine. In those states, an employee going to another employer did not actually have to misappropriate secrets in order to be found guilty of a trade secret violation. Rather, it is assumed that the employee will inevitably disclose trade secrets. In this way, employees are prevented from taking jobs at rival firms or sometimes even at firms in distantly related industries. Empirical research finds that these laws diminish not only employee mobility but innovation.[46]

Increasingly, employers are requiring employees to sign agreements that control what they do after they leave a company, prohibiting them from taking a job in the same industry and from soliciting clients or fellow workers. There is a recent and rapidly growing empirical literature evaluating the impacts of these policies. One recent reviewer concludes that "post-employment restrictive covenants likely contributed to declining economic dynamism."[47] Researchers who looked at what happened when Hawaii banned noncompete agreements in 2015 find that employee mobility rose 11 percent and that the pay of new hires rose 4 percent.[48] Another study of a Florida change that made it easier to enforce noncompete agreements finds that the effect was to reduce new firm entry.[49]

As technology has shifted toward using software and other intangibles, firms have increasingly looked for ways to exert ownership rights over employee knowledge, to own minds. Although new technology provided the impetus, lobbying and campaign contributions appear to have contributed to changing the law. Lawrence Lessig, writing in 2011, notes that since 1995, Congress has enacted thirty-two separate statutes to refine and strengthen copyright protection.[50] At the same time, advocates for expanded copyright spent $1.3 billion on lobbying and campaign contributions, compared to just $1 million spent by opponents.[51] Regardless of whether money has swayed views, it appears that courts, regulators, and legislators have tended to adopt the corporate view on these issues. That is, there appears to be cultural or ideological capture whereby policy makers have tended to acquire the outlook and concerns of the most-affected corporate interests.

Policy makers and courts tend to privilege IP owners over the broader needs of society. Where policy might encourage firms to open their platforms to the benefit of society, the tendency has been to favor intellectual property rights excessively. When only industry representatives are invited to the table to negotiate copyright legislation, the broader needs of society get short shrift. When judges at the main patent court spend all day communicating with patent owners, they appear to lose sight of the needs of follow-on innovators.[52] Hence, policy tilts to favor the rights of owners over the social need for technology diffusion.

Over the past two decades, the diffusion of technology has slowed, resulting in slower productivity growth, rising inequality, and a host of related problems. Although this change is not solely the result of policy shifts, it is now crucial for policy to support greater diffusion in order to encourage firms to unbundle. Yet the pro-rights-owner mind-set of the courts and regulators appears to be further weakening diffusion for each of the policies that might encourage opening platforms:

Compulsory opening. Courts have ordered compulsory licensing of patents much less frequently in recent years. The courts appear to have accepted arguments that undermining patent owners' rights will reduce innovation. For example, U.S. pharmaceutical companies argue that the compulsory licensing of AIDS drugs by Brazil, India, and Thailand reduces incentives to develop new drugs. But the evidence suggests that in significant cases, compulsory licensing has actually served to increase innovation by increasing diffusion. The U.S. government antitrust lawsuit against Bell Telephone was settled with a consent decree requiring Bell to license all of its patents without royalty, including Bell's patents on the transistor. This action hastened the development of the semiconductor industry. A careful economic study finds that this compulsory licensing increased innovation in fields outside of telecommunications.[53] Economic historian Petra Moser, along with coauthors, has explored what happened when the United States allowed the royalty-free licensing of enemy-owned patents during World War I.[54] They find that this action increased innovation in the United States and also, after the war, that it increased innovation by German firms whose patents had been licensed. Apparently, the diffusion of these technologies boosted long-run innovation. There is little reason to think that policies to selectively encourage firms to open proprietary platforms will have a negative effect on innovation, yet there appears to be resistance to this perspective.

Open standards. Open platforms work well when large communities of independent parties use a common standard to access and improve technology. Platforms using open standards are often successful because they entice independent users with a promise of a low-cost interface. Yet technology companies sometimes renege on explicit or implicit promises to keep interface costs low. This problem arises with standard setting organizations, the groups of engineers from different companies who jointly work out common standards used to coordinate activity in many digital technologies including the Internet, Wi-Fi, and cell phones. Sometimes the participating companies have patents covering the emerging standard. To participate in the standards body, these companies give assurances that they will not charge too much to license their patents—that is, they will provide fair, reasonable, and non-discriminatory licenses. Yet once a large number of independent parties invest in adopting the new standard, all too often companies exert their patents and attempt to extract money from these users. Economists Cesare Righi and Timothy Simcoe find that firms tend to file patents *after* standard-setting organizations publish elements of an emerging standard and that these patents are disproportionately likely to be litigated after the standard is issued.[55] Unfortunately, in a couple of recent decisions—*Qualcomm v. FTC* and *Oracle v. Google*—the courts have sided with the IP owners over the needs of the broader community of users, asserting the primacy of innovation incentives over the need for diffusing technology. Fortunately, the Supreme Court recently reversed the lower courts in *Oracle v. Google*.

Worker mobility. Legal action by firms against departing employees often combines trade secrecy actions and actions regarding postemployment agreements. Lawsuits involving trade secrets or noncompete agreements have almost quadrupled since 2000, with reported annual decisions rising from 1,162 to 4,187.[56] Firms are increasingly acting to limit employee mobility and courts often support these efforts, including developing new doctrines such as inevitable disclosure to assert the primacy of employer investments over concerns about technology diffusion and basic worker freedoms.

The detrimental effects of superstar capitalism might not persist indefinitely but restoring the balance between incentives to innovate and incentives to diffuse innovation can only hasten the remedy. More generally, changes in antitrust, intellectual property, and employment policy can go a long way toward nudging firms to unbundle and to promote diffusion of technology.

11

A New Information Economy

Almost sixty years have passed since Fritz Machlup wrote about the Knowledge Economy.[1] Following his work and that of subsequent scholars such as Peter Drucker and Daniel Bell, it became commonplace to speak of a transition to an Information Society or Postindustrial Society. Machlup focused on the rising role of the production and distribution of knowledge and information in the economy. Others tied the new developments more broadly to the relative rise of the service and professional sectors. Yet these scholars, focusing as they did on information workers, could not anticipate the troubling features that information *technology* would bring to society.

The original vision of the information society was an optimistic one tied to the growing role of the professional, managerial, and other educated classes. In an information society, decisions would be made by enlightened individuals backed by data analysis and expertise rather than by inflamed political passions or autocratic robber barons. This was also a deeply meritocratic society where individuals of humble origin could work hard, get educated, and become influential decision makers. Notions of a New Economy that emerged in the 1990s based on inexpensive computers and software only enhanced this optimism. Now talented, hard-working individuals could form their own companies, thanks to this technology, and grow to challenge and disrupt industry incumbents.

Optimistic views of the information economy were largely based on a liberal policy framework that prized the value of information held by private individuals. Hayek argued that the challenge to constructing a rational economic order was the dispersion of knowledge necessary for economic activity.[2] Economists have since come to see information as central to the way the economy operates. Individuals know what they value and what resources are available; they know the quality of their actions and the alternative actions available to them. Socialist central planners could not effectively run an economy because they lacked this decentralized information. But private firms could respond to individual needs and communicate economic valuations through market prices. The inherent assumption behind this arrangement is that private firms would use private information to maximize their profits and, by doing so, that they would maximize output, thus furthering social goals. Private incentives were assumed to be more or less aligned with public incentives. To the extent that growing profits created socially undesirable inequality, taxes or subsidies could be used to redistribute wealth.

This logic about private information also extended to the creation and distribution of knowledge itself. Private parties were seen as having the knowledge needed to create inventions or artistic works. Property rights provided inventors with the strongest incentives to create new technologies that would benefit society. As knowledge of new technologies became ever more economically important, it was propertized and ownership ceded from individual creators to firms. Patents were extended to cover software, abstract concepts, and genetic information; copyrights were extended to cover a panoply of new media; and a variety of extensions allowed owners to maintain these rights for much longer durations and in many more circumstances. At the same time, rights that had been routinely granted to employee-inventors were ceded to employers and changes in employment, and trade secrecy law allowed firms to limit the mobility of employees who might have acquired valuable technical skills or know-how.

There is no doubt that this policy regime has been successful. Yet it has worked well only because new knowledge spread widely and quickly through society. Innovation, meritocratic rewards, and the application of expert judgment all depend on access to information, and when access is restricted, as I have argued here, we see slower productivity growth, greater inequality, and ineffective regulation. A new generation of large, software-enabled systems has given rise to a superstar capitalism that exposes two important contradictions in the information society: (1) large firms also face challenges dealing with decentralized information; and (2) the incentives of large firms are not necessarily aligned with the goals of society, particularly when firms are focused on differentiating themselves from rivals. Both play a role in the critical decline in the pace of technology diffusion.

Large firms, too, not just socialist planners, engage in centralized planning, of course. Particularly with the introduction of technologies exhibiting strong economies of scale during the latter half of the nineteenth century, large business enterprises emerged that engaged in varying degrees of centralized planning.[3] In many cases, these businesses standardized products and services to reduce the informational burden, to reduce the costs of discovering consumer demand or the costs of communicating quality to consumers, and to reduce the costs of meeting those disparate needs. Retailers like A&P standardized the merchandise sold in their stores; large manufacturers of products ranging from textiles to steel standardized goods. While mass production didn't necessarily mean "any color so long as it's black," it did imply highly restricted variety. Standardization reduced information costs and brought production efficiencies, but it also meant that local, decentralized information was often ignored.

Today, new technologies and organizational forms have permitted leading firms to better meet disparate consumer needs, making them more dominant in their markets. But these systems do not fix all the problems raised by dispersed knowledge. Importantly, they do not solve the challenge that dispersed knowledge poses for innovation. Centralized control of technology is especially a problem for innovation because no large firm has a monopoly on new ideas. Innovation works best when disparate individuals or companies can develop different ideas and license them or build disruptive companies based on them. And that process depends very much on the active diffusion of technical knowledge. Yet when large firms become more dominant, they may choose to limit diffusion, slowing innovation and productivity growth.

The reason for this is that when firms profit by using proprietary technology to differentiate their products from rivals' offerings, their interests are not necessarily aligned with the social good. They can use their technology to increase their share of the economic pie without necessarily increasing the overall size of the pie. They have strong incentives not to license their technology and to prevent its diffusion in other ways. And so, it is no surprise that the evidence shows a slowing rate of diffusion accompanying the rise of superstar capitalism.

It is this slowdown that is responsible for the growing dominance of leading firms across industries and for other troubling trends. Slower diffusion is responsible for much of the more sluggish growth of productive smaller firms, contributing to lower aggregate productivity growth. And when only select firms have the most advanced systems, only some workers can access the technology and learn the associated skills. Pay gaps emerge between different groups of workers, between employees of different companies, between different occupations, between people living in select large cities and the rest. Income inequality rises partly for reasons unrelated to workers' effort and education, undermining meritocratic rationalizations of inequality and fueling a politics of resentment against elites. Social division increases as the meritocratic ideal is corrupted. And the power of the new generation of superstar firms is not effectively countered by government. From the Volkswagen diesel emissions scandal to the subprime mortgage collapse, regulators have been outmatched at a drastic penalty to society. Indeed, the complexity of technology aids firms in capturing regulators, in confusing them, or in outright deceiving them. The common good is undermined.

Yet the large firms have only gained extensive economic power because they have harnessed technology to satisfy consumer demand so well. This power can be tamed, but not easily. The policy challenge is to preserve the benefits while reinvigorating competition, increasing the diffusion of technology, and restoring a balanced role for regulation.

The public and politicians have been expressing growing concerns about the role of large firms in society, but the nature of those concerns is highly varied. Some are concerned with the supposed liberal bias of Big Tech firms; others are concerned with Big Tech because of the special problems posed by digital platforms. Some call for breaking up Big Tech firms. But these viewpoints fail to comprehend the real nature of what has changed. Without a better understanding, they risk inadequate, misdirected, or harmful policy responses.

The problems documented in this book are not confined to a handful of Big Tech firms; they are seen in every major sector of the economy. And the problems are not inherent in platform technology itself. They are not determined by the technology per se but rather by how dominant firms are using the technology, specifically the extent to which they are keeping proprietary control of new knowledge.

Platform technologies are used throughout the economy, but many or most of those platforms are used within companies. Walmart has a very powerful logistics and inventory platform, but it is a closed, internal platform, as opposed to the open platforms of Amazon. Both sorts of platforms are very powerful because they deliver substantial economic benefits. They meet individual consumer needs, they create jobs, many of which are highly paid, and they increase productivity. But to the extent that platform companies limit access to their technologies and knowledge, they contribute to slowing diffusion.

In this sense, open platforms are more desirable than closed ones. Open platforms allow access to at least part of the technology and, by doing so, help restore industry dynamism. While open platforms pose problems for antitrust enforcement and therefore deserve closer antitrust scrutiny, there is strong evidence of their potential benefits. For example, open cloud platforms have been a big boost to innovative startups and other firms. For this reason, opening up the technology of large firms is highly preferable to breaking up the firms. Breakups risk destroying the benefits that come with large platforms—there are strong economies of scale with these technologies, so large size is a prerequisite—and it is not clear what breakups accomplish. Because the benefits of large systems remain, other firms will soon enter the breach and reemerge as dominant replacements. That is nothing new. The breakup of AT&T created Baby Bells that merged to generate a phone industry that is dominated by large players and is no more dynamic than what came before.

In contrast, a policy of encouraging or, in some cases, compelling firms to make parts of their platforms, data, or software code accessible to other parties promises to preserve the benefits of the technology while ameliorating the social costs of slow diffusion. Unbundling has proved to be a potent source of economic dynamism in the past, and that continues today. The semiconductor industry arose when Bell Labs licensed its patents; the modern packaged software industry grew up when IBM unbundled its hardware and software; the cloud computing industry was created when

Amazon unbundled its IT infrastructure; and hundreds of thousands of sellers grew when Amazon opened its Marketplace. If this and other open-knowledge practices were to spread across industries, it could reverse many of the detrimental social impacts of superstar capitalism.

Of course, unbundling might diminish the private returns to new technology and thus reduce firms' incentives to invest in developing the technology in the first place. This is an important concern, but it is not too worrisome for two reasons. First, unbundling can be hugely profitable to the unbundling firm. Although IBM executives did not anticipate the gains that software unbundling would bring, the government's nudge from the threat of antitrust litigation proved to be highly beneficial for IBM. Second, the strong bent of policy over the past few decades has been to favor innovation incentives at the expense of diffusion. Innovation policy needs to strike a balance between incenting firms to invest in developing new ideas and encouraging the distribution of those innovations and associated knowledge. The evidence of slowing diffusion indicates that the policy framework is out of balance. A policy to encourage diffusion, judiciously applied to preserve innovation incentives where possible, can help restore that balance.

We appear to be groping toward a new information economy as superstar capitalism challenges some of the foundations of the old one. A sustainable information economy involves more than a large share of people working with information; it is also one in which new knowledge is actively developed and widely shared. It is one that delivers the benefits of large-scale production and large-scale data, that addresses individual needs, and that also encourages the broadest access to the most advanced technology to encourage competition, innovation, greater economic opportunity, and a fairer society. One can imagine an economic order populated by big firms and small, large platform companies and innovative small companies. To get there, we need policies that encourage open access to technology, even if that sometimes comes at the expense of some proprietary control.

Notes

1. Introduction

1. Wildman, "First Barcode Scan in History"; Stokel-Walker, "Beep Beep."
2. Christensen, *Innovator's Dilemma*.
3. Ellickson, "Evolution of the Supermarket Industry"; Tedlow and Jones, *Rise and Fall of Mass Marketing*; Beniger, *Control Revolution: Technological and Economic Origins of the Information Society*.
4. Beniger, *Control Revolution*.
5. Brown, *Revolution at the Checkout Counter*.
6. Basker, Klimek, and Hoang Van, "Supersize It"; Basker, "Change at the Checkout."
7. Levin, Levin, and Meisel, "Dynamic Analysis of the Adoption of a New Technology"; Basker, Klimek, and Hoang Van, "Supersize It." Basker, "Change at the Checkout," notes that the large chains tended to experiment, at first placing scanners in a few stores and only gradually rolling them out thereafter.
8. Knee, "Dick's Supermarkets Expand in Wisconsin."
9. Basker, "Change at the Checkout."
10. Basker, Klimek, and Hoang Van, "Supersize It."
11. Tanner, "Modern Day General Store."
12. Tanner.
13. Schafer, "How Information Technology Is Leveling the Playing Field."
14. The term "desktop publishing" was coined by Paul Brainerd a couple of years later.
15. Liebling, "Wayward Press," 109; Bove and Rhodes, "Editorial."
16. Hicks, "Annual Survey of Economic Theory," 8.
17. Stalk, Evans, and Shulman, "Competing on Capabilities," 57.
18. Basker, "Job Creation or Destruction?"
19. Jia, "What Happens When Wal-Mart Comes to Town."

20. Kmart was also an early adopter of scanners, but it fell behind on related computer technologies and on integrating the disparate components and suppliers into an effective system. Baselinemag, "How Kmart Fell Behind."

21. Basker, "Change at the Checkout."

22. "Walmart History."

23. Wal-Mart Stores, *Annual Report* (1991), 3.

24. Wal-Mart Stores, *Annual Report* (1994), 7.

25. Pew Research Center poll conducted in 2005 and cited in Basker, "Change at the Checkout."

26. Chiou, "Empirical Analysis of Retail Competition," cited in Basker, "Causes and Consequences of Wal-Mart's Growth."

27. Stalk, Evans, and Shulman, "Competing on Capabilities."

28. Basker and Noel, "Evolving Food Chain."

29. Mises, "Die Wirtschaftsrechnung im Sozialistischen Gemeinwesen"; Hayek, *Collectivist Economic Planning;* Hayek, "Use of Knowledge in Society."

30. Hayek, "Use of Knowledge in Society," 519–20.

31. Hayek, 527.

32. Most directly by Leonid Hurwicz, "On Informationally Decentralized Systems." Using Hurwicz's mathematical tools, economists have revisited Hayek's original critique of socialist central planning. See Myerson, "Fundamental Theory of Institutions."

33. This might not be such a problem if manufacturers offered full warranties that spelled out the exact nature of the quality. However, this is often not possible, there are strong informational problems to concluding a warranty contract, and most products that have warranties have only limited warranties, leaving residual concerns about quality.

34. Baldwin and Clark, *Design Rules.*

35. Sutton, *Sunk Costs and Market Structure.*

2. Disruption Lost

1. "Clayton Christensen's Insights Will Outlive Him."

2. Lepore, "What the Gospel of Innovation Gets Wrong."

3. Schumpeter, *Capitalism, Socialism and Democracy,* 82–83.

4. This figure uses publicly listed global firms ranked by sales in NAICS six-digit industries. See Bessen et al., "Declining Industrial Disruption," for more details and other measures.

5. Wiggins and Ruefli, "Schumpeter's Ghost"; Gschwandtner, "Evolution of Profit Persistence in the USA"; Brynjolfsson et al., "Scale without Mass." Brynjolfsson et al. find that the decrease in persistence is related to IT. Other researchers, using a different method, find no evidence of decreased persistence of profits: McNamara, Vaaler, and Devers, "Same as It Ever Was."

6. Similar changes in persistence were found by Autor et al., "Fall of the Labor Share," fig. A24. Philippon, *Great Reversal;* Bennett, "Changes in Persistence of Performance over Time."

7. Bresnahan and Trajtenberg, "General Purpose Technologies 'Engines of Growth'?"

8. Devine, "From Shafts to Wires"; David, "The Dynamo and the Computer."

9. As Ben Rosen put it in 1979, "VisiCalc could some day become the software tail that wags (and sells) the personal computer dog." This account draws on Liebowitz, Margolis, and Hirshleifer, *Winners, Losers and Microsoft,* chap. 8, and on Dan Bricklin's web history at www.bricklin.com/visicalc.htm.

10. *PC Magazine,* October 27, 1987, 94.

11. Baldwin and Clark, *Design Rules.*

12. Marginal costs are not zero. For instance, support costs will increase with the number of customers.

13. Bessen and Maskin, "Sequential Innovation, Patents, and Imitation."

14. Cusumano and Selby, *Microsoft Secrets,* 218.

15. Economists also highlight the roles of "network effects" in solidifying Microsoft's dominance. There is benefit to consumers in purchasing the product with the largest customer base because users may want to interchange documents with other users or because more training resources might be available. However, other programs can read Microsoft Excel files, and Lotus's dominance in the marketplace was not ultimately a high barrier to being replaced by Microsoft.

16. Thus software does much more than generate economies of scope—that is, efficiencies in producing multiple products.

17. Charette, "This Car Runs on Code"; Shea, "Why Does It Cost So Much?"

18. "Car Company in Front."

19. Womack, "Why Toyota Won."

20. See, e.g., Iyengar, "Fiat Chrysler Proposes Merger with Renault."

21. Stock, "Explaining the Differing U.S. and EU Positions."

22. Varian, "Beyond Big Data."

23. U.S. Bureau of Economic Analysis, "National Income and Product Accounts," table 9.4U. Software investment and prices, July 31, 2020, revision.

24. See, e.g., Bartel, Ichniowski, and Shaw, "How Does Information Technology Affect Productivity?"; Bloom, Sadun, and Van Reenen, "Americans Do IT Better"; Bloom et al., "Distinct Effects of Information Technology"; Greenstein and Bresnahan, "Technical Progress and Coinvention in Computing"; Bresnahan, Brynjolfsson, and Hitt, "Information Technology, Workplace Organization"; and Crespi, Criscuolo, and Haskel, "Information Technology, Organisational Change and Productivity."

25. This section is drawn from Bessen et al., "Declining Industrial Disruption."

26. We measure acquisitions both by the number of acquisitions each firm makes each year and also by balance sheet Goodwill, which includes the amount the firm paid for the acquired company less the book value of that company. We measure software development by the employment of software developers derived from LinkedIn data. We measure lobbying using data from the Center for Responsive Politics. The figure shows stock, cumulated over time but depreciated, rather than investment flows in order to

capture the effect of past investments. The software figure excludes industries where software is a major part of the product. While proprietary software includes both own-developed software and custom contracted software, this measure only captures own-developed software. However, own-developed software is highly correlated with custom software, so the measure reflects total proprietary software reasonably well. See Bessen, "Information Technology and Industry Concentration," sec. 4.2.

27. Haskel and Westlake, *Capitalism without Capital;* Corrado, Hulten, and Sichel, "Intangible Capital and U.S. Economic Growth"; Corrado et al., "Intangible Investment in the EU and US."

28. Bessen et al., "Declining Industrial Disruption." The study looks specifically at the probability that a firm ranked fifth through eighth by sales enters the top four, displacing an incumbent firm. In one regression, patent stocks also have a statistically significant effect.

29. From Bessen, "Information Technology and Industry Concentration."

30. Calligaris, Criscuolo, and Marcolin, "Mark-Ups in the Digital Era"; Crouzet and Eberly, "Intangibles, Investment, and Efficiency"; Hsieh and Rossi-Hansberg, "Industrial Revolution in Services."

31. Specifically, Bessen et al., "Declining Industrial Disruption," use two instrumental variable estimations to assess the causal impact on leapfrogging. First, we instrument firm intangible investments with the five-year lag of intangible investments. Coefficients change little, ruling out all but very long-term factors. Second, we instrument U.S. industry software investment with software investment data from European countries. The effect persists, ruling out any U.S.-specific policy or other factors. Bessen, "Information Technology and Industry Concentration," uses three instrumental variable estimations to assess the causal impact on industry concentration. These are the share of sedentary jobs (more likely to adopt computers) in the industry in 1980, the share of software developers in the industry workforce in 1980, and the share of software in total investment in eighteen European countries. This paper also conducts placebo tests.

32. See, e.g., Grullon, Larkin, and Michaely, "Are US Industries Becoming More Concentrated?"; and Khan, "Amazon's Antitrust Paradox."

33. De Loecker, Eeckhout, and Unger, "Rise of Market Power"; Barkai, "Declining Labor and Capital Shares"; Hall, "New Evidence on the Markup of Prices." These estimates are contested by some: see Basu, "Are Price-Cost Markups Rising?"; and Syverson, "Macroeconomics and Market Power."

34. Bajgar et al., "Industry Concentration in Europe and North America"; Grullon, Larkin, and Michaely, "Are US Industries Becoming More Concentrated?"; Autor et al., "Fall of the Labor Share"; Gutierrez and Philippon, "Declining Competition and Investment"; Philippon, "Economics and Politics of Market Concentration"; Bessen, "Information Technology and Industry Concentration." While industry concentration has been rising at the national level, it has been *falling* when measured at the local level: see Rinz, "Labor Market Concentration, Earnings Inequality, and Earnings Mobility"; Rossi-Hansberg, Sarte, and Trachter, "Diverging Trends in National and Local Concentration"; and Berry, Gaynor, and Morton, "Do Increasing Markups Matter?"

35. See Bessen et al., "Declining Industrial Disruption," fig. 4. Firms ranked in the top four by sales in their industries acquired 1–1.5 firms per year on average in the late 1990s, falling to about 0.8 per year on average.

36. Bajgar et al., "Industry Concentration in Europe and North America"; Philippon, *Great Reversal*.

37. Disruption of industry leaders is greater on average in industries with *higher* markups. This may be because markups may reflect the returns to a firm's technological advantage. Bessen et al., "Declining Industrial Disruption."

38. See, e.g., Kades, "State of U.S. Federal Antitrust Enforcement"; Kwoka, *Mergers, Merger Control, and Remedies;* Wollmann, "Stealth Consolidation."

39. Liu, Mian, and Sufi, "Low Interest Rates, Market Power, and Productivity Growth."

40. Hopenhayn, Neira, and Singhania, "From Population Growth to Firm Demographics."

3. The Superstar Economy

1. Chen, "Cold War Competition and Food Production in China."

2. Chen, 64.

3. Chandler, *Scale and Scope*.

4. With recycling of used steel, the first stage is eliminated.

5. This section draws on Temin, *Iron and Steel Industry*.

6. Chandler, *Visible Hand*.

7. Large vessels can be heated more efficiently than smaller ones because they have less surface area relative to their volume. For a spherical vessel, for instance, the volume increases as the cube of the diameter, but the surface area increases only proportional to the square of the diameter. Since heat dissipates from the surface and the rate of dissipation is proportional to the surface area, the cost per volume of heating the contents of the vessel declines as the volume increases.

8. Karlson, "Modeling Location and Production."

9. Christensen and Greene, "Economies of Scale in U.S. Electric Power Generation."

10. Bain, *Barriers to New Competition*.

11. In the 1970s, when the minimum efficient steel mill was estimated to have 6 million tons capacity, national production was around 120 million tons. And the emergence of steel mini-mills, which use a different technology fed by recycled steel, has further reduced plant scale relative to the market size.

12. Sutton, *Sunk Costs and Market Structure*, 4.

13. This is U.S. production of steel and net imports of steel rails. U.S. Bureau of the Census, *Historical Statistics of the United States;* Temin, *Iron and Steel Industry*, 282.

14. Chandler, *Scale and Scope*, 128–32.

15. Nash, "Amazon, Alphabet and Walmart," reporting on estimates from IDC of IT spending, includes hardware, software, IT services, telecommunications services, and internal IT spending, including personnel. The capital expenditure data are from

Compustat. The IT expenditures are also relatively small compared to the cash flow firms generate from operations. In standard models of scale economies, firms will enter an industry until they can no longer profit from additional capital investments. For this reason, in industries with noted scale economies, such as petroleum refining and electric power generation, capital expenditures are large compared to earnings before income taxes, depreciation, and amortization (EBITDA)—from 2014 through 2019, capital expenditures by the top firms in these industries average 89 percent of EBITDA. For the top ten IT spenders in 2018, IT expenditures were only 24 percent of EBITDA.

16. Bessen et al., "Declining Industrial Disruption," app. A2.

17. While not dispositive, the correlation between the change in market share of the top four firms and the growth of industry shipments is .325 in four-digit NAICS industries between 2002 and 2007.

18. Rosen, "Economics of Superstars," 845.

19. Rosen, 846.

20. Frank and Cook, *Winner-Take-All Society,* observe this change in many aspects of society. They argue that we have become a winner-take-all society.

21. Flint, "Netflix's Reed Hastings Deems Remote Work 'a Pure Negative.' "

22. Sutton, *Sunk Costs and Market Structure.* A series of papers with Avner Shaked develop this model of vertical differentiation: Shaked and Sutton, "Relaxing Price Competition through Product Differentiation"; Shaked and Sutton, "Natural Oligopolies"; and Shaked and Sutton, "Product Differentiation and Industrial Structure."

23. Firms can also differentiate horizontally—that is, they can appeal to consumers who have different senses of quality and receive different value for different qualities. Horizontal differentiation complicates the analysis, but the same results can obtain with both vertical and horizontal differentiation. See Ellickson, "Quality Competition in Retailing."

24. Shaked and Sutton, "Product Differentiation and Industrial Structure."

25. Ellickson, "Does Sutton Apply to Supermarkets?"; Latcovich and Smith, "Pricing, Sunk Costs, and Market Structure Online"; Berry and Waldfogel, "Product Quality and Market Size."

26. This isn't the only thing firms use their large proprietary IT investments for, nor is it the only benefit they receive, but it is a key aspect of many of these investments.

27. Ellickson, "Does Sutton Apply to Supermarkets?"; Ellickson, "Quality Competition in Retailing."

28. Neiman and Vavra, "Rise of Niche Consumption."

29. Brand, "Differences in Differentiation."

30. Norman, "Economies of Scale in the Cement Industry"; Syverson, "Market Structure and Productivity"; Ellickson, "Does Sutton Apply to Supermarkets?"

31. There are 252 industries included, mostly at the four-digit NAICS level. The excluded industries include NAICS 5112, Software Publishers; 5181, Internet Service Providers and Web Search Portals; 5182, Data Processing, Hosting, and Related Services; 5191, Other Information Services; 5415, Computer Systems Design and

Related Services; 3341, Computer and Peripheral Equipment Manufacturing; 3342, Communications Equipment Manufacturing; 3344, Semiconductor and Other Electronic Component Manufacturing; and 3345, Navigational, Measuring, Electromedical, and Control Instruments Manufacturing. Note that some industries might be software-intensive, but not vertically differentiated, natural oligopolies.

32. Mueller, "Persistence of Profits above the Norm"; Syverson, "What Determines Productivity?"

33. Syverson, "What Determines Productivity?"

34. Decker et al., "Declining Business Dynamism: What We Know"; Decker et al., "Declining Business Dynamism: Implications for Productivity."

35. Coad and Rao, "Innovation and Firm Growth in High-Tech Sectors"; Autor et al., "Fall of the Labor Share."

4. From Open to Closed Capitalism

1. Severson, "Hydra-Matic History"; Wikipedia contributors, "Automatic Transmission."

2. SAE International, "About SAE International."

3. Laws, "Fairchild, Fairchildren, and the Family Tree of Silicon Valley."

4. Cohen et al., "Industry and the Academy."

5. Andrews, Criscuolo, and Gal, "The Best versus the Rest"; Calligaris, Criscuolo, and Marcolin, "Mark-Ups in the Digital Era."

6. Akcigit and Ates, "What Happened to U.S. Business Dynamism?"

7. A similar gap can be seen comparing the top four firms and the rest for domestic producers using comprehensive data from the quinquennial economic censuses.

8. The top four firms are defined using 6-digit NAICS industries and the 5 percent tails are trimmed.

9. Bessen, "Information Technology and Industry Concentration," 19.

10. This section draws broadly from Bessen, *Learning by Doing.*

11. Bessen, chap. 11; Bessen and Nuvolari, "Knowledge Sharing among Inventors"; Bessen and Nuvolari, "Diffusing New Technology without Dissipating Rents."

12. Thomson, *Structures of Change in the Mechanical Age;* Meyer, *Networked Machinists.*

13. Porter, editorial. See also Bessen, *Learning by Doing,* chap. 12.

14. U.S. Bureau of the Census, *Historical Statistics of the United States,* 2:810.

15. In 1885, 411 patents were granted per million residents; 384 of these were granted to domestic inventors.

16. Lamoreaux and Sokoloff, "Long-Term Change in the Organization of Inventive Activity"; Lamoreaux and Sokoloff, "Inventors, Firms, and the Market for Technology."

17. Lamoreaux and Sokoloff, "Long-Term Change in the Organization of Inventive Activity"; Lamoreaux and Sokoloff, "Market Trade in Patents." In order for the sale of a patent to be legally binding, a copy of the contract had to be deposited with the Patent Office in Washington, recording the reassignment of rights. A substantial

number of patents were also reassigned after the patent was issued. Many were reassigned multiple times, and many of the rights were transferred to a geographically restricted area. Because of these complications, researchers use the share assigned at issue as a basic measure of the trade in patents, although it represents a lower bound of the share of patents ever traded.

18. Lamoreaux and Sokoloff, "Long-Term Change in the Organization of Inventive Activity"; Lamoreaux and Sokoloff, "Inventors, Firms, and the Market for Technology"; Lamoreaux and Sokoloff, "Market Trade in Patents"; Khan and Sokoloff, "Early Development of Intellectual Property Institutions"; Khan and Sokoloff, "Institutions and Democratic Invention in 19th-Century America"; Khan, *Democratization of Invention*.

19. Arora and Gambardella, "Market for Technology"; Winder, "Before the Corporation and Mass Production"; Lamoreaux and Sokoloff, "Inventors, Firms, and the Market for Technology."

20. Lamoreaux and Sokoloff, "Inventors, Firms, and the Market for Technology," 40.

21. Lamoreaux and Sokoloff, 53.

22. Fisk, *Working Knowledge*.

23. Lamoreaux and Sokoloff, "Inventors, Firms, and the Market for Technology," 50.

24. Mass, "Mechanical and Organizational Innovation"; Bessen, *Learning by Doing*.

25. Draper, "Present Development of the Northrop Loom," 88.

26. Draper, 88.

27. Not all of these patents were used: some were to fence off the technology—that is, to cover alternative designs that rivals might seek to use.

28. Arora, "Contracting for Tacit Knowledge," argues that patents can facilitate licensing of tacit knowledge, but that does not mean that markets for patents can work as well for complex technologies as for simple ones.

29. Mass, "Mechanical and Organizational Innovation."

30. There is also an active market for patents, although patent transactions are often distinct from actual technology transfer. Patents can exclude others from practicing or using an invention, but they do not necessarily correspond to an actual diffusion of useful knowledge. A great many patents are used by firms as strategic tools to block competitors from innovating or by patent trolls to extort money from firms that are using technology. See, e.g., Lemley and Feldman, "Patent Licensing, Technology Transfer, and Innovation."

31. Arora and Gambardella, "Changing Technology of Technological Change"; Arora, Fosfuri, and Gambardella, *Markets for Technology;* Arora and Gambardella, "Ideas for Rent."

32. See, e.g., Mowery et al., *Ivory Tower and Industrial Innovation;* and Corredoira et al., "Impact of Intellectual Property Rights."

33. Thursby, Jensen, and Thursby, "Objectives, Characteristics and Outcomes of University Licensing"; Valdivia, "University Start-Ups."

34. Agrawal, Cockburn, and Zhang, "Deals Not Done."

35. Zucker, Darby, and Armstrong, "Commercializing Knowledge"; Zucker and Darby, "Defacto and Deeded Intellectual Property."

36. Arora et al., "Changing Structure of American Innovation," 39.

37. A standard result of theoretical models of product differentiation is that this kind of competition can produce more product variety than is socially optimal. See Salop, "Monopolistic Competition with Outside Goods."

5. The Automation Paradox

1. "Geoff Hinton: On Radiology."

2. Winick, "Every Study We Could Find."

3. Bessen et al., "Automation: A Guide for Policymakers," provide an overview of the issue.

4. Wood, "8 Trends Affecting Radiologist Jobs in 2019."

5. Topol, "High-Performance Medicine."

6. Roberts et al., "Common Pitfalls and Recommendations," 199.

7. Marcus and Little, "Advancing AI in Health Care."

8. Ruggles et al., "IPUMS USA: Version 8.0 [Dataset]." IPUMS has mapped these occupations to the 1990 and 2010 Census classifications. When occupations become too small, they are combined with other occupations, so I looked at all instances where the 1950 occupation was either renamed or combined into a broader category.

9. Arntz, Gregory, and Zierahn, "Revisiting the Risk of Automation."

10. Using census data, the number of full-time-equivalent cashiers increased from 1.4 percent of the workforce in 1980 to 1.6 percent in 2000 and 1.7 percent in 2016; absolute numbers also increased.

11. The number of bank tellers per branch office decreased, but the number of bank branches grew to more than offset this loss. See Bessen, *Learning by Doing*, 107–9. See also Bessen, "Automation and Jobs"; and Bessen, "AI and Jobs."

12. Bessen, "Automation and Jobs."

13. Bessen et al., "Firm-Level Automation"; Bessen et al., "Automatic Reaction."

14. An exception is the Accommodation and Food Service industry, where income effects are not significant.

15. Studies that look at automation generally or specifically at IT or robots at the firm level include Acemoglu, Lelarge, and Restrepo, "Competing with Robots"; Aghion et al., "What Are the Labor and Product Market Effects of Automation?"; Akerman, Gaarder, and Mogstad, "Skill Complementarity of Broadband Internet"; Bessen and Righi, "Information Technology and Firm Employment"; Cirera and Sabetti, "Effects of Innovation on Employment in Developing Countries"; Dixon, Hong, and Wu, "Robot Revolution"; Domini et al., "Threats and Opportunities in the Digital Era"; Gaggl and Wright, "Short-Run View of What Computers Do"; Humlum, "Robot Adoption and Labor Market Dynamics"; Koch, Manuylov, and Smolka, "Robots and Firms"; and Mann and Püttmann, "Benign Effects of Automation."

16. See, e.g., Acemoglu, Lelarge, and Restrepo, "Competing with Robots"; and Aghion et al., "What Are the Labor and Product Market Effects of Automation?"

17. Autor and Salomons, "Is Automation Labor-Displacing?"; Dauth et al., "German Robots"; Graetz and Michaels, "Robots at Work." Acemoglu and Restrepo, "Robots and Jobs," find that they do.

18. Hardoy and Schøne, "Displacement and Household Adaptation." In part, this is by law: unemployment benefits in the Netherlands have a replacement rate of 75 percent in the first two months of unemployment, which then decreases to 70 percent. Further, there is a maximum ceiling, such that workers with higher wages earn lower replacement rates than the 70 or 75 percent maximum.

19. Abbring et al., "Displaced Workers."

20. Crevier, *AI*, 108–9.

21. Agrawal, Gans, and Goldfarb, *Economics of Artificial Intelligence*.

22. U.S. Census Bureau, "Capital Expenditures for Robotic Equipment."

23. U.S. Bureau of Economic Analysis, "National Income and Product Accounts," table 5.3.5, September 30, 2020, revision.

24. Many of the automation events are substantially investments in information technology—that is, IT is used for automation and the major automation investments occur at the same time as major investments in computers. To study the effect of computers alone, we looked only at events where major computer investments occurred without similar increases in automation expenditures.

25. Bessen and Righi, "Information Technology and Firm Employment." We studied what happened at firms that made major investments in software compared to equivalent firms that did not invest at the same time. We identified these events as years when the share of software developers in the firm workforce increased substantially, using LinkedIn résumé data to identify these changes. The results shown correct for endogenous selection of investment decisions by controlling for firm productivity. See the paper for details. As above, firms that make investments may increase their employment yet aggregate employment could decline. There is no evidence that this is happening, however.

26. Bessen et al., "Business of AI Startups."

27. Keynes, "Economic Possibilities for Our Grandchildren."

28. Also, many new products have enhanced our leisure time, including automating tasks such as washing clothes and dishes.

6. The Productivity Gap

1. ScanSoft, "ScanSoft and Nuance to Merge."

2. The saying of board member Bill Janeway was "Buy if you can, build if you must."

3. Nuance, "Nuance Dragon Dictation App 2.0."

4. MacMillan, "Amazon Says It Has over 10,000 Employees."

5. Kinsella, "Amazon Alexa Has 100k Skills."

6. Amadeo, "New Android OEM Licensing Terms Leak."

7. Faulkner, "Data Panel Presentation."

8. Merced, Metz, and Weise, "Microsoft to Buy Nuance."

9. Bureau of Labor Statistics, "Productivity Growth by Major Sector." For manufacturing, annual labor productivity growth fell from 4.4 percent per year to 0.5 percent per year.

10. Or output per worker hour. Multifactor productivity is the ratio of output to some combination of inputs, including labor.

11. Gordon, *Rise and Fall of American Growth.*

12. Sellars, "Twenty Years of Web Scraping."

13. Faulkner, "Data Panel Presentation."

14. Bessen et al., "GDPR and the Importance of Data to AI Startups."

15. The absolute number of startups has also gone up substantially; however, because Crunchbase has lags in reporting new firms, I use the ratio of startups in this field to the number of all software startups.

16. Panzarino, "Samsung Acquires Viv."

17. Schwartz, "Apple Acquires Voice AI Startup Voysis."

18. Ku, "Microsoft Acquires Semantic Machines."

19. Gartner, "Gartner Says Worldwide Robotic Process"; Gartner, "Market Share Analysis."

20. Lamanna, "Robotic Process Automation"; Taulli, "Microsoft Races Ahead on RPA"; SAPInsider, "Intelligent Robotic Process Automation (RPA) Capabilities"; Oracle Corporation, "Oracle Integration Cloud's Process Automation with RPA."

21. Large vendors have an advantage in that they have well-established sales channels and customer relationships. However, UiPath has large partners that provide these relationships.

22. See Bill Janeway's lectures at www.econ.cam.ac.uk/graduate/mphil/modules/F530.pdf.

23. PitchBook, "Q2 2020 PitchBook."

24. Hathaway, "Time to Exit."

25. Ewens, Nanda, and Rhodes-Kropf, "Cost of Experimentation."

26. Guzman and Stern, "State of American Entrepreneurship."

27. While it is possible to, say, count innovations, it is hard to compare the quality of different innovations. Some researchers have used patents or citation-weighted patents to measure innovation, but there are well-known problems with this approach. For instance, some industries and firms are simply much more likely to obtain patents on their innovations than others.

28. Bessen and Denk, "From Productivity to Firm Growth."

29. The figure is a binned scatterplot showing average firm annual growth rate in constant-dollar revenues after controlling for industry and year.

30. Bessen and Denk, "From Productivity to Firm Growth."

31. See, e.g., Innovation Enterprise, "Why Small Companies Can Out Innovate Big Corporations."

32. Schumpeter, *Capitalism, Socialism and Democracy,* chap. 8. See also Atkinson and Lind, *Big Is Beautiful.*

33. Cohen, "Fifty Years of Empirical Studies."

34. Cohen, 137.

35. Cohen and Klepper, "Reprise of Size and R & D," provide a rationale for this division.

36. Cunningham, Ederer, and Ma, "Killer Acquisitions."

37. Without such patents covering the innovation, if one startup is removed from the market, other firms and other researchers can still pursue that line of innovation. This is often the case, for instance, in software-related fields. With well-defined patents, the acquisition of *the patents* can prevent further research.

38. Hicks, "Annual Survey of Economic Theory."

39. Shapiro, "Competition and Innovation," 376. See also Gilbert, "Looking for Mr. Schumpeter." Aghion et al., "Competition and Innovation," argue that the relation between innovation and competition is an inverted U. In their view, innovation increases with greater competition until the level of competition becomes too high and subsequent increases decrease innovation. Significantly, these authors measure static price competition rather than the dynamic contestability that Shapiro alludes to.

40. Syverson, "Market Structure and Productivity."

41. Bain, *Barriers to New Competition*.

42. Bresnahan, "Empirical Studies of Industries with Market Power"; Schmalensee, "Inter-Industry Studies of Structure and Performance."

43. Demsetz, "Industry Structure, Market Rivalry, and Public Policy."

44. Baumol, Panzar, and Willig, *Contestable Markets and the Theory of Industry Structure*.

45. Nelson and Winter, *Evolutionary Theory of Economic Change;* Gort and Klepper, "Time Paths in the Diffusion of Product Innovations."

46. Haltiwanger, Hathaway, and Miranda, "Declining Business Dynamism in the U.S. High-Technology Sector"; Decker et al., "Declining Business Dynamism: What We Know"; Decker et al., "Declining Business Dynamism: Implications for Productivity"; Decker et al., "Where Has All the Skewness Gone?"; Decker et al., "Declining Dynamism, Allocative Efficiency, and the Productivity Slowdown"; Decker et al., "Changing Business Dynamism and Productivity."

47. Cicilline, "Investigation of Competition in Digital Markets," 46–47.

48. U.S. Census Bureau, "BDS Data Tables."

49. This figure is an update of fig. 3 in Haltiwanger, Hathaway, and Miranda, "Declining Business Dynamism in the U.S. High-Technology Sector." Following them, I define high-tech firms as those in NAICS 4-digit industries 3341, 3342, 3344, 3345, 5112, 5161, 5179, 5181, 5182, 5415, 3254, 3364, 5413, and 5417.

50. PitchBook, "Q2 2020 PitchBook"; CB Insights Research, "Venture Capital Funding Report Q2 2020."

51. In PitchBook, the number of early stage investments almost quadrupled since 2006; in CB Insights, the number of early stage deals almost quadrupled since 1995. Average deal size has increased.

52. Kamepalli, Rajan, and Zingales, "Kill Zone." See also Wen and Zhu, "Threat of Platform-Owner Entry and Complementor Responses," where entry into a market

segment by a Big Tech firm caused smaller firms to direct their innovation to other market segments.

53. Phillips and Zhdanov, "R&D and the Incentives from Merger and Acquisition Activity."

54. Guzman and Stern, "State of American Entrepreneurship."

55. Krugman, *Age of Diminished Expectations,* 11.

56. Coyle, *GDP.*

57. Coyle, 130.

58. Court, "Hedonic Price Indexes with Automotive Examples"; Goodman, "Andrew Court and the Invention of Hedonic Price Analysis."

59. Griliches, "Hedonic Price Indexes for Automobiles."

60. Coyle, *GDP,* chap. 6; Cox and Alm, "Right Stuff"; Bils and Klenow, "Acceleration of Variety Growth."

61. Coyle, *GDP,* 128.

62. Syverson, "Challenges to Mismeasurement Explanations." Syverson's focus is on whether mismeasurement can explain the productivity slowdown, a slightly different question. Moreover, I am not suggesting that there is no actual productivity slowdown, just that measurement problems are getting worse as firm investments in proprietary software increase.

7. Divided Society

1. See, e.g., Katz and Murphy, "Changes in Relative Wages, 1963–1987."

2. For a review of this literature, see Acemoglu, "Technical Change, Inequality, and the Labor Market."

3. Goldin and Katz, *The Race between Education and Technology;* Tinbergen, "Substitution of Graduate by Other Labour."

4. Card, Heining, and Kline, "Workplace Heterogeneity"; Song et al., "Firming up Inequality." See also Lachowska et al., "Do Firm Effects Drift?"

5. The focus here is on broad income inequality. I am not specifically concerned about the inequality between the top 1 percent and the rest or with inequality of wealth.

6. For a recent overview, see Boushey, *Unbound.* For a technical study and review, see Aiyar and Ebeke, "Inequality of Opportunity, Inequality of Income and Economic Growth."

7. Sandel, *Tyranny of Merit,* 34. See also Markovits, *Meritocracy Trap.*

8. See, e.g., Chetty et al., "Opportunity Atlas."

9. Sandel, *Tyranny of Merit,* 25.

10. Sandel, 71–72.

11. Bessen, *Learning by Doing.*

12. The 2019 survey covered 24,419 employers across six industry sectors in forty-four countries. ManpowerGroup, "What Workers Want."

13. Cappelli, *Why Good People Can't Get Jobs.* This section draws from my article "Employers Aren't Just Whining."

14. Krugman, "Jobs and Skills and Zombies."

15. Yglesias, " 'Skills Gap' Was a Lie."

16. Editorial Board, "Don't Blame the Work Force."

17. See, e.g., Kocherlakota, "Inside the FOMC." Contrary to this view, employer reports of talent scarcity have grown even as unemployment has fallen.

18. Sigelman et al., "Hybrid Job Economy."

19. This paragraph paraphrases from another Burning Glass study: Markow et al., *Quant Crunch*.

20. Harvey Nash/KPMG, "CIO Survey 2018."

21. Markow et al., *Quant Crunch*, 21.

22. Restuccia, Taska, and Bittle, "Different Skills, Different Gaps."

23. Deming and Noray, "STEM Careers and the Changing Skill Requirements of Work."

24. Deming, "Growing Importance of Social Skills in the Labor Market."

25. Burning Glass (BGT) scrapes, deduplicates, and cleans the near-universe of online job advertisements. A previous analysis of the data set showed that this BGT accounts for 60–70 percent of all job openings and 80–90 percent of openings requiring a bachelor's degree or more; Carnevale, Jayasundera, and Repnikov, "Understanding Online Job Ads Data." To analyze skills, I used a sample drawn from the Burning Glass data from 2010 to 2019 that consists of more than 2 million help wanted ads and excludes IT jobs, public sector jobs, internships, and part-time jobs, firms that have posted fewer than one hundred jobs, and firms that do not post salary, experience, or education required.

26. The top three most frequently requested skills were Communication, Customer Service, and Teamwork/Collaboration; the most frequently requested IT skills were SQL, Java, and Software Development; the top AI skills were Machine Learning, Artificial Intelligence, and Image Processing; and the most frequently requested soft skills were Communication, Teamwork/Collaboration, and Problem-Solving.

27. I measured IT intensity as the share of software developer jobs in the share of total help wanted ads for the firm. To make the comparison apples-to-apples, these differences in required skills were estimated in a regression that includes controls for occupation, industry, state, year, and a measure of labor market tightness. The measure of labor market tightness is the ratio between Job Openings and Labor Turnover Survey (JOLTS) statewide openings for the nonfarm sector and the state unemployment rate. It is important to control for tightness because posted skill requirements change with the business cycle. Modestino, Shoag, and Ballance, "Downskilling"; Modestino, Shoag, and Ballance, "Upskilling."

28. Tambe, Ye, and Cappelli, "Paying to Program?"

29. And differences between establishments likely correspond to differences between firms. See Dunne et al., "Wage and Productivity Dispersion."

30. The total sample for wage analysis consists of more than ten million help-wanted ads from 2010 to 2019, excluding public sector jobs, internships, part-time jobs, and jobs that did not list a firm. The wage variable used is the log of salary; if a range of salaries was listed, then the mean of the range was used. Only a minority of ads listed

salary information, raising possible issues of selection bias. However, evidence from an exogenous change in the economics of listing salaries (legislation that bans the use of salary histories by employers) suggests that selection effects do not significantly bias salary levels. Bessen, Meng, and Denk, "Perpetuating Inequality."

31. This is the difference in means of log salary advertised excluding IT jobs. I excluded IT jobs because they tend to pay higher salaries and will be more prevalent in the top quartile group by construction.

32. See, e.g., Slichter, "Notes on the Structure of Wages."

33. These figures are derived from regressions using the Current Population Survey March supplements from 1989 to 2019 with controls for industry, education, experience, experience squared, state, year, union coverage, full year/full-time status, and worker fixed effects. Worker fixed effects are identified by tracking worker ids across consecutive annual surveys. Without these controls, the large firm premiums are even larger: 17 percent for secretaries, 20 percent for janitors, and 25 percent for truck drivers.

34. One explanation, *rent sharing*, proposes that when firms earn rents—that is, they earn extra profits because they are not in perfectly competitive product markets—workers can bargain for a share of those rents, raising wages. For example, Rose, "Labor Rent Sharing and Regulation," finds that union wages at trucking firms fell when the trucking industry was deregulated, thus reducing firm rents. Because different firms may earn different rents and because workers' bargaining power may vary across firms, the wages of comparable workers will differ across firms.

Another explanation argues that firms have *monopsony* power in setting wages. Manning, *Monopsony in Motion;* Card et al., "Firms and Labor Market Inequality." This means that firms do not merely take the market wage but will have to pay more if they want to hire more workers. For example, when workers have heterogeneous preferences for working at different employers, more will choose to work at a given employer for a higher wage. In this case, more profitable firms will pay more for comparable workers.

A third set of models provide *efficiency wage* explanations. Katz, "Efficiency Wage Theories," provides an overview of this literature. For example, if firms cannot monitor workers' performance, they may pay higher wages to elicit greater effort. More profitable firms may pay higher-efficiency wages.

A *search* model by Burdett and Mortensen, "Wage Differentials, Employer Size, and Unemployment," considers what happens when workers looking for a new job have to search through different employers. Some will accept a job offer sooner than others, but more productive workers will continue searching because they know they can command a higher wage. Then firms that hire more productive workers will be more productive and will also pay higher wages.

35. Card et al., "Firms and Labor Market Inequality," review this empirical literature.

36. Specifically, I ran a fixed effects panel regression on a sample of 3,193,877 ads that listed salary information, experience, and education required. Firm fixed effects were estimated along with controls for education, experience, experience squared,

labor market tightness, state, year, occupation, and industry. The regression R-squared was .689. Note that this approach results in firm fixed effects that are conceptually slightly different from those obtained using the AKM method; Abowd, Kramarz, and Margolis, "High Wage Workers and High Wage Firms." Because I am using help-wanted ads, the fixed effects I obtained for each firm reflect both the AKM fixed effect and the average firm pay premium associated with unobserved worker characteristics.

37. The correlation between firm fixed effects and firm IT intensity is .351. This is the simple correlation coefficient between the fixed effect and a best-fit quadratic form in the IT share. A simple linear correlation coefficient is .303.

38. Song et al., "Firming Up Inequality." I use the term "sorting" here to mean both the effect that Song et al. call sorting and the effect they call segregation.

39. I calculated partial correlations after controlling for detailed occupation (six-digit) and labor market tightness. All correlations were highly significant. The partial correlation coefficients are 0.038 for the number of skills, 0.059 for IT skills, 0.020 for AI skills, –0.002 for soft skills, 0.067 for experience, and 0.034 for education.

40. Bessen, Denk, and Meng, "Firm Differences."

41. This table excludes IT jobs and outsourced jobs. I define outsourced jobs as jobs in the administrative and support services industry, transportation jobs in the general freight industry, and food service workers in the food service industry.

42. Weil, *Fissured Workplace,* cites trucking jobs as an example where computers promoted outsourcing. Following George Baker and Thomas Hubbard, he argues that onboard computers have had two distinct effects on truckers. Because these computers report the location of trucks in real time, they reduce the costs of monitoring drivers. Monitoring is significant because employers otherwise have difficulty observing whether a driver is working diligently or shirking or worse. To the extent that drivers were paid more to encourage them to work diligently (called efficiency wages), onboard computers might have tended to decrease their pay. But also, computers allow third-party trucking companies to coordinate pickups and deliveries more efficiently when customers have partial loads. This makes outsourcing more attractive, especially for companies with highly paid inhouse drivers. The combination of these two effects can explain why IT-intensive firms might have outsourced trucking more (column 1) and also paid their own drivers less (columns 2 and 3). Baker and Hubbard, "Make versus Buy in Trucking."

43. Kremer and Maskin, "Wage Inequality and Segregation by Skill."

44. For software developers, the estimate is 13 percent. A sample of 1.8 million job changers was assembled from LinkedIn résumé data for new hires in 2012–13. Regression estimates controlled for experience, job tenure, recommendations, connections, education, occupation, and inferred ethnicity.

45. Controlling for year, industry, job tenure, U.S. firm, and R&D intensity.

46. The top ten metropolitan statistical areas are New York, Los Angeles, Chicago, Dallas, Houston, Washington, D.C., Miami, Philadelphia, Atlanta, and Phoenix.

47. They are New York, Washington, D.C., San Francisco, Chicago, Los Angeles, Dallas–Fort Worth, Seattle–Tacoma, Boston–Cambridge, Atlanta, and San Jose.

48. Eckert, Ganapati, and Walsh, "Skilled Tradable Services."

8. Regulating Complexity

1. Bigelow, "West Virginia Researcher Describes How Volkswagen Got Caught"; Ewing, "Researchers Who Exposed VW Gain Little Reward."

2. Grescoe, "Dirty Truth about 'Clean Diesel.' "

3. U.S. Environmental Protection Agency, "Notice of Violation," September 18, 2015.

4. Geuss, "Year of Digging through Code."

5. Geuss.

6. Release, "EFF Wins Petition to Inspect and Modify Car Software."

7. King, "Fewer Than 10 VW Engineers."

8. Wikipedia contributors, "Diesel Emissions Scandal."

9. Moore, "Volkswagen CEO Quits amid Emissions-Cheating Scandal."

10. Wikipedia contributors, "Volkswagen Emissions Scandal."

11. Corporate Europe Observatory, "Dieselgate Report Slams Commission and National Governments."

12. MacLellan, "Electric Dream."

13. Taleb, *Antifragile;* Clearfield and Tilcsik, *Meltdown.*

14. MacGillis, "Case against Boeing"; Langewiesche, "What Really Brought Down the Boeing 737 Max?"; Hamby, "How Boeing's Responsibility in a Deadly Crash 'Got Buried.' "

15. Kaplan, Austen, and Gebrekidan, "Boeing Planes Are Grounded in U.S."

16. Lewis, *Big Short,* chap. 4.

17. Lewis, 31.

18. See generally, Fishback, *Government and the American Economy.*

19. Olmstead and Rhode, "Origins of Economic Regulation in the United States."

20. Pigou, *Economics of Welfare.*

21. Gilligan, Marshall, and Weingast, "Regulation and the Theory of Legislative Choice"; Friedman, *Free to Choose.*

22. Friedman, *Free to Choose,* 196.

23. For an overview, see Carpenter and Moss, *Preventing Regulatory Capture.*

24. Friedman, *Free to Choose,* 196.

25. This development followed directly in response to Hayek's paper on knowledge. Hurwicz, "Informationally Decentralized Systems."

26. Laffont and Tirole, *Theory of Incentives in Procurement and Regulation.*

27. McAfee and McMillan, "Analyzing the Airwaves Auction."

28. Goulder, "Markets for Pollution Allowances."

29. Truth in lending laws date from the early twentieth century but were not initially seen as a substitute for usury laws. See Fleming, "Long History of 'Truth in Lending.'"

30. Thaler and Sunstein, *Nudge.*

31. McCarty, "Regulation and Self-Regulation."

32. MacGillis, "Case against Boeing."

33. Gates, "Inspector General Report."

34. Laris, "Messages Show Boeing Employees Knew."

35. Alm et al., "New Technologies and the Evolution of Tax Compliance."

36. See, e.g., Barton, Turner-Lee, and Resnick, "Algorithmic Bias Detection and Mitigation."

37. Plungis, "Volkswagen Used Special Software."

38. Boudette, "Tesla Faults Brakes."

39. Ben-Shahar and Schneider, *More Than You Wanted to Know*, 3.

40. Winston, "Efficacy of Information Policy."

41. Willis, "Decisionmaking and the Limits of Disclosure," 712.

42. Citing the Federal Reserve; see Ben-Shahar and Schneider, *More Than You Wanted to Know*, 7.

43. Warren quoted in Ben-Shahar and Schneider, 8.

44. Al-Ubaydli and McLaughlin, "RegData."

45. Mancur Olson, for instance, argues that lobbying tends to increase the complexity of regulation by creating exceptions and loopholes. Olson, *Rise and Decline of Nations*.

46. Elliehausen and Kurtz, "Scale Economies in Compliance Costs for Federal Consumer Credit Regulations"; Elliehausen, "Cost of Bank Regulation"; Dahl, Meyer, and Neely, "Bank Size, Compliance Costs"; Dahl et al., "Compliance Costs, Economies of Scale and Compliance Performance"; Hughes and Mester, "Who Said Large Banks Don't Experience Scale Economies?"

47. Dahl et al., "Compliance Costs, Economies of Scale and Compliance Performance."

48. Dahl et al. Some of that rise may also be due to the implementation of new regulations related to Dodd-Frank.

49. Because of this relative advantage, large firms, although frequently complaining about the high cost of regulation, sometimes welcome the advantages that come with greater regulation. For instance, the Philip Morris company welcomed FDA regulation of tobacco partly for this reason. See Flanigan, "Philip Morris' Tactic."

50. Llaguno, "2017 Coverity Scan Report."

51. Raymond, *Cathedral and the Bazaar*, chap. 2.

52. Van Loo, "Technology Regulation by Default," 542–43.

53. Clarke, Dorwin, and Nash, "Is Open Source Software More Secure?"

54. Hawkins, "We're Never Going to Get Meaningful Data."

55. MacGillis, "Case against Boeing."

56. Hettinga, "Open Source Framework for Powertrain Simulation."

57. Brandeis, "What Publicity Can Do," 10.

9. Platforms and Antitrust

1. Kang, Nicas, and McCabe, "Amazon, Apple, Facebook and Google Prepare."

2. Hilts, "Tobacco Chiefs Say Cigarettes Aren't Addictive."

3. Tracy, "After Big Tech Hearing, Congress Takes Aim."

4. Newton, "This Is How Much Americans Trust Facebook."

5. Cohen, "Surprise!"

6. Sauter and Stebbins, "America's Most Hated Companies."

7. Mylan's CEO was called before a hearing of the House Committee on Oversight and Government Reform in 2016.

8. Short tons of steel per worker hour rose from .0205 in 1900 to .0482 in 1930, a 135 percent increase. Deflated prices declined 23 percent, from $338 per gross ton in 1987 dollars to $262.

9. Azar, Marinescu, and Steinbaum, "Labor Market Concentration"; Azar et al., "Concentration in US Labor Markets"; Benmelech, Bergman, and Kim, "Strong Employers and Weak Employees."

10. Brown and Medoff, "Employer Size-Wage Effect."

11. Brandeis, *Curse of Bigness*, 118.

12. Schumpeter, *Capitalism, Socialism and Democracy*.

13. Lamoreaux, "Problem of Bigness."

14. Wu, "Be Afraid of Economic 'Bigness' "; Wu, "Curse of Bigness"; Stapp, "Tim Wu's Bad History."

15. Using data from the Current Population Survey from 1988–2019, the workforces at firms with more than one thousand employees are 48.8 percent female and 11.9 percent Black on average; smaller firms have workforces that are 47.4 percent female and 8.8 percent Black.

16. This analysis uses the same Current Population Survey data, matching workers across sequential surveys to construct a longitudinal panel of 1.4 million observations one year apart. This allowed controlling for person fixed effect to capture unobserved worker characteristics in regressions on log hourly wage. In addition the regressions controlled for marital status, full-time/full-year status, experience, experience squared, occupation, education, industry, state, and year.

17. Arguing big = good, see Atkinson and Lind, *Big Is Beautiful*.

18. Temin, *Iron and Steel Industry in Nineteenth-Century America*.

19. Tarbell, *History of the Standard Oil Company*.

20. Tarbell, 63.

21. Tarbell, 164.

22. Brandeis, *Curse of Bigness*, 131.

23. Brandeis did not view large firms as necessarily illegal; he just believed that the large firms of his day had not achieved their size by natural growth. He argued that (p. 115) "There are no natural monopolies in the industrial world. The Oil Trust and the Steel Trust have sometimes been called 'natural monopolies,' but they are both most unnatural monopolies. The Oil Trust acquired its control of the market by ruthless conduct which was not only a sin against society, but in large part involved flagrant violations of law. Without the aid of criminal rebating the Standard Oil would not have acquired the vast wealth and power which enabled it to destroy its smaller competitors by price-cutting and similar processes. The course of the Tobacco Trust was similar in character. The Steel Trust, while apparently free from the coarser forms of suppressing competition, acquired control of the market not through greater efficiency, but by buying up existing plants and particularly ore supplies at fabulous prices, and by controlling

strategic transportation systems" (*Curse of Bigness,* 115). He argued, much as I do in chapter 3, that the steel industry far exceeded minimum efficient plant size, so the size of U.S. Steel was not determined purely by efficiency.

24. Also in *Addyston Pipe & Steel Co. v. United States,* 175 U.S. 211 (1899).

25. *Chicago Board of Trade v. United States,* 246 U.S. 231 (1918).

26. Lamoreaux, "Problem of Bigness."

27. Bain, *Barriers to New Competition.*

28. *United States v. Aluminum Co. of America,* 148 F.2d 416 (2d Cir. 1945).

29. Demsetz, "Industry Structure, Market Rivalry, and Public Policy"; Schmalensee, "Inter-Industry Studies of Structure and Performance"; Bresnahan, "Empirical Studies of Industries with Market Power."

30. Posner, "Rule of Reason and the Economic Approach," 14.

31. Grullon, Larkin, and Michaely, "Are US Industries Becoming More Concentrated?"; Gutierrez and Philippon, "Declining Competition and Investment in the U.S."; Philippon, *Great Reversal*; Bessen, "Information Technology and Industry Concentration."

32. Cooper et al., "The Price Ain't Right?"; Dafny, Duggan, and Ramanarayanan, "Paying a Premium on Your Premium?"; Miller and Weinberg, "Understanding the Price Effects of the MillerCoors Joint Venture."

33. Kwoka, *Mergers, Merger Control, and Remedies;* Vita and Osinski, "John Kwoka's Mergers, Merger Control, and Remedies."

34. Kovacic, Marshall, and Meurer, "Serial Collusion by Multi-Product Firms."

35. Digital markets: Furman et al., "Unlocking Digital Competition"; digital platforms: Scott Morton et al., "Committee for the Study of Digital Platforms"; multi-sided platforms: OECD, *Rethinking Antitrust Tools for Multi-Sided Platforms.*

36. Ohio v. American Express Co., 585 U.S. 2274 (2018). See Hovenkamp, "Antitrust Policy for Two-Sided Markets"; and Hovenkamp, "Platforms and the Rule of Reason."

37. This is an *indirect* network effect because what matters is the size of the network on the *other* side of the two-sided platform.

38. Dirks, Van Essen, & April, "History of Ownership Consolidation."

39. On desktop computers, Windows has 67 percent of the U.S. market and OS X (Apple) has 27 percent; on all computing platforms, Apple has 43 percent (iOS and OS X), Windows has 33 percent, and Android has 20 percent. StatCounter Global Stats, "Desktop Operating System Market Share."

40. Cicilline, "Investigation of Competition in Digital Markets."

41. Khan, "Amazon's Antitrust Paradox."

42. Rey, "Amazon and Walmart Are in an All-Out Price War."

43. Cavallo, "More Amazon Effects."

44. On August 19, 2020, I checked for Newborn/Size 1 (8–14 lb.), 198 Count—Pampers Swaddlers Disposable Baby Diapers.

45. Collins, "Google + Amazon."

46. Quidsi might have been a competitive threat in other ways, possibly as a platform that could expand into other product lines. But Amazon did not monopolize either

the market for diapers or even the market for online diaper sales if they could be considered separately.

47. Mitchell, Freed, and Knox, "Report: Amazon's Monopoly Tollbooth." The ILSR report contends: "Amazon has leveraged its captive base of sellers to build a dominant logistics business. It's now delivering half of the items ordered on its site and a growing share of those purchased on other sites. Amazon has already overtaken the U.S. Postal Service in the large e-commerce parcel market, and it's expected to surpass UPS and FedEx by 2022." But the source cited for this projection actually projects only that Amazon will overtake UPS and FedEx in the shipment of *Amazon* parcels. Cosgrove, "Amazon Logistics Parcel Volume Will Surpass UPS and FedEx by 2022." In fact, most of the business of UPS and FedEx comes from other shippers; Amazon accounts for only about 5–8 percent of UPS revenues and 1.3 percent of FedEx revenues. Solomon, "Despite Talk of Budding Rivalry."

48. UPS had 57 percent market share, and FedEx had 25 percent. Gasparini and Cotton, "Report: United Parcel Service."

49. Alec Stapp reports that only about 1 percent of Amazon's revenues are from private-label goods, but 15–46 percent of the revenues of major brick-and-mortar retailers come from private-label items. Stapp, "Amazon, Antitrust, and Private Label Goods." The European Commission began antitrust action against Amazon, contending: "As a marketplace service provider, Amazon has access to non-public business data of third party sellers such as the number of ordered and shipped units of products, the sellers' revenues on the marketplace, the number of visits to sellers' offers, data relating to shipping, to sellers' past performance, and other consumer claims on products, including the activated guarantees." European Commission, "Antitrust." Much of this data is also available to brick-and-mortar retailers. Moreover, companies like Nielsen make scanner data from a variety of competing retailers available, something not available for online sellers. It is hard to see that the data make a fundamental difference here.

50. The two largest battery sellers in the United States are Duracell (46.4 percent share) and Energizer (28.5 percent share). Barker, "Energizer Buying Rayovac Batteries for $2 Billion."

51. Evans, "What's Amazon's Market Share?"

52. Fifty-six percent also sell on eBay, 47 percent on a personal website, 35 percent on Walmart.com, 23 percent at a brick-and-mortar store, and 19 percent on Shopify. Droesch, "Amazon's Marketplace Is Growing."

53. Greene and Bhattarai, "Amazon's Virus Stumbles."

54. Furman et al., "Unlocking Digital Competition"; Scott Morton et al., "Committee for the Study of Digital Platforms."

55. Jaffe and Lerner, *Innovation and Its Discontents.*

10. The Next Unbundling

1. Boyle, "Wal-Mart to Discount 1 Million Online Items."

2. Johnson, "Creating the Software Industry."

3. Object code is the machine language code that can be loaded on to a computer and directly run. This is what is delivered when one buys a software package. Source code consists of high-level programming instructions that developers use to create a program. The source code is highly modifiable and can be readily copied. For this reason, it is typically not made available to customers except with open-source software.

4. Welke, "Founding the ICP Directories."

5. Steinmueller, "U.S. Software Industry."

6. Grad, "Personal Recollection."

7. Grad; Usselman, "Unbundling IBM."

8. In December, Control Data Corporation filed a private antitrust lawsuit.

9. Grad, "Personal Recollection," 70.

10. Steinmueller, "U.S. Software Industry," 28.

11. Fisher, "IBM and Microsoft Cases," 180.

12. Grad, "Personal Recollection," 65; Humphrey, "Software Unbundling."

13. Grad, "Personal Recollection"; Usselman, "Unbundling IBM."

14. Grad, "Personal Recollection," 70.

15. Usselman, "Unbundling IBM," 267.

16. Dunne, "15 Amazon Statistics."

17. Murphy, "Amazon Suddenly Became a Massive Threat."

18. Miller, "How AWS Came to Be"; Furrier, "Story of AWS"; Clark, "How Amazon Exposed Its Guts."

19. Miller, "How AWS Came to Be."

20. Wilke, "2020 Amazon SMB Impact Report."

21. Jin and McElheran, "Economies before Scale."

22. "Wal-Mart Agrees to Settle Lawsuit against Amazon."

23. The settlement involved reassigning one Amazon employee and placing limits on the projects that others could work on so that knowledge they acquired while working at Walmart would not be used at Amazon.

24. Interview with former Amazon engineer/scientist, October 13, 2020.

25. Bezos, "Amazon 2014 Letter to Shareholders."

26. Wilke, "2020 Amazon SMB Impact Report."

27. Evans, "What's Amazon's Market Share?"

28. In 2012, Amazon created the AWS Marketplace, where third-party developers could sell apps built on the AWS platform, making it a two-sided market.

29. Bezos, "Amazon 2014 Letter to Shareholders."

30. Interview with former Amazon engineer/scientist, October 13, 2020.

31. Zhu and Furr, "Products to Platforms"; Hagiu and Altman, "Finding the Platform in Your Product"; Hagiu and Wright, "Multi-Sided Platforms."

32. Hagiu and Altman, "Finding the Platform in Your Product," 94.

33. Van Loo, "Rise of the Digital Regulator"; Rudegeair and Huang, "Bank of America Cut Off Finance Sites."

34. Pandy, "Developments in Open Banking and APIs."

35. 12 US Code, Section 5533 (a), (d).

36. Eversheds Sutherland, "CFPB Data Access Rule." Legal scholar Rory van Loo argues that this poor response is the result of regulatory fragmentation. Multiple agencies separately regulate different aspects of the industry. The CFPB mission is financial stability while competition policy—the policy area most closely related to data sharing—is handled by the Department of Justice. Van Loo, "Technology Regulation by Default"; Van Loo, "Making Innovation More Competitive."

37. Contreras, "Brief History of FRAND," 45.

38. Contreras.

39. Council of Economic Advisers, "2015 Economic Report of the President," 136ff.

40. Fisk, *Working Knowledge.*

41. Lobel, "New Cognitive Property."

42. Bessen and Meurer, *Patent Failure;* Bessen and Meurer, "Patent Litigation Explosion"; Bessen, Ford, and Meurer, "Private and Social Costs of Patent Trolls"; Bessen and Meurer, "Direct Costs from NPE Disputes."

43. Tucker, "Patent Trolls and Technology Diffusion"; Cohen, Gurun, and Kominers, "Patent Trolls."

44. Galasso and Schankerman, "Patents and Cumulative Innovation."

45. Litman, *Digital Copyright,* 23.

46. Contigiani, Hsu, and Barankay, "Trade Secrets and Innovation"; Png and Samila, "Trade Secrets Law and Mobility."

47. Starr, "Dynamism and the Fine Print."

48. Balasubramanian et al., "Locked in?"

49. Kang and Fleming, "Non-Competes, Business Dynamism, and Concentration."

50. Lessig, *Republic, Lost,* 56.

51. Lessig, 59.

52. Jaffe and Lerner, *Innovation and Its Discontents.*

53. Watzinger et al., "How Antitrust Enforcement Can Spur Innovation."

54. Moser and Voena, "Compulsory Licensing"; Baten, Bianchi, and Moser, "Compulsory Licensing and Innovation."

55. Righi and Simcoe, "Patenting Inventions or Inventing Patents?"

56. Beck, "New Trade Secret and Noncompete Case Growth Graph."

11. A New Information Economy

1. Machlup, *Production and Distribution of Knowledge in the United States.*

2. Hayek, "Use of Knowledge in Society."

3. Chandler, *Scale and Scope;* Beniger, *Control Revolution.*

Bibliography

Abbring, Jaap, Gerard van den Berg, Pieter Gautier, A. G. C. van Lomwel, Jan van Ours, and Christopher Ruhm. "Displaced Workers in the United States and the Netherlands." In *Losing Work, Moving On: International Perspectives on Worker Displacement,* ed. Peter Joseph Kuhn, 105–94. Kalamazoo, Mich.: W. E. Upjohn Institute, 2002.

Abowd, John M., Francis Kramarz, and David N. Margolis. "High Wage Workers and High Wage Firms." *Econometrica* 67, no. 2 (1999): 251–333.

Acemoglu, Daron. "Technical Change, Inequality, and the Labor Market." *Journal of Economic Literature* 40, no. 1 (2002): 7–72.

Acemoglu, Daron, Claire Lelarge, and Pascual Restrepo. "Competing with Robots: Firm-Level Evidence from France." *AEA Papers and Proceedings* 110 (2020): 383–88.

Acemoglu, Daron, and Pascual Restrepo. "Robots and Jobs: Evidence from US Labor Markets." *Journal of Political Economy* 128, no. 6 (2020): 2188–244.

Aghion, Philippe, Céline Antonin, Simon Bunel, and Xavier Jaravel. "What Are the Labor and Product Market Effects of Automation? New Evidence from France." Cato Institute, Research Briefs in Economic Policy 225, 2020.

Aghion, Philippe, Nick Bloom, Richard Blundell, Rachel Griffith, and Peter Howitt. "Competition and Innovation: An Inverted-U Relationship." *Quarterly Journal of Economics* 120, no. 2 (2005): 701–28.

Agrawal, Ajay, Iain Cockburn, and Laurina Zhang. "Deals Not Done: Sources of Failure in the Market for Ideas." *Strategic Management Journal* 36, no. 7 (2015): 976–86.

Agrawal, Ajay, Joshua Gans, and Avi Goldfarb. *The Economics of Artificial Intelligence: An Agenda.* Chicago: University of Chicago Press, 2019.

Aiyar, Shekhar, and Christian Ebeke. "Inequality of Opportunity, Inequality of Income and Economic Growth." *World Development* 136 (2020): 105115.

Akcigit, Ufuk, and Sina T. Ates. "What Happened to U.S. Business Dynamism?" National Bureau of Economic Research, Working Paper 25756, 2019.

Akerman, Anders, Ingvil Gaarder, and Magne Mogstad. "The Skill Complementarity of Broadband Internet." *Quarterly Journal of Economics* 130, no. 4 (2015): 1781–824.

Alm, James, Joyce Beebe, Michael S. Kirsch, Omri Marian, and Jay A. Soled. "New Technologies and the Evolution of Tax Compliance." *Virginia Tax Review* 39, no. 3 (2019): 287.

Al-Ubaydli, Omar, and Patrick A. McLaughlin. "RegData: A Numerical Database on Industry-Specific Regulations for All United States Industries and Federal Regulations, 1997–2012." *Regulation and Governance* 11, no. 1 (2017): 109–23.

Amadeo, Ron. "New Android OEM Licensing Terms Leak; 'Open' Comes with a Lot of Restrictions." *Ars Technica,* February 13, 2014. https://arstechnica.com/gadgets/2014/02/new-android-oem-licensing-terms-leak-open-comes-with-restrictions/.

Andrews, Dan, Chiara Criscuolo, and Peter N. Gal. "The Best versus the Rest: The Global Productivity Slowdown, Divergence across Firms and the Role of Public Policy." OECD Productivity Working Papers 5, 2016.

Arntz, Melanie, Terry Gregory, and Ulrich Zierahn. "Revisiting the Risk of Automation." *Economics Letters* 159 (2017): 157–60.

Arora, Ashish. "Contracting for Tacit Knowledge: The Provision of Technical Services in Technology Licensing Contracts." *Journal of Development Economics* 50, no. 2 (1996): 233–56.

Arora, Ashish, Sharon Belenzon, Andrea Patacconi, and Jungkyu Suh. "The Changing Structure of American Innovation: Some Cautionary Remarks for Economic Growth." *Innovation Policy and the Economy* 20, no. 1 (2020): 39–93.

Arora, Ashish, Andrea Fosfuri, and Alfonso Gambardella. *Markets for Technology: The Economics of Innovation and Corporate Strategy.* Cambridge, Mass.: MIT Press, 2004.

Arora, Ashish, and Alfonso Gambardella. "The Changing Technology of Technological Change: General and Abstract Knowledge and the Division of Innovative Labour." *Research Policy* 23, no. 5 (1994): 523–32.

———. "Ideas for Rent: An Overview of Markets for Technology." *Industrial and Corporate Change* 19, no. 3 (2010): 775–803.

———. "The Market for Technology." In *Handbook of the Economics of Innovation,* ed. Bronwyn H. Hall and Nathan Rosenberg, 1:641–78. Amsterdam: Elsevier, 2010.

Atkinson, Robert D., and Michael Lind. *Big Is Beautiful: Debunking the Myth of Small Business.* Cambridge, Mass.: MIT Press, 2018.

Autor, David, David Dorn, Lawrence F. Katz, Christina Patterson, and John Van Reenen. "The Fall of the Labor Share and the Rise of Superstar Firms." *Quarterly Journal of Economics* 135, no. 2 (2020): 645–709.

Autor, David, and Anna Salomons. "Is Automation Labor-Displacing? Productivity Growth, Employment, and the Labor Share." Brookings Papers on Economic Activity, Spring 2018.

Azar, José, Ioana Marinescu, and Marshall Steinbaum. "Labor Market Concentration." *Journal of Human Resources* (2020): 1218–9914R1.

Azar, José, Ioana Marinescu, Marshall Steinbaum, and Bledi Taska. "Concentration in US Labor Markets: Evidence from Online Vacancy Data." *Labour Economics* 66, no. 1 (2020): 101886.

Bain, Joe Staten. *Barriers to New Competition: The Character and Consequences in Manufacturing Industries.* Cambridge, Mass.: Harvard University Press, 1956.

Bajgar, Matej, Giuseppe Berlingieri, Sara Calligaris, Chiara Criscuolo, and Jonathan Timmis. "Industry Concentration in Europe and North America." OECD Productivity Working Papers 18, 2019.

Baker, George P., and Thomas N. Hubbard. "Make versus Buy in Trucking: Asset Ownership, Job Design, and Information." *American Economic Review* 93, no. 3 (2003): 551–72.

Balasubramanian, Natarajan, Jin Woo Chang, Mariko Sakakibara, Jagadeesh Sivadasan, and Evan Starr. "Locked in? The Enforceability of Covenants Not to Compete and the Careers of High-Tech Workers." *Journal of Human Resources* (2020): 1218–9931R1.

Baldwin, Carliss Young, and Kim B. Clark. *Design Rules: The Power of Modularity.* Vol. 1. Cambridge, Mass.: MIT Press, 2000.

Barkai, Simcha. "Declining Labor and Capital Shares." *Journal of Finance* 75, no. 5 (2020): 2421–63.

Barker, Jacob. "Energizer Buying Rayovac Batteries for $2 Billion." *STLtoday.com,* January 16, 2018. www.stltoday.com/business/local/energizer-buying-rayovac-batteries-for-2-billion/article_ac1d41d3-abod-5407-8f14-8a57dd594ee3.html.

Bartel, Ann, Casey Ichniowski, and Kathryn Shaw. "How Does Information Technology Affect Productivity? Plant-Level Comparisons of Product Innovation, Process Improvement, and Worker Skills." *Quarterly Journal of Economics* 122, no. 4 (2007): 1721–58.

Barton, Genie, Nicol Turner-Lee, and Paul Resnick. "Algorithmic Bias Detection and Mitigation: Best Practices and Policies to Reduce Consumer Harms." *Brookings* (blog), May 22, 2019. www.brookings.edu/research/algorithmic-bias-detection-and-mitigation-best-practices-and-policies-to-reduce-consumer-harms/.

Baselinemag. "How Kmart Fell Behind." *Baseline,* December 10, 2001. www.baselinemag.com/c/a/Projects-Supply-Chain/How-Kmart-Fell-Behind.

Basker, Emek. "The Causes and Consequences of Wal-Mart's Growth." *Journal of Economic Perspectives* 21, no. 3 (2007): 177–98.

———. "Change at the Checkout: Tracing the Impact of a Process Innovation." *Journal of Industrial Economics* 63, no. 2 (2015): 339–70.

———. "Job Creation or Destruction? Labor Market Effects of Wal-Mart Expansion." *Review of Economics and Statistics* 87, no. 1 (2005): 174–83.

Basker, Emek, Shawn Klimek, and Pham Hoang Van. "Supersize It: The Growth of Retail Chains and the Rise of the 'Big-Box' Store." *Journal of Economics and Management Strategy* 21, no. 3 (2012): 541–82.

Basker, Emek, and Michael Noel. "The Evolving Food Chain: Competitive Effects of Wal-Mart's Entry into the Supermarket Industry." *Journal of Economics and Management Strategy* 18, no. 4 (2009): 977–1009.

Basu, Susanto. "Are Price-Cost Markups Rising in the United States? A Discussion of the Evidence." *Journal of Economic Perspectives* 33, no. 3 (2019): 3–22.

Baten, Joerg, Nicola Bianchi, and Petra Moser. "Compulsory Licensing and Innovation—Historical Evidence from German Patents after WWI." *Journal of Development Economics* 126 (2017): 231–42.

Baumol, William, John Panzar, and Robert Willig. *Contestable Markets and the Theory of Industry Structure*. New York: Harcourt Brace Jovanovich, 1982.

Beck, Russell. "New Trade Secret and Noncompete Case Growth Graph (Updated June 7, 2020)." *Fair Competition Law* (blog), June 7, 2020. www.faircompetitionlaw.com/2020/06/07/new-trade-secret-and-noncompete-case-growth-graph-updated-june-7-2020/.

Beniger, James R. *The Control Revolution: Technological and Economic Origins of the Information Society*. Cambridge, Mass.: Harvard University Press, 1986.

Benmelech, Efraim, Nittai Bergman, and Hyunseob Kim. "Strong Employers and Weak Employees: How Does Employer Concentration Affect Wages?" National Bureau of Economic Research, Working Paper 24307, 2018.

Bennett, Victor Manuel. "Changes in Persistence of Performance over Time (February 12, 2020)." *Strategic Management Journal* 41, no. 10 (2020): 1745–69.

Ben-Shahar, Omri, and Carl E. Schneider. *More Than You Wanted to Know: The Failure of Mandated Disclosure*. Princeton, N.J.: Princeton University Press, 2014.

Berry, Steven, Martin Gaynor, and Fiona Scott Morton. "Do Increasing Markups Matter? Lessons from Empirical Industrial Organization." *Journal of Economic Perspectives* 33, no. 3 (2019): 44–68.

Berry, Steven, and Joel Waldfogel. "Product Quality and Market Size." *Journal of Industrial Economics* 58, no. 1 (2010): 1–31.

Bessen, James. "AI and Jobs: The Role of Demand." In *The Economics of Artificial Intelligence: An Agenda*, ed. Ajay Agarwal, Joshua Gans, and Avi Goldfarb, 291–307. Chicago: University of Chicago Press, 2019.

———. "Automation and Jobs: When Technology Boosts Employment." *Economic Policy* 34, no. 100 (2019): 589–626.

———. "Employers Aren't Just Whining—the 'Skills Gap' Is Real." *Harvard Business Review*, June 2014.

———. "Information Technology and Industry Concentration." *Journal of Law and Economics* 63, no. 3 (2020): 531–55.

———. *Learning by Doing: The Real Connection between Innovation, Wages, and Wealth*. New Haven: Yale University Press, 2015.

Bessen, James, and Erich Denk. "From Productivity to Firm Growth." Working paper, 2021. Available at SSRN: https://ssrn.com/abstract=3862796.

Bessen, James, Erich Denk, Joowon Kim, and Cesare Righi. "Declining Industrial Disruption." Boston University School of Law, Law and Economics Research Paper 20-28, 2020. Available at SSRN: https://ssrn.com/abstract= 3682745.

Bessen, James, Erich Denk, and Chen Meng. "Firm Differences: Skill Sorting and Software." Working paper, 2021. Available at SSRN: https://ssrn.com/ abstract=3862782.

Bessen, James, Jennifer Ford, and Michael J. Meurer. "The Private and Social Costs of Patent Trolls." *Regulation* 34 (Winter 2011–12): 26–35.

Bessen, James E., Maarten Goos, Anna Salomons, and Wiljan van den Berge. "Automatic Reaction: What Happens to Workers at Firms That Automate?" Boston University School of Law, Law and Economics Research Paper, 2019. Available at SSRN: https://ssrn.com/abstract=3328877.

———. *Automation: A Guide for Policymakers.* Washington, D.C.: Brookings Institution Press, 2020.

———. "Firm-Level Automation: Evidence from the Netherlands." *AEA Papers and Proceedings* 110 (2020): 389–93.

Bessen, James E., Stephen Michael Impink, Lydia Reichensperger, and Robert Seamans. "The Business of AI Startups." Boston University School of Law, Law and Economics Research Paper 18–28, 2018. Available at SSRN: https://ssrn. com/abstract=3293275.

———. "GDPR and the Importance of Data to AI Startups." Working paper, 2020. Available at SSRN: https://ssrn.com/abstract=3576714.

Bessen, James, and Eric Maskin. "Sequential Innovation, Patents, and Imitation." *RAND Journal of Economics* 40, no. 4 (2009): 611–35.

Bessen, James, Chen Meng, and Erich Denk. "Perpetuating Inequality: What Salary History Bans Reveal about Wages." Working paper, 2020. Available at SSRN: https://ssrn.com/abstract=3628729.

Bessen, James, and Michael J. Meurer. "The Direct Costs from NPE Disputes." *Cornell Law Review* 99 (2013): 387.

———. "The Patent Litigation Explosion." *Loyola University of Chicago Law Journal* 45, no. 2 (2013): 401–40.

———. *Patent Failure: How Judges, Bureaucrats, and Lawyers Put Innovators at Risk.* Princeton, N.J.: Princeton University Press, 2008.

Bessen, James, and Alessandro Nuvolari. "Diffusing New Technology without Dissipating Rents: Some Historical Case Studies of Knowledge Sharing." *Industrial and Corporate Change* 28, no. 2 (2019): 365–88.

———. "Knowledge Sharing among Inventors: Some Historical Perspectives." *Revolutionizing Innovation: Users, Communities and Open Innovation.* Cambridge, Mass.: MIT Press, 2016.

Bessen, James E., and Cesare Righi. "Information Technology and Firm Employment." Boston Univ. School of Law, Law and Economics Research Paper 19–6 (2019). Available at SSRN: https://ssrn.com/abstract=3371016.

Bezos, Jeffrey. "Amazon 2014 Letter to Shareholders." Amazon.com, 2014. https://s2.q4cdn.com/299287126/files/doc_financials/annual/AMAZON-2014-Shareholder-Letter.pdf.

Bigelow, Pete. "West Virginia Researcher Describes How Volkswagen Got Caught." *Autoblog,* September 15, 2015. www.autoblog.com/2015/09/23/researcher-how-vw-got-caught/.

Bils, Mark, and Peter J. Klenow. "The Acceleration of Variety Growth." *American Economic Review* 91, no. 2 (2001): 274–80.

Bloom, Nicholas, Luis Garicano, Raffaella Sadun, and John Van Reenen. "The Distinct Effects of Information Technology and Communication Technology on Firm Organization." *Management Science* 60, no. 12 (2014): 2859–85.

Bloom, Nicholas, Raffaella Sadun, and John Van Reenen. "Americans Do IT Better: US Multinationals and the Productivity Miracle." *American Economic Review* 102, no. 1 (2012): 167–201.

Boudette, Neal E. "Tesla Faults Brakes, but Not Autopilot, in Fatal Crash." *New York Times,* July 29, 2016.

Boushey, Heather. *Unbound: How Inequality Constricts Our Economy and What We Can Do about It.* Cambridge, Mass.: Harvard University Press, 2019.

Bove, Tony, and Cheryl Rhodes. "Editorial." *Desktop Publishing,* October 1985.

Boyle, Matthew. "Wal-Mart to Discount 1 Million Online Items Picked Up in Stores." Bloomberg, April 12, 2017. www.bloomberg.com/news/articles/2017-04-12/wal-mart-to-discount-1-million-online-items-picked-up-in-stores.

Brand, James. "Differences in Differentiation: Rising Variety and Markups in Retail Food Stores." Working paper, 2021. Available at SSRN: https://ssrn.com/abstract=3712513.

Brandeis, Louis D. *The Curse of Bigness: Miscellaneous Papers of Louis D. Brandeis.* New York: Viking Press, 1934.

———. "What Publicity Can Do." *Harper's Weekly,* December 20, 1913, 92.

Bresnahan, Timothy F. "Empirical Studies of Industries with Market Power." In *Handbook of Industrial Organization,* ed. R. Schmalensee and R. D. Willig, 2:1011–57. Amsterdam: Elsevier, 1989.

Bresnahan, Timothy F., Erik Brynjolfsson, and Lorin M. Hitt. "Information Technology, Workplace Organization, and the Demand for Skilled Labor: Firm-Level Evidence." *Quarterly Journal of Economics* 117, no. 1 (2002): 339–76.

Bresnahan, Timothy F., and Manuel Trajtenberg. "General Purpose Technologies 'Engines of Growth'?" *Journal of Econometrics* 65, no. 1 (1995): 83–108.

Brown, Charles, and James Medoff. "The Employer Size-Wage Effect." *Journal of Political Economy* 97, no. 5 (1989): 1027–59.

Brown, Stephen Allen. *Revolution at the Checkout Counter.* Cambridge, Mass.: Harvard University Press, 1997.

Brynjolfsson, Erik, Andrew McAfee, Michael Sorell, and Feng Zhu. "Scale without Mass: Business Process Replication and Industry Dynamics." Harvard Business

School Technology and Operations Management Unit Research Paper 07-016, 2008.

Burdett, Kenneth, and Dale T. Mortensen. "Wage Differentials, Employer Size, and Unemployment." *International Economic Review* 39, no. 2 (1998): 257–73.

Calligaris, Sara, Chiara Criscuolo, and Luca Marcolin. "Mark-Ups in the Digital Era." OECD Science, Technology and Industry Working Papers, 2018.

Cappelli, Peter. *Why Good People Can't Get Jobs: The Skills Gap and What Companies Can Do about It.* Philadelphia: Wharton Digital Press, 2012.

"The Car Company in Front." *Economist,* January 27, 2005. https://www.econo mist.com/special-report/2005/01/27/the-car-company-in-front.

Card, David, Ana Rute Cardoso, Joerg Heining, and Patrick Kline. "Firms and Labor Market Inequality: Evidence and Some Theory." *Journal of Labor Economics* 36, no. S1 (2018): S13–70.

Card, David, Jörg Heining, and Patrick Kline. "Workplace Heterogeneity and the Rise of West German Wage Inequality." *Quarterly Journal of Economics* 128, no. 3 (2013): 967–1015.

Carnevale, Anthony P., Tamara Jayasundera, and Dmitri Repnikov. "Understanding Online Job Ads Data." Georgetown University, Center on Education and the Workforce, Technical Report (April), 2014.

Carpenter, Daniel, and David A. Moss. *Preventing Regulatory Capture: Special Interest Influence and How to Limit It.* Cambridge: Cambridge University Press, 2013.

Cavallo, Alberto. "More Amazon Effects: Online Competition and Pricing Behaviors." National Bureau of Economic Research, Working Paper 25138, 2018.

CB Insights Research. "Venture Capital Funding Report Q2 2020 with PwC MoneyTree." Accessed October 9, 2020. www.cbinsights.com/research/report/ venture-capital-q2-2020/.

Chandler, Alfred, Jr. *Scale and Scope: The Dynamics of Industrial Capitalism.* Cambridge, Mass: Belknap Press of Harvard University Press, 1990.

———. *The Visible Hand.* Cambridge, Mass.: Harvard University Press, 1993.

Charette, Robert N. "This Car Runs on Code." *IEEE Spectrum* 46, no. 3 (2009): 3.

Chen, Yixin. "Cold War Competition and Food Production in China, 1957–1962." *Agricultural History* 83, no. 1 (2009): 51–78.

Chetty, Raj, John N. Friedman, Nathaniel Hendren, Maggie R. Jones, and Sonya R. Porter. "The Opportunity Atlas: Mapping the Childhood Roots of Social Mobility." National Bureau of Economic Research, Working Paper 25147, 2018.

Chiou, Lesley. 2005. "Empirical Analysis of Retail Competition: Spatial Differentiation at Wal-Mart, Amazon.com, and Their Competitors." Working paper.

Christensen, Clayton. *The Innovator's Dilemma: When New Technologies Cause Great Firms to Fail.* Boston, Mass.: Harvard Business School Press, 1997.

Christensen, Laurits R., and William H. Greene. "Economies of Scale in U.S. Electric Power Generation." *Journal of Political Economy* 84, no. 4, part 1 (1976): 655–76.

Cicilline, David N. "Investigation of Competition in Digital Markets." Subcommittee on Antitrust Commercial and Administrative Law of the Committee on the Judiciary, October 2020. https://int.nyt.com/data/documenttools/house-anti trust-report-on-big-tech/b2ec22cf340e1af1/full.pdf.

Cirera, Xavier, and Leonard Sabetti. "The Effects of Innovation on Employment in Developing Countries: Evidence from Enterprise Surveys." *Industrial and Corporate Change* 28, no. 1 (2019): 161–76.

Clark, Jack. "How Amazon Exposed Its Guts: The History of AWS's EC2." *ZDNet,* June 7, 2012. www.zdnet.com/article/how-amazon-exposed-its-guts-the-history-of-awss-ec2/.

Clarke, Russell, David Dorwin, and Rob Nash. *Is Open Source Software More Secure?* Homeland Security/Cyber Security, 2009.

"Clayton Christensen's Insights Will Outlive Him." *Economist,* January 30, 2020. www.economist.com/business/2020/01/30/clayton-christensens-insights-will-outlive-him.

Clearfield, Chris, and András Tilcsik. *Meltdown: Why Our Systems Fail and What We Can Do about It.* London: Penguin, 2018.

Coad, Alex, and Rekha Rao. "Innovation and Firm Growth in High-Tech Sectors: A Quantile Regression Approach." *Research Policy* 37, no. 4 (2008): 633–48.

Cohen, Arianne. "Surprise! The Big Tech Antitrust Hearing Was a PR Boost for Amazon, Facebook, Google, and Apple." *Fast Company,* August 5, 2020. www.fastcompany.com/90536550/surprise-the-big-tech-antitrust-hearing-was-a-pr-boost-for-amazon-facebook-google-and-apple.

Cohen, Lauren, Umit G. Gurun, and Scott Duke Kominers. "Patent Trolls: Evidence from Targeted Firms." *Management Science* 65, no. 12 (2019): 5461–86.

Cohen, Wesley M. "Fifty Years of Empirical Studies of Innovative Activity and Performance." In *Handbook of the Economics of Innovation,* ed. Bronwyn H. Hall and Nathan Rosenberg, 1:129–213. Amsterdam: Elsevier, 2010.

Cohen, Wesley M., Richard Florida, Lucien Randazzese, and John Walsh. "Industry and the Academy: Uneasy Partners in the Cause of Technological Advance." *Challenges to Research Universities* 171, no. 200 (1998): 59.

Cohen, Wesley M., and Steven Klepper. "A Reprise of Size and R & D." *Economic Journal* 106, no. 437 (1996): 925–51.

Collins, Kimberly. "Google + Amazon: Data on Market Share, Trends, Searches from Jumpshot." Search Engine Watch, August 1, 2019. www.searchenginewatch.com/2019/08/01/amazon-google-market-share/.

Contigiani, Andrea, David H. Hsu, and Iwan Barankay. "Trade Secrets and Innovation: Evidence from the 'Inevitable Disclosure' Doctrine." *Strategic Management Journal* 39, no. 11 (2018): 2921–42.

Contreras, Jorge L. "A Brief History of FRAND: Analyzing Current Debates in Standard Setting and Antitrust through a Historical Lens." *Antitrust Law Journal* 80, no. 1 (2015): 39–120.

Cooper, Zack, Stuart V. Craig, Martin Gaynor, and John Van Reenen. "The Price Ain't Right? Hospital Prices and Health Spending on the Privately Insured." *Quarterly Journal of Economics* 134, no. 1 (2019): 51–107.

Corporate Europe Observatory. "Dieselgate Report Slams Commission and National Governments for Maladministration." December 20, 2016. https://corporateeurope.org/en/power-lobbies/2016/12/dieselgate-report-slams-commission-and-national-governments-maladministration.

Corrado, Carol, Jonathan Haskel, Cecilia Jona-Lasinio, and Massimiliano Iommi. "Intangible Investment in the EU and US before and since the Great Recession and Its Contribution to Productivity Growth." EIB Working Papers, 2016.

Corrado, Carol, Charles Hulten, and Daniel Sichel. "Intangible Capital and U.S. Economic Growth." *Review of Income and Wealth* 55, no. 3 (2009): 661–85.

Corredoira, Rafael A., Brent D. Goldfarb, Seojin Kim, and Anne Marie Knott. "The Impact of Intellectual Property Rights on Commercialization of University Research." 2020. Available at SSRN: https://ssrn.com/abstract=3399626.

Cosgrove, Emma. "Amazon Logistics Parcel Volume Will Surpass UPS and FedEx by 2022, Morgan Stanley Says." Supply Chain Dive, December 13, 2019. www.supplychaindive.com/news/amazon-logistics-volume-surpass-ups-fedex-2022-morgan-stanley/569044/.

Council of Economic Advisers. "2015 Economic Report of the President." The White House. https://obamawhitehouse.archives.gov/administration/eop/cea/economic-report-of-the-President/2015.

Court, A. T. "Hedonic Price Indexes with Automotive Examples." In *The Dynamics of Automobile Demand*, 99–118. New York: General Motors, 1939.

Cox, W. Michael, and Richard Alm. "The Right Stuff: America's Move to Mass Customization." Economic Review, Federal Reserve Bank of Dallas, 1998.

Coyle, Diane. *GDP: A Brief but Affectionate History*. Rev. and expanded ed. Princeton, N.J.: Princeton University Press, 2015.

Crespi, Gustavo, Chiara Criscuolo, and Jonathan Haskel. "Information Technology, Organisational Change and Productivity." CEPR Discussion Paper DP6105, 2007.

Crevier, Daniel. *AI: The Tumultuous History of the Search for Artificial Intelligence*. New York: Basic Books, 1993.

Crouzet, Nicolas, and Janice Eberly. "Intangibles, Investment, and Efficiency." *AEA Papers and Proceedings* 108 (2018): 426–31.

Cunningham, Colleen, Florian Ederer, and Song Ma. "Killer Acquisitions." *Journal of Political Economy* 129, no. 3 (2021): 649–702.

Cusumano, Michael A., and Richard W. Selby. *Microsoft Secrets: How the World's Most Powerful Software Company Creates Technology, Shapes Markets, and Manages People*. New York: Simon and Schuster, 1998.

Dafny, Leemore, Mark Duggan, and Subramaniam Ramanarayanan. "Paying a Premium on Your Premium? Consolidation in the US Health Insurance Industry." *American Economic Review* 102, no. 2 (2012): 1161–85.

Dahl, Drew, J. Fuchs, A. P. Meyer, and M. C. Neely. *Compliance Costs, Economies of Scale and Compliance Performance: Evidence from a Survey of Community Banks.* Federal Reserve Bank of St. Louis, April 2018.

Dahl, Drew, Andrew Meyer, and Michelle Neely. "Bank Size, Compliance Costs and Compliance Performance in Community Banking." In Federal Reserve Bank of St. Louis Manuscript, www.communitybanking.org/~/media/files/communitybanking/2016/session2_paper2_neely.pdf, 2016.

Dauth, Wolfgang, Sebastian Findeisen, Jens Südekum, and Nicole Wößner. "German Robots—The Impact of Industrial Robots on Workers." Institute for Employment Research, IAB-Discussion Paper 30/2017, 2017.

David, Paul A. "The Dynamo and the Computer: An Historical Perspective on the Modern Productivity Paradox." *American Economic Review* 80, no. 2 (1990): 355–61.

Decker, Ryan A., John C. Haltiwanger, Ron S. Jarmin, and Javier Miranda. "Changing Business Dynamism and Productivity: Shocks vs. Responsiveness." *American Economic Review* 110, no. 12 (2020): 3952–990.

———. "Declining Business Dynamism: Implications for Productivity." *Brookings Institution, Hutchins Center Working Paper,* 2016.

———. "Declining Business Dynamism: What We Know and the Way Forward." *American Economic Review* 106, no. 5 (2016): 203–7.

———. "Declining Dynamism, Allocative Efficiency, and the Productivity Slowdown." *American Economic Review* 107, no. 5 (2017): 322–26.

———. "Where Has All the Skewness Gone? The Decline in High-Growth (Young) Firms in the U.S." *European Economic Review* 86, no. C (2016): 4–23.

De Loecker, Jan, Jan Eeckhout, and Gabriel Unger. "The Rise of Market Power and the Macroeconomic Implications." *Quarterly Journal of Economics* 135, no. 2 (2020): 561–644.

Deming, David J. "The Growing Importance of Social Skills in the Labor Market." *Quarterly Journal of Economics* 132, no. 4 (2017): 1593–640.

Deming, David J., and Kadeem L. Noray. "STEM Careers and the Changing Skill Requirements of Work." National Bureau of Economic Research, Working Paper 25065, 2018.

Demsetz, Harold. "Industry Structure, Market Rivalry, and Public Policy." *Journal of Law and Economics* 16, no. 1 (1973): 1–9.

Devine, Warren D., Jr. "From Shafts to Wires: Historical Perspective on Electrification." *Journal of Economic History* 43, no. 2 (1983): 347–72.

Dirks, Van Essen, & April. "History of Ownership Consolidation." March 31, 2017. http://dirksvanessen.com/articles/view/223/history-of-ownership-consolidation-.

Dixon, Jay, Bryan Hong, and Lynn Wu. "The Robot Revolution: Managerial and Employment Consequences for Firms." NYU Stern School of Business, 2020.

Domini, Giacomo, Marco Grazzi, Daniele Moschella, and Tania Treibich. "Threats and Opportunities in the Digital Era: Automation Spikes and Employment Dynamics." LEM Working Paper Series, Scuola Superiore Sant'Anna, 2019.

Draper, George Otis. "The Present Development of the Northrop Loom." *Transactions of the National Association of Cotton Manufacturers* 59 (1895): 88–104.

Droesch, Blake. "Amazon's Marketplace Is Growing, but Most of Its Sellers Are Active on eBay, Too." *eMarketer,* June 25, 2019. www.emarketer.com/content/amazon-s-marketplace-is-growing-but-most-of-its-sellers-are-active-on-ebay-too.

Dunne, Chris. "15 Amazon Statistics You Need to Know in 2020 (September 2020)." *RepricerExpress* (blog), March 27, 2019. www.repricerexpress.com/amazon-statistics/.

Dunne, Timothy, Lucia Foster, John Haltiwanger, and Kenneth R. Troske. "Wage and Productivity Dispersion in United States Manufacturing: The Role of Computer Investment." *Journal of Labor Economics* 22, no. 2 (2004): 397–429.

Eckert, Fabian, Sharat Ganapati, and Conor Walsh. "Skilled Tradable Services: The Transformation of US High-Skill Labor Markets." Federal Reserve Bank of Minneapolis, Opportunity and Inclusive Growth Institute Working Papers 25, 2019.

Editorial Board. "Don't Blame the Work Force." *New York Times,* June 15, 2013.

Electronic Frontier Foundation. "EFF Wins Petition to Inspect and Modify Car Software." Press release, October 27, 2015. www.eff.org/press/releases/eff-wins-petition-inspect-and-modify-car-software.

Ellickson, Paul B. "Does Sutton Apply to Supermarkets?" *RAND Journal of Economics* 38, no. 1 (2007): 43–59.

———. "The Evolution of the Supermarket Industry: From A&P to Walmart." In *Handbook on the Economics of Retailing and Distribution,* Emek Basker, 368–91. Cheltenham, UK: Edward Elgar, 2016.

———. "Quality Competition in Retailing: A Structural Analysis." *International Journal of Industrial Organization* 24, no. 3 (2006): 521–40.

Elliehausen, Gregory E. "The Cost of Bank Regulation: A Review of the Evidence." *Federal Reserve Bulletin* 84 (1998): 252.

Elliehausen, Gregory E., and Robert D. Kurtz. "Scale Economies in Compliance Costs for Federal Consumer Credit Regulations." *Journal of Financial Services Research* 1, no. 2 (1988): 147–59.

European Commission. "Antitrust: Commission Sends Statement of Objections to Amazon for the Use of Non-Public Independent Seller Data and Opens Second Investigation into Its E-Commerce Business Practices." Press release, November 10, 2020. https://ec.europa.eu/commission/presscorner/detail/en/ip_20_2077.

Evans, Benedict. "What's Amazon's Market Share?" Benedict Evans, December 19, 2019. www.ben-evans.com/benedictevans/2019/12/amazons-market-share19.

Eversheds Sutherland. "A CFPB Data Access Rule Could Be a Win for Open Banking in the US." September 8, 2020. https://us.eversheds-sutherland.com/

NewsCommentary/Legal-Alerts/235010/A-CFPB-data-access-rule-could-be-a-win-for-open-banking-in-the-US.

Ewens, Michael, Ramana Nanda, and Matthew Rhodes-Kropf. "Cost of Experimentation and the Evolution of Venture Capital." *Journal of Financial Economics* 128, no. 3 (2018): 422–42.

Ewing, Jack. "Researchers Who Exposed VW Gain Little Reward from Success." *New York Times,* July 24, 2016.

Faulkner, Dan. "Data Panel Presentation." Paper presented at the Technology and Declining Economic Dynamism Conference, TPRI, Boston University Law School, September 12, 2020. http://sites.bu.edu/tpri/files/2020/10/Faulkner-Data_Panel-Dan-Faulkner_Plannuh.pptx.

Fishback, Price V. *Government and the American Economy: A New History.* Chicago: University of Chicago Press, 2008.

Fisher, Franklin M. "The IBM and Microsoft Cases: What's the Difference?" *American Economic Review* 90, no. 2 (2000): 180–83.

Fisk, Catherine L. *Working Knowledge: Employee Innovation and the Rise of Corporate Intellectual Property, 1800–1930.* Chapel Hill: University of North Carolina Press, 2009.

Flanigan, James. "Philip Morris' Tactic: FDA Regulation," April 22, 2001. www.latimes.com/archives/la-xpm-2001-apr-22-fi-54048-story.html.

Fleming, Anne. "The Long History of 'Truth in Lending.' " *Journal of Policy History* 30, no. 2 (2018): 236–71.

Flint, Joe. "Netflix's Reed Hastings Deems Remote Work 'a Pure Negative.' " *Wall Street Journal,* September 7, 2020.

Frank, Robert H. *The Winner-Take-All Society: Why the Few at the Top Get So Much More Than the Rest of Us.* New York: Penguin, 1996.

Friedman, Milton. *Free to Choose: A Personal Statement.* New York: Harcourt Brace Jovanovich, 1980.

Furman, Jason, Diane Coyle, Amelia Fletcher, Derek McAuley, and Philip Marsden. *Unlocking Digital Competition: Report of the Digital Competition Expert Panel.* London: HM Treasury, 2019.

Furrier, John. "The Story of AWS and Andy Jassy's Trillion Dollar Baby." *Medium,* January 30, 2015. https://medium.com/@furrier/original-content-the-story-of-aws-and-andy-jassys-trillion-dollar-baby-4e8a35fd7ed.

Gaggl, Paul, and Greg C. Wright. "A Short-Run View of What Computers Do: Evidence from a UK Tax Incentive." *American Economic Journal: Applied Economics* 9, no. 3 (2017): 262–94.

Galasso, Alberto, and Mark Schankerman. "Patents and Cumulative Innovation: Causal Evidence from the Courts." *Quarterly Journal of Economics* 130, no. 1 (2015): 317–69.

Gartner. "Gartner Says Worldwide Robotic Process Automation Software Market Grew 63% in 2018." June 24, 2019. www.gartner.com/en/newsroom/press-releases/2019-06-24-gartner-says-worldwide-robotic-process-automation-sof.

————. "Market Share Analysis: Robotic Process Automation, Worldwide, 2019." May 6, 2020. www.gartner.com/en/documents/3985614/market-share-analysis-robotic-process-automation-worldwi.

Gasparini, Steven, and Joseph Cotton. *Report: United Parcel Service.* November 18, 2016. https://smf.business.uconn.edu/wp-content/uploads/sites/818/2016/12/UPS-1-Page-Report.pdf.

Gates, Dominic. "Inspector General Report Details How Boeing Played Down MCAS in Original 737 MAX Certification—and FAA Missed It." *Seattle Times,* June 30, 2020.

"Geoff Hinton: On Radiology." Creative Destruction Lab, November 24, 2016. https://www.youtube.com/watch?v=2HMPRXstSvQ&t=29s.

Geuss, Megan. "A Year of Digging through Code Yields 'Smoking Gun' on VW, Fiat Diesel Cheats." *Ars Technica,* May 28, 2017. https://arstechnica.com/cars/2017/05/volkswagen-bosch-fiat-diesel-emissions-cheats-cracked-open-in-new-research/.

Gilbert, Richard. "Looking for Mr. Schumpeter: Where Are We in the Competition—Innovation Debate?" In *Innovation Policy and the Economy,* ed. Adam B. Jaffe, Josh Lerner, and Scott Stern, 6:159–215. Cambridge, Mass.: MIT Press, 2006.

Gilligan, Thomas W., William J. Marshall, and Barry R. Weingast. "Regulation and the Theory of Legislative Choice: The Interstate Commerce Act of 1887." *Journal of Law and Economics* 32, no. 1 (1989): 35–61.

Goldin, Claudia Dale, and Lawrence F. Katz. *The Race between Education and Technology.* Cambridge, Mass.: Harvard University Press, 2009.

Goodman, Allen C. "Andrew Court and the Invention of Hedonic Price Analysis." *Journal of Urban Economics* 44, no. 2 (1998): 291–98.

Gordon, Robert J. *The Rise and Fall of American Growth: The U.S. Standard of Living since the Civil War.* Princeton, N.J.: Princeton University Press, 2017.

Gort, Michael, and Steven Klepper. "Time Paths in the Diffusion of Product Innovations." *Economic Journal* 92, no. 367 (1982): 630–53.

Goulder, Lawrence H. "Markets for Pollution Allowances: What Are the (New) Lessons?" *Journal of Economic Perspectives* 27, no. 1 (2013): 87–102.

Grad, Burton. "A Personal Recollection: IBM's Unbundling of Software and Services." *IEEE Annals of the History of Computing* 24, no. 1 (2002): 64–71.

Graetz, Georg, and Guy Michaels. "Robots at Work." *Review of Economics and Statistics* 100, no. 5 (2018): 753–68.

Greene, Jay, and Abha Bhattarai. "Amazon's Virus Stumbles Have Been a Boon for Walmart and Target." *Washington Post,* July 30, 2020.

Greenstein, Shane, and Timothy F. Bresnahan. "Technical Progress and Co-Invention in Computing and in the Uses of Computers." Brookings Papers on Economic Activity, 1996.

Grescoe, Taras. "The Dirty Truth About 'Clean Diesel.' " *New York Times,* January 2, 2016.

Griliches, Zvi. "Hedonic Price Indexes for Automobiles: An Econometric of Quality Change." In Price Statistics Review Committee, *The Price Statistics of the Federal Government*, 173–96. Cambridge, Mass.: National Bureau of Economic Research, 1961.

Grullon, Gustavo, Yelena Larkin, and Roni Michaely. "Are US Industries Becoming More Concentrated?" *Review of Finance* 23, no. 4 (2019): 697–743.

Gschwandtner, Adelina. "Evolution of Profit Persistence in the USA: Evidence from Three Periods." *Manchester School* 80, no. 2 (2012): 172–209.

Gutierrez, German, and Thomas Philippon. "Declining Competition and Investment in the U.S." National Bureau of Economic Research, Working Paper 23583, 2017.

Guzman, Jorge, and Scott Stern. "The State of American Entrepreneurship: New Estimates of the Quantity and Quality of Entrepreneurship for 32 US States, 1988–2014." *American Economic Journal: Economic Policy* 12, no. 4 (2020): 212–43.

Hagiu, Andrei, and Elizabeth J. Altman. "Finding the Platform in Your Product." *Harvard Business Review* 95, no. 4 (2017): 94–100.

Hagiu, Andrei, and Julian Wright. "Multi-Sided Platforms." *International Journal of Industrial Organization* 43 (November 2015): 162–74.

Hall, Robert E. "New Evidence on the Markup of Prices over Marginal Costs and the Role of Mega-Firms in the US Economy." National Bureau of Economic Research, Working Paper 24574, 2018.

Haltiwanger, John, Ian Hathaway, and Javier Miranda. "Declining Business Dynamism in the U.S. High-Technology Sector." 2014. Available at SSRN: https://ssrn.com/abstract=2397310.

Hamby, Chris. "How Boeing's Responsibility in a Deadly Crash 'Got Buried.' " *New York Times*, June 15, 2020.

Hardoy, Inés, and Paal Schøne. "Displacement and Household Adaptation: Insured by the Spouse or the State?" *Journal of Population Economics* 27, no. 3 (2014): 683–703.

Harvey Nash/KPMG. *CIO Survey 2018*. 2018. https://assets.kpmg/content/dam/kpmg/dk/pdf/DK-2018/07/harvey-nash-kpmg-cio-survey-2018.pdf.

Haskel, Jonathan, and Stian Westlake. *Capitalism without Capital: The Rise of the Intangible Economy*. Princeton, N.J.: Princeton University Press, 2018.

Hathaway, Ian. "Time to Exit." Ian Hathaway (blog), January 9, 2019. www.ianhathaway.org/blog/2019/1/9/time-to-exit.

Hawkins, Andrew J. "We're Never Going to Get Meaningful Data on Self-Driving Car Testing." *The Verge*, June 15, 2020. www.theverge.com/2020/6/15/21292014/dot-nhtsa-self-driving-car-test-data-voluntary.

Hayek, Friedrich August. "The Use of Knowledge in Society." *American Economic Review* 35, no. 4 (1945): 519–30.

———, ed. *Collectivist Economic Planning: Critical Studies on the Possibilities of Socialism by N. G. Pierson, Ludwig von Mises, Georg Halm, and Enrico Barone*. London: Routledge and Kegan Paul, 1935.

Hettinga, Wissa. "Open Source Framework for Powertrain Simulation." *eeNews Automotive*, May 18, 2019. www.eenewsautomotive.com/news/open-source-framework-powertrain-simulation.

Hicks, John R. "Annual Survey of Economic Theory: The Theory of Monopoly." *Econometrica: Journal of the Econometric Society* 3, no. 1 (1935): 1–20.

Hilts, Philip J. "Tobacco Chiefs Say Cigarettes Aren't Addictive." *New York Times,* April 15, 1994.

Hopenhayn, Hugo, Julian Neira, and Rish Singhania. "From Population Growth to Firm Demographics: Implications for Concentration, Entrepreneurship and the Labor Share." National Bureau of Economic Research, Working Paper 25382, 2018.

Hovenkamp, Erik. "Antitrust Policy for Two-Sided Markets." 2018. Available at SSRN: https://ssrn.com/abstract=3121481.

Hovenkamp, Herbert. "Platforms and the Rule of Reason: The *American Express* Case." *Columbia Business Law Review*, 2019, no. 1 (2019): 35–92.

Hsieh, Chang-Tai, and Esteban Rossi-Hansberg. "The Industrial Revolution in Services." National Bureau of Economic Research, Working Paper 25968, 2019.

Hughes, Joseph P., and Loretta J. Mester. "Who Said Large Banks Don't Experience Scale Economies? Evidence from a Risk-Return-Driven Cost Function." *Journal of Financial Intermediation* 22, no. 4 (2013): 559–85.

Humlum, Anders. "Robot Adoption and Labor Market Dynamics." Working Paper, 2019.

Humphrey, Watts S. "Software Unbundling: A Personal Perspective." *IEEE Annals of the History of Computing* 24, no. 1 (2002): 59–63.

Hurwicz, Leonid. "On Informationally Decentralized Systems." In *Decision and Organization: A Volume in Honor of J. Marschak,* ed. C. B. McGuire and Roy Radner, 297–336. Amsterdam: North-Holland, 1972.

Innovation Enterprise. "Why Small Companies Can Out Innovate Big Corporations." Accessed October 12, 2020. https://channels.theinnovationenterprise.com/articles/why-small-companies-can-out-innovate-big-corporations.

Iyengar, Rishi. "Fiat Chrysler Proposes Merger with Renault to Create Carmaking Powerhouse." *CNN Business,* May 28, 2019. www.cnn.com/2019/05/27/business/fiat-chrysler-renault-merger/index.html.

Jaffe, Adam B., and Josh Lerner. *Innovation and Its Discontents: How Our Broken Patent System Is Endangering Innovation and Progress, and What to Do about It.* Princeton, N.J.: Princeton University Press, 2004.

Jia, Panle. "What Happens When Wal-Mart Comes to Town: An Empirical Analysis of the Discount Retailing Industry." *Econometrica* 76, no. 6 (2008): 1263–316.

Jin, Wang, and Kristina McElheran. "Economies before Scale: Survival and Performance of Young Plants in the Age of Cloud Computing." Rotman School of Management Working Paper 3112901, 2017.

Johnson, Luanne. "Creating the Software Industry—Recollections of Software Company Founders of the 1960s." *IEEE Annals of the History of Computing* 24, no. 1 (2002): 14–42.

Kades, Michael. "The State of U.S. Federal Antitrust Enforcement." *Equitable Growth* (blog), September 17, 2019. www.equitablegrowth.org/research-paper/the-state-of-u-s-federal-antitrust-enforcement/.

Kamepalli, Sai Krishna, Raghuram G. Rajan, and Luigi Zingales. "Kill Zone." University of Chicago, Becker Friedman Institute for Economics Working Paper 2020-19. Available at SSRN: https://ssrn.com/abstract=3555915.

Kang, Cecilia, Jack Nicas, and David McCabe. "Amazon, Apple, Facebook and Google Prepare for Their 'Big Tobacco Moment.' " *New York Times*, July 29, 2020.

Kang, Hyo, and Lee Fleming. "Non-Competes, Business Dynamism, and Concentration: Evidence from a Florida Case Study." *Journal of Economics and Management Strategy* 29, no. 3 (2020): 663–85.

Kaplan, Thomas, Ian Austen, and Selam Gebrekidan. "Boeing Planes Are Grounded in U.S. after Days of Pressure." *New York Times*, March 13, 2019.

Karlson, Stephen H. "Modeling Location and Production: An Application to U.S. Fully-Integrated Steel Plants." *Review of Economics and Statistics* 65, no. 1 (1983): 41–50.

Katz, Lawrence F. "Efficiency Wage Theories: A Partial Evaluation." *NBER Macroeconomics Annual* 1 (1986): 235–76.

Katz, Lawrence F., and Kevin M. Murphy. "Changes in Relative Wages, 1963–1987: Supply and Demand Factors." *Quarterly Journal of Economics* 107, no. 1 (1992): 35–78.

Keynes, John Maynard. "Economic Possibilities for Our Grandchildren." In *Essays in Persuasion*, 321–32. London: Palgrave Macmillan, 2010.

Khan, B. Zorina. *The Democratization of Invention: Patents and Copyrights in American Economic Development, 1790–1920*. New York: Cambridge University Press, 2005.

Khan, B. Zorina, and Kenneth L. Sokoloff. "The Early Development of Intellectual Property Institutions in the United States." *Journal of Economic Perspectives* 15, no. 3 (2001): 233–46.

———. "Institutions and Democratic Invention in 19th-Century America: Evidence from 'Great Inventors,' 1790–1930." *American Economic Review* 94, no. 2 (2004): 395–401.

Khan, Lina M. "Amazon's Antitrust Paradox." *Yale Law Journal* 126, no. 3 (2016): 710–805.

King, Danny. "Fewer than 10 VW Engineers May Have Worked to Defeat Diesel Tests." *Autoblog*, October 23, 2015. www.autoblog.com/2015/10/23/fewer-than-10-vw-engineers-may-have-been-involved-in-diesel-defe/.

Kinsella, Bret. "Amazon Alexa Has 100k Skills but Momentum Slows Globally; Here Is the Breakdown by Country." *Voicebot.ai*, October 1, 2019. https://voicebot.ai/2019/10/01/amazon-alexa-has-100k-skills-but-momentum-slows-globally-here-is-the-breakdown-by-country/.

Knee, Bill. "Dick's Supermarkets Expand in Wisconsin; Someday Dubuque?" *Telegraph-Herald* (Dubuque, Iowa), December 17, 1978.

Koch, Michael, Ilya Manuylov, and Marcel Smolka. "Robots and Firms." CESifo
    Working Paper, 2019.
Kocherlakota, Narayana. "Inside the FOMC." Federal Reserve Bank of Minneapolis,
    2010. www.minneapolisfed.org:443/speeches/2010/inside-the-fomc.
Kovacic, William E., Robert C. Marshall, and Michael J. Meurer. "Serial Collusion
    by Multi-Product Firms." *Journal of Antitrust Enforcement* 6, no. 3 (2018):
    296–354.
Kremer, Michael, and Eric Maskin. "Wage Inequality and Segregation by Skill."
    National Bureau of Economic Research, Working Paper 5718, 1996.
Krugman, Paul. "Jobs and Skills and Zombies." *New York Times,* March 30,
    2014.
———. *The Age of Diminished Expectations: U.S. Economic Policy in the 1990s.*
    Cambridge, Mass.: MIT Press, 1997.
Ku, David. "Microsoft Acquires Semantic Machines, Advancing the State of
    Conversational AI." Official Microsoft Blog, May 21, 2018. https://blogs.micro
    soft.com/blog/2018/05/20/microsoft-acquires-semantic-machines-advancing-
    the-state-of-conversational-ai/.
Kwoka, John. *Mergers, Merger Control, and Remedies: A Retrospective Analysis of
    U.S. Policy.* Cambridge, Mass.: MIT Press, 2014.
Lachowska, Marta, Alexandre Mas, Raffaele D. Saggio, and Stephen A. Woodbury.
    "Do Firm Effects Drift? Evidence from Washington Administrative Data."
    National Bureau of Economic Research, Working Paper 26653, 2020.
Laffont, Jean-Jacques, and Jean Tirole. *A Theory of Incentives in Procurement and
    Regulation.* Cambridge, Mass.: MIT Press, 1993.
Lamanna, Charles. "Robotic Process Automation Now in Preview in Microsoft
    Power Automate." November 4, 2019. https://flow.microsoft.com/en-us/blog/
    robotic-process-automation-now-in-preview-in-microsoft-power-automate/.
Lamoreaux, Naomi R. "The Problem of Bigness: From Standard Oil to Google."
    Journal of Economic Perspectives 33, no. 3 (2019): 94–117.
Lamoreaux, Naomi R., and Kenneth L. Sokoloff. "Inventors, Firms, and the Market
    for Technology in the Late Nineteenth and Early Twentieth Centuries." In
    Learning by Doing in Markets, Firms, and Countries, ed. Naomi R. Lamoreaux,
    Daniel M. G. Raff, and Peter Temin, 19–60. Chicago: University of Chicago
    Press, 1999.
———. "Long-Term Change in the Organization of Inventive Activity." *Proceedings
    of the National Academy of Sciences* 93, no. 23 (1996): 12686–92.
———. "Market Trade in Patents and the Rise of a Class of Specialized Inventors in
    the 19th-Century United States." *American Economic Review* 91, no. 2 (2001):
    39–44.
Langewiesche, William. "What Really Brought Down the Boeing 737 Max?" *New
    York Times,* September 16, 2020.
Laris, Michael. "Messages Show Boeing Employees Knew in 2016 of Problems That
    Turned Deadly on the 737 Max." *Washington Post,* October 18, 2019.

Latcovich, Simon, and Howard Smith. "Pricing, Sunk Costs, and Market Structure Online: Evidence from Book Retailing." *Oxford Review of Economic Policy* 17, no. 2 (2001): 217–34.

Laws, David. "Fairchild, Fairchildren, and the Family Tree of Silicon Valley." Computer History Museum, December 20, 2016. https://computerhistory.org/blog/fairchild-and-the-fairchildren/.

Lemley, Mark A., and Robin Feldman. "Patent Licensing, Technology Transfer, and Innovation." *American Economic Review* 106, no. 5 (2016): 188–92.

Lepore, Jill. "What the Gospel of Innovation Gets Wrong." *New Yorker,* June 16, 2014.

Lessig, Lawrence. *Republic, Lost: How Money Corrupts Congress—and a Plan to Stop It.* London: Hachette UK, 2011.

Levin, Sharon G., Stanford L. Levin, and John B. Meisel. "A Dynamic Analysis of the Adoption of a New Technology: The Case of Optical Scanners." *Review of Economics and Statistics* 69, no. 1 (1987): 12–17.

Lewis, Michael. *The Big Short: Inside the Doomsday Machine.* New York: W. W. Norton, 2010.

Liebling, A. J. "The Wayward Press: Do You Belong in Journalism?" *New Yorker,* May 16, 1960.

Liebowitz, Stanley J., Stephen Margolis, and Jack Hirshleifer. *Winners, Losers and Microsoft: Competition and Antitrust in High Technology.* Oakland, Calif.: Independent Institute, 1999.

Litman, Jessica. *Digital Copyright.* Amherst, N.Y.: Prometheus Books, 2001.

Liu, Ernest, Atif Mian, and Amir Sufi. "Low Interest Rates, Market Power, and Productivity Growth." National Bureau of Economic Research, Working Paper 25505, 2019.

Llaguno, Mel. "2017 Coverity Scan Report. Open Source Software—The Road Ahead." Synopsys, undated. www.synopsys.com/content/dam/synopsys/sig-assets/reports/SCAN-Report-2017.pdf.

Lobel, Orly. "The New Cognitive Property: Human Capital Law and the Reach of Intellectual Property." *Texas Law Review* 93 (2014): 789.

MacGillis, Alex. "The Case against Boeing." *New Yorker,* November 11, 2019.

Machlup, Fritz. *The Production and Distribution of Knowledge in the United States.* Princeton, N.J.: Princeton University Press, 1962.

MacLellan, Kylie. "Electric Dream: Britain to Ban New Petrol and Hybrid Cars from 2035." *Reuters,* February 4, 2020.

MacMillan, Douglas. "Amazon Says It Has Over 10,000 Employees Working on Alexa, Echo." *Wall Street Journal,* November 13, 2018.

Mann, Katja, and Lukas Püttmann. "Benign Effects of Automation: New Evidence from Patent Texts." 2018. Available at SSRN: https://ssrn.com/abstract=2959584.

Manning, Alan. *Monopsony in Motion: Imperfect Competition in Labor Markets.* Princeton, N.J.: Princeton University Press, 2003.

ManpowerGroup. "What Workers Want 2019 Talent Shortage Study." 2020. https://go.manpowergroup.com/talent-shortage.

Marcus, Gary, and Max Little. "Advancing AI in Health Care: It's All about Trust." *STAT* (blog), October 23, 2019. www.statnews.com/2019/10/23/advancing-ai-health-care-trust/.

Markovits, Daniel. *The Meritocracy Trap: How America's Foundational Myth Feeds Inequality, Dismantles the Middle Class, and Devours the Elite.* New York: Penguin, 2019.

Markow, Will, Souyma Braganza, Bledi Taska, Steven M. Miller, and Debbie Hughes. *The Quant Crunch: How the Demand for Data Science Skills Is Disrupting the Job Market.* Burning Glass Technologies, 2017. www.burning-glass.com/wp-content/uploads/The_Quant_Crunch.pdf.

Mass, William. "Mechanical and Organizational Innovation: The Drapers and the Automatic Loom." *Business History Review* 63, no. 4 (1989): 876–929.

McAfee, R. Preston, and John McMillan. "Analyzing the Airwaves Auction." *Journal of Economic Perspectives* 10, no. 1 (1996): 159–75.

McCarty, Nolan. "The Regulation and Self-Regulation of a Complex Industry." *Journal of Politics* 79, no. 4 (2017): 1220–36.

McNamara, Gerry, Paul M. Vaaler, and Cynthia Devers. "Same as It Ever Was: The Search for Evidence of Increasing Hypercompetition." *Strategic Management Journal* 24, no. 3 (2003): 261–78.

Merced, Michael J. de la, Cade Metz, and Karen Weise. "Microsoft to Buy Nuance for $16 Billion to Focus on Health Care Tech." *New York Times,* April 12, 2021.

Meyer, David R. *Networked Machinists: High-Technology Industries in Antebellum America.* Baltimore: Johns Hopkins University Press, 2006.

Miller, Nathan H., and Matthew C. Weinberg. "Understanding the Price Effects of the MillerCoors Joint Venture." *Econometrica* 85, no. 6 (2017): 1763–91.

Miller, Ron. "How AWS Came to Be." *TechCrunch* (blog), July 2, 2016. https://social.techcrunch.com/2016/07/02/andy-jassys-brief-history-of-the-genesis-of-aws/.

Mises, Ludwig von. "Die Wirtschaftsrechnung im Sozialistischen Gemeinwesen." *Archiv für Sozialwissenschaft und Sozialpolitik* 47, no. 1 (1920): 86–121.

Mitchell, Stacy, Zach Freed, and Ron Knox. "Report: Amazon's Monopoly Tollbooth." Institute for Local Self-Reliance, July 28, 2020. https://ilsr.org/amazons_tollbooth/.

Modestino, Alicia Sasser, Daniel Shoag, and Joshua Ballance. "Downskilling: Changes in Employer Skill Requirements over the Business Cycle." *Labour Economics* 41 (2016): 333–47.

———. "Upskilling: Do Employers Demand Greater Skill When Workers Are Plentiful?" *Review of Economics and Statistics* 102, no. 4 (2020): 793–805.

Moore, Thad. "Volkswagen CEO Quits amid Emissions-Cheating Scandal." *Washington Post,* September 23, 2015.

Moser, Petra, and Alessandra Voena. "Compulsory Licensing: Evidence from the Trading with the Enemy Act." *American Economic Review* 102, no. 1 (2012): 396–427.

Mowery, David C., Richard R. Nelson, Bhaven N. Sampat, and Arvids A. Ziedonis. *Ivory Tower and Industrial Innovation: University-Industry Technology Transfer before and after the Bayh-Dole Act.* Stanford, Calif.: Stanford University Press, 2015.

Mueller, Dennis C. "The Persistence of Profits above the Norm." *Economica* 44, no. 176 (1977): 369–80.

Murphy, Bill. "Amazon Suddenly Became a Massive Threat to Target; Then Target Did Something Brilliant." *Inc.com,* September 7, 2019. www.inc.com/bill-mur phy-jr/amazon-suddenly-became-a-massive-threat-to-target-then-target-did-something-brilliant.html.

Myerson, Roger B. "Fundamental Theory of Institutions: A Lecture in Honor of Leo Hurwicz." *Review of Economic Design* 13, no. 1–2 (2009): 59–75.

Nash, Kim S. "Amazon, Alphabet and Walmart Were Top IT Spenders in 2018." *Wall Street Journal,* January 17, 2019.

Neiman, Brent, and Joseph Vavra. "The Rise of Niche Consumption." National Bureau of Economic Research, Working Paper 26134, 2020.

Nelson, Richard R., and Sidney G. Winter. *An Evolutionary Theory of Economic Change.* Cambridge, Mass.: Harvard University Press, 1982.

Newton, Casey. "This Is How Much Americans Trust Facebook, Google, Apple, and Other Big Tech Companies." *The Verge,* March 2, 2020. www.theverge.com/2020/3/2/21144680/verge-tech-survey-2020-trust-privacy-security-face-book-amazon-google-apple.

Norman, George. "Economies of Scale in the Cement Industry." *Journal of Industrial Economics* 27, no. 4 (1979): 317–37.

Nuance. "Nuance Dragon Dictation App 2.0 Now Live in iTunes App Store." Press release, July 23, 2010. https://web.archive.org/web/20110927093234/http://www.nuance.com/company/news-room/press-releases/ND_003871.

OECD. *Rethinking Antitrust Tools for Multi-Sided Platforms.* Paris: OECD, 2018. www.oecd.org/competition/rethinking-antitrust-tools-for-multi-sided-platforms.htm.

Olmstead, Alan L., and Paul W. Rhode. "The Origins of Economic Regulation in the United States: The Interstate Commerce and Bureau of Animal Industry Acts." Working paper, 2017.

Olson, Mancur. *The Rise and Decline of Nations: Economic Growth, Stagflation, and Social Rigidities.* New Haven: Yale University Press, 2008.

Oracle Corporation. "Oracle Integration Cloud's Process Automation with RPA." 2017. www.oracle.com/a/ocom/docs/oracle-process-automation-with-rpa.pdf.

Pandy, Susan M. "Developments in Open Banking and APIs: Where Does the U.S. Stand?" Federal Reserve Bank of Boston, March 17, 2020. www.bostonfed.org/publications/payment-strategies/developments-in-open-banking-and-apis-where-does-the-us-stand.aspx.

Panzarino, Matthew. "Samsung Acquires Viv, a Next-Gen AI Assistant Built by the Creators of Apple's Siri." *TechCrunch* (blog), October 5, 2016. https://social. techcrunch.com/2016/10/05/samsung-acquires-viv-a-next-gen-ai-assistant-built-by-creators-of-apples-siri/.

Philippon, Thomas. "The Economics and Politics of Market Concentration." *NBER Reporter,* no. 4 (2019): 10–12.

———. *The Great Reversal: How America Gave Up on Free Markets.* Cambridge, Mass.: Harvard University Press, 2019.

Phillips, Gordon M., and Alexei Zhdanov. "R&D and the Incentives from Merger and Acquisition Activity." *Review of Financial Studies* 26, no. 1 (2013): 34–78.

Pigou, A. C. *The Economics of Welfare.* London: Macmillan, 1920.

PitchBook. "Q2 2020 PitchBook-NVCA Venture Monitor." July 13, 2020. https:// pitchbook.com/news/reports/q2-2020-pitchbook-nvca-venture-monitor.

Plungis, Jeff. "Volkswagen Used Special Software to Exaggerate Fuel-Economy Claims, EPA Says." *Consumer Reports,* August 30, 2019.

Png, Ivan P. L., and Sampsa Samila. "Trade Secrets Law and Mobility: Evidence from 'Inevitable Disclosure.' " 2015. Available at SSRN: https://ssrn.com/abstract=1986775.

Porter, Rufus. Editorial. *Scientific American,* August 28, 1845, 1. Available at http://en.wikisource.org/wiki/Scientific_American/Series_1/Volume_1/Issue_1/Front_page.

Posner, Richard A. "The Rule of Reason and the Economic Approach: Reflections on the Sylvania Decision." *University of Chicago Law Review* 45, no. 1 (1977): 1–20.

Raymond, Eric S. *The Cathedral and the Bazaar: Musings on Linux and Open Source by an Accidental Revolutionary.* Boston: O'Reilly Media, 1999.

Restuccia, Dan, Bledi Taska, and Scott Bittle. *Different Skills, Different Gaps: Measuring and Closing the Skills Gap.* Burning Glass Technologies, 2018. www. burning-glass.com/wp-content/uploads/Skills_Gap_Different_Skills_Different_Gaps_FINAL.pdf.

Rey, Jason Del. "Amazon and Walmart Are in an All-Out Price War That Is Terrifying America's Biggest Brands." *Vox,* March 30, 2017. www.vox. com/2017/3/30/14831602/amazon-walmart-cpg-grocery-price-war.

Righi, Cesare, and Timothy Simcoe. "Patenting Inventions or Inventing Patents? Strategic Use of Continuations at the USPTO." National Bureau of Economic Research, Working Paper 27686, 2020.

Rinz, Kevin. "Labor Market Concentration, Earnings Inequality, and Earnings Mobility." Center for Administrative Records Research and Applications Working Paper 10, 2018.

Roberts, Michael, Derek Driggs, Matthew Thorpe, Julian Gilbey, Michael Yeung, Stephan Ursprung, Angelica I. Aviles-Rivero, et al. "Common Pitfalls and

Recommendations for Using Machine Learning to Detect and Prognosticate for COVID-19 Using Chest Radiographs and CT Scans." *Nature Machine Intelligence* 3, no. 3 (2021): 199–217.

Rose, Nancy L. "Labor Rent Sharing and Regulation: Evidence from the Trucking Industry." *Journal of Political Economy* 95, no. 6 (1987): 1146–78.

Rosen, Sherwin. "The Economics of Superstars." *American Economic Review* 71, no. 5 (1981): 845–58.

Rossi-Hansberg, Esteban, Pierre-Daniel Sarte, and Nicholas Trachter. "Diverging Trends in National and Local Concentration." National Bureau of Economic Research, Working Paper 25066, 2018.

Rudegeair, Peter, and Daniel Huang. "Bank of America Cut Off Finance Sites from Its Data." *Wall Street Journal,* November 10, 2015.

Ruggles, Steven, Sarah Flood, Ronald Goeken, Josiah Grover, Erin Meyer, Jose Pacas, and Matthew Sobek. "IPUMS USA: Version 8.0 [Dataset]." Minneapolis: University of Minnesota, 2018. https://www.ipums.org/projects/ipums-usa/do10.v8.0.

SAE International. "About SAE International." https://www.sae.org/about/history.

Salop, Steven C. "Monopolistic Competition with Outside Goods." *Bell Journal of Economics* (1979): 141–56.

Sandel, Michael. *The Tyranny of Merit: What's Become of the Common Good?* New York: Farrar, Straus and Giroux, 2020.

SAPInsider. "What Intelligent Robotic Process Automation (RPA) Capabilities Are on the Horizon for SAP Customers." January 28, 2019. www.sapinsideronline.com/blogs/what-intelligent-robotic-process-automation-rpa-capabilities-are-on-the-horizon-for-sap-customers/.

Sauter, Michael, and Samuel Stebbins. "America's Most Hated Companies." *24/7 Wall St.* (blog), January 12, 2020. https://247wallst.com/special-report/2019/01/10/americas-most-hated-companies-6/.

ScanSoft. "ScanSoft and Nuance to Merge, Creating Comprehensive Portfolio of Enterprise Speech Solutions and Expertise; Combined Company Poised to Accelerate Technology Innovation for Customers and Partners around the World." May 9, 2005. https://sec.report/Document/0000950135-05-002726/.

Schafer, Sarah. "How Information Technology Is Leveling the Playing Field." *Inc.com,* December 15, 1995. www.inc.com/magazine/19951215/2660.html.

Schmalensee, Richard. "Inter-Industry Studies of Structure and Performance." In *Handbook of Industrial Organization,* ed. Richard Schmalensee and Robert Willig, 2:951–1009. Amsterdam: North-Holland, 1989.

Schumpeter, Joseph A. *Capitalism, Socialism and Democracy.* New York: Harper and Brothers, 1942.

Schwartz, Eric Hal. "Apple Acquires Voice AI Startup Voysis." *Voicebot.ai,* April 6, 2020. https://voicebot.ai/2020/04/06/apple-acquires-voice-ai-startup-voysis/.

Scott Morton, Fiona, Pascal Bouvier, Ariel Ezrachi, Bruno Jullien, Roberta Katz, Gene Kimmelman, A. Douglas Melamed, and Jamie Morgenstern. *Committee for the Study of Digital Platforms: Market Structure and Antitrust Subcommittee Report*. Chicago: Stigler Center for the Study of the Economy and the State, University of Chicago Booth School of Business, 2019.

Sellars, Andrew. "Twenty Years of Web Scraping and the Computer Fraud and Abuse Act." *Boston University Journal of Science and Technology Law* 24 (2018): 372–415.

Severson, Aaron. "Hydra-Matic History: GM's First Automatic Transmission." Ate Up with Motor, May 29, 2010. https://ateupwithmotor.com/terms-technology-definitions/hydramatic-history-part-1/view-all.

Shaked, Avner, and John Sutton. "Natural Oligopolies." *Econometrica: Journal of the Econometric Society* (1983): 1469–83.

———. "Product Differentiation and Industrial Structure." *Journal of Industrial Economics* (1987): 131–46.

———. "Relaxing Price Competition through Product Differentiation." *Review of Economic Studies* 49, no. 1 (1982): 3–13.

Shapiro, Carl. "Competition and Innovation: Did Arrow Hit the Bull's Eye?" In *The Rate and Direction of Inventive Activity Revisited*, 361–404. Chicago: University of Chicago Press, 2011.

Shea, Terry. "Why Does It Cost So Much for Automakers to Develop New Models?" *Autoblog*, July 27, 2010. www.autoblog.com/2010/07/27/why-does-it-cost-so-much-for-automakers-to-develop-new-models/.

Sigelman, Matthew, Scott Bittle, Will Markow, and Benjamin Francis. *The Hybrid Job Economy: How New Skills Are Rewriting the DNA of the Job Market*. Burning Glass Technologies, 2019. www.burning-glass.com/wp-content/uploads/hybrid_jobs_2019_final.pdf.

Slichter, Sumner H. "Notes on the Structure of Wages." *Review of Economics and Statistics* 32, no. 1 (1950): 80–91.

Solomon, Mark. "Despite Talk of Budding Rivalry, Amazon and UPS May Find They're Stuck with Each Other." *FreightWaves*, June 20, 2019. www.freight-waves.com/news/despite-talk-of-budding-rivalry-amazon-and-ups-may-find-theyre-stuck-with-each-other.

Song, Jae, David J. Price, Fatih Guvenen, Nicholas Bloom, and Till Von Wachter. "Firming Up Inequality." *Quarterly Journal of Economics* 134, no. 1 (2019): 1–50.

Stalk, George, Philip Evans, and Lawrence E. Shulman. "Competing on Capabilities: The New Rules of Corporate Strategy." *Harvard Business Review* 70, no. 2 (1992): 57–69.

Stapp, Alec. "Amazon, Antitrust, and Private Label Goods." *Medium*, April 27, 2020. https://medium.com/@progressivepolicyinstitute/amazon-antitrust-and-private-label-goods-bf8b8ccooe99.

———. "Tim Wu's Bad History: Big Business and the Rise of Fascism." Niskanen Center, March 11, 2019. www.niskanencenter.org/big-business-rise-fascism-bad-history-tim-wu/.

Starr, Evan. "Dynamism and the Fine Print." Paper presented at the Technology and Declining Economic Dynamism, Boston University School of Law, September 11, 2020. http://sites.bu.edu/tpri/files/2020/09/Starr_BU_Dynamism_9_11_2020.pdf.

StatCounter Global Stats. "Desktop Operating System Market Share United States of America." Accessed August 21, 2020. https://gs.statcounter.com/os-market-share/desktop/united-states-of-america.

Steinmueller, William Edward. "The U.S. Software Industry: An Analysis and Interpretive History." In *The International Computer Software Industry: A Comparative Study of Industry Evolution and Structure*, ed. David C. Mowery, 15–52. New York: Oxford University Press, 1996.

Stock, Eric J. "Explaining the Differing U.S. and EU Positions on the Boeing/McDonnell-Douglas Merger: Avoiding Another Near-Miss." *University of Pennsylvania Journal of International Law* 20, no. 4 (1999): 825–909.

Stokel-Walker, Chris. "Beep Beep: The History of George Laurer and the Barcode." *Medium,* December 20, 2019. https://onezero.medium.com/beep-beep-the-history-of-george-laurer-and-the-barcode-3522a15405ea.

Sutton, John. *Sunk Costs and Market Structure: Price Competition, Advertising, and the Evolution of Concentration.* Cambridge, Mass.: MIT Press, 1991.

Syverson, Chad. "Challenges to Mismeasurement Explanations for the U.S. Productivity Slowdown." *Journal of Economic Perspectives* 31, no. 2 (2017): 165–86.

———. "Macroeconomics and Market Power: Context, Implications, and Open Questions." *Journal of Economic Perspectives* 33, no. 3 (2019): 23–43.

———. "Market Structure and Productivity: A Concrete Example." *Journal of Political Economy* 112, no. 6 (2004): 1181–222.

———. "What Determines Productivity?" *Journal of Economic Literature* 49, no. 2 (2011): 326–65.

Taleb, Nassim Nicholas. *Antifragile: Things That Gain from Disorder.* New York: Random House, 2012.

Tambe, Prasanna, Xuan Ye, and Peter Cappelli. "Paying to Program? Engineering Brand and High-Tech Wages." *Management Science* 66, no. 7 (2020): 3010–28.

Tanner, Ronald. "The Modern Day General Store." *Progressive Grocer,* February 1, 1987.

Tarbell, Ida M. *The History of the Standard Oil Company.* New York: McClure, Phillips, 1904.

Taulli, Tom. "Microsoft Races Ahead on RPA (Robotic Process Automation)." *Forbes,* September 22, 2020. www.forbes.com/sites/tomtaulli/2020/09/22/microsoft-races-ahead-on-rpa-robotic-process-automation/.

Tedlow, Richard S., and Geoffrey G. Jones. *The Rise and Fall of Mass Marketing.* London: Routledge, 2014.

Temin, Peter. *Iron and Steel Industry in Nineteenth-Century America: An Economic Inquiry.* Cambridge, Mass: MIT Press, 1964.

Thaler, Richard H., and Cass R. Sunstein. *Nudge: Improving Decisions about Health, Wealth, and Happiness*. New York: Penguin, 2009.

Thomson, Ross. *Structures of Change in the Mechanical Age: Technological Innovation in the United States, 1790–1865*. Baltimore: Johns Hopkins University Press, 2009.

Thursby, Jerry G., Richard Jensen, and Marie C. Thursby. "Objectives, Characteristics and Outcomes of University Licensing: A Survey of Major U.S. Universities." *Journal of Technology Transfer* 26, no. 1–2 (2001): 59–72.

Tinbergen, Jan. "Substitution of Graduate by Other Labour." *Kyklos: International Review for Social Sciences* 27, no. 2 (1974): 217–26.

Topol, Eric J. "High-Performance Medicine: The Convergence of Human and Artificial Intelligence." *Nature Medicine* 25, no. 1 (2019): 44–56.

Tracy, Ryan. "After Big Tech Hearing, Congress Takes Aim but from Different Directions." *Wall Street Journal*, July 30, 2020.

Transactions of the New England Cotton Manufacturers' Association. Vol. 59. Waltham, Mass.: E. L. Berry, 1895.

Tucker, Catherine E. "Patent Trolls and Technology Diffusion: The Case of Medical Imaging." 2014. Available at SSRN: https://ssrn.com/abstract=1976593.

U.S. Bureau of the Census. *Historical Statistics of the United States: Colonial Times to 1970*. Washington, D.C.: U.S. Department of Commerce, 1975.

U.S. Bureau of Economic Analysis. "National Income and Product Accounts." Accessed October 3, 2020. https://apps.bea.gov/iTable/index_nipa.cfm.

U.S. Bureau of Labor Statistics. "Productivity Growth by Major Sector, 1947–2017. Bar Chart." Accessed October 12, 2020. www.bls.gov/lpc/prodybar.htm.

U.S. Census Bureau. "BDS Data Tables." Accessed October 14, 2020. www.census.gov/data/tables/time-series/econ/bds/bds-tables.html.

———. "Capital Expenditures for Robotic Equipment: 2018." Accessed October 6, 2020. www.census.gov/library/publications/2019/econ/2018-robotic-equipment.html.

U.S. Environmental Protection Agency. "Notice of Violation." September 18, 2015. www.epa.gov/sites/production/files/2015-10/documents/vw-nov-caa-09-18-15.pdf.

Usselman, Steven W. "Unbundling IBM: Antitrust and the Incentives to Innovation in American Computing." In *The Challenge of Remaining Innovative: Insights from Twentieth-Century American Business*, ed. Sally H. Clarke, Naomi R. Lamoreaux, and Steven W. Usselman, 249–79. Stanford, Calif.: Stanford University Press, 2009.

Valdivia, Walter D. *University Start-Ups: Critical for Improving Technology Transfer.* Washington, DC: Brookings Institution, 2013.

Van Loo, Rory. "Making Innovation More Competitive: The Case of Fintech." *UCLA Law Review* 65 (2018): 232.

———. "Rise of the Digital Regulator." *Duke Law Journal* 66, no. 6 (2016): 1267–329.

———. "Technology Regulation by Default: Platforms, Privacy, and the CFPB." *Georgetown Law Technology Review* 2, no. 2 (2018): 531.

Varian, Hal R. "Beyond Big Data." *Business Economics* 49, no. 1 (2014): 27–31.

Vita, Michael, and F. David Osinski. "John Kwoka's Mergers, Merger Control, and Remedies: A Critical Review." 2016. Available at SSRN: https://ssrn.com/abstract=2888485.

"Wal-Mart Agrees to Settle Lawsuit against Amazon." *New York Times,* April 6, 1999.

"Walmart History." http://www.wal-martchina.com/english/walmart/history.htm.

Wal-Mart Stores, Inc. *Annual Report.* 1991.

———. *Annual Report.* 1994.

Watzinger, Martin, Thomas A. Fackler, Markus Nagler, and Monika Schnitzer. "How Antitrust Enforcement Can Spur Innovation: Bell Labs and the 1956 Consent Decree." *American Economic Journal: Economic Policy* 12, no. 4 (2020): 328–59.

Weil, David. *The Fissured Workplace.* Cambridge, Mass.: Harvard University Press, 2014.

Welke, Lawrence. "Founding the ICP Directories." *IEEE Annals of the History of Computing* 24, no. 1 (2002): 85–89.

Wen, Wen, and Feng Zhu. "Threat of Platform-Owner Entry and Complementor Responses: Evidence from the Mobile App Market." *Strategic Management Journal* 40, no. 9 (2019): 1336–67.

Wiggins, Robert R., and Timothy W. Ruefli. "Schumpeter's Ghost: Is Hypercompetition Making the Best of Times Shorter?" *Strategic Management Journal* 26, no. 10 (2005): 887–911.

Wikipedia contributors. "Automatic Transmission." *Wikipedia,* August 2, 2021. https://en.wikipedia.org/wiki/Automatic_transmission.

———. "Diesel Emissions Scandal." *Wikipedia,* July 25, 2020. https://en.wikipedia.org/w/index.php?title=Diesel_emissions_scandal&oldid=969432451.

———. "Volkswagen Emissions Scandal." *Wikipedia,* September 22, 2020. https://en.wikipedia.org/w/index.php?title=Volkswagen_emissions_scandal&oldid=979657167.

Wildman, Jim. "The First Barcode Scan in History and What It Tells Us about How Some Stories Make Us Care." *Medium,* November 12, 2017. https://medium.com/sharon-and-clyde/the-first-barcode-scan-in-history-and-what-it-tells-us-about-how-some-stories-make-us-care-90a8123875ab.

Wilke, Jeff. "2020 Amazon SMB Impact Report." Amazon.com, 2020. https://d39w7f4ix9f5s9.cloudfront.net/4d/8a/3831c73e4cf484def7a5a8e0d684/amazon-2020-smb-report.pdf.

Willis, Lauren E. "Decisionmaking and the Limits of Disclosure: The Problem of Predatory Lending: Price." *Maryland Law Review* 65, no. 3 (2006): 707–840.

Winder, Gordon M. "Before the Corporation and Mass Production: The Licensing

Regime in the Manufacture of North American Harvesting Machinery, 1830–1910." *Annals of the Association of American Geographers* 85, no. 3 (1995): 521–52.

Winick, Erin. "Every Study We Could Find on What Automation Will Do to Jobs, in One Chart." *Technology Review,* January 25, 2018. https://www.technologyreview.com/2018/01/25/146020/every-study-we-could-find-on-what-automation-will-do-to-jobs-in-one-chart/.

Winston, Clifford. "The Efficacy of Information Policy: A Review of Archon Fung, Mary Graham, and David Weil's Full Disclosure: The Perils and Promise of Transparency." *Journal of Economic Literature* 46, no. 3 (2008): 704–17.

Wollmann, Thomas G. "Stealth Consolidation: Evidence from an Amendment to the Hart-Scott-Rodino Act." *American Economic Review: Insights* 1, no. 1 (2019): 77–94.

Womack, James P. "Why Toyota Won." *Wall Street Journal,* February 13, 2006.

Wood, Debra. "8 Trends Affecting Radiologist Jobs in 2019." *Staff Care,* July 29, 2019.

Wu, Tim. "Be Afraid of Economic 'Bigness'; Be Very Afraid." *New York Times,* November 10, 2018.

———. *The Curse of Bigness: Antitrust in the New Gilded Age.* New York: Columbia Global Reports, 2018.

Yglesias, Matthew. "The 'Skills Gap' Was a Lie." *Vox,* January 7, 2019. www.vox.com/2019/1/7/18166951/skills-gap-modestino-shoag-ballance.

Zhu, Feng, and Nathan Furr. "Products to Platforms: Making the Leap." *Harvard Business Review* 94, no. 4 (2016): 72–78.

Zucker, Lynne G., and Michael R. Darby. "Defacto and Deeded Intellectual Property: Knowledge-Driven Co-Evolution of Firm Collaboration Boundaries and IPR Strategy." National Bureau of Economic Research, Working Paper 20249, 2014.

Zucker, Lynne G., Michael R. Darby, and Jeff S. Armstrong. "Commercializing Knowledge: University Science, Knowledge Capture, and Firm Performance in Biotechnology." *Management Science* 48, no. 1 (2002): 138–53.

Index

Page numbers followed by an f indicate a figure, those followed by a t indicate a table.